Autobiographical International Relations

This volume provides a novel approach to International Relations. In the course of 15 essays, scholars write about how life events brought them to their subject matter. They place their narratives in the larger context of world politics, culture, and history.

Autobiographical International Relations believes that the fictive distancing associated with academic prose creates disaffection in both readers and writers. In contrast, these essays demonstrate how to reengage the "I" while simultaneously sustaining theoretical precision and historical awareness. Authors highlight their motives, their desires, and their wounds. By connecting their theoretical and practical engagements with their needs and wounds, and by working within the overlap between theory, history, and autobiography, these essays aim to increase the clarity, urgency, and meaningfulness of academic work.

These essays are *autobiographical*, but focused on the academic aspect of authors' lives. Specifically, they are set within the domain of international relations/global politics. They are *theoretical*, but geared to demonstrate that theoretical decisions emerge from theorists' needs and wounds. Theoretical precision, rather than being explicitly deduced, is instead immanent to the autobiographical and the historical/cultural narrative each author portrays. And, these essays are framed in *historical/cultural* terms, but seek to bind together theory, history, culture, and the personal into a differentiated and vibrant whole.

This book moves the field of International Relations towards greater candidness about how personal narrative influences theoretical articulations. No such volume currently exists in the field of international relations.

Naeem Inayatullah is Associate Professor at Ithaca College, USA. With David Blaney, he has co-authored *Savage Economics* (Routledge 2010) and *International Relations and the Problem of Difference* (Routledge 2004). He is the co-editor, with Robin Riley, of *Interrogating Imperialism* (Palgrave 2006).

Interventions
Edited by Jenny Edkins
Aberystwyth University
and Nick Vaughan-Williams
University of Warwick

As Michel Foucault has famously stated, "knowledge is not made for understanding; it is made for cutting." In this spirit The Edkins–Vaughan-Williams Interventions series solicits cutting edge, critical works that challenge mainstream understandings in international relations. It is the best place to contribute post disciplinary works that think rather than merely recognize and affirm the world recycled in IR's traditional geopolitical imaginary.

Michael J. Shapiro, University of Hawai'i at Mānoa, USA

The series aims to advance understanding of the key areas in which scholars working within broad critical post-structural and post-colonial traditions have chosen to make their interventions, and to present innovative analyses of important topics.

Titles in the series engage with critical thinkers in philosophy, sociology, politics and other disciplines and provide situated historical, empirical and textual studies in international politics.

Critical Theorists and International Relations
Edited by Jenny Edkins and Nick Vaughan-Williams

Ethics as Foreign Policy
Britain, the EU and the other
Dan Bulley

Universality, Ethics and International Relations
A grammatical reading
Véronique Pin-Fat

The Time of the City
Politics, philosophy, and genre
Michael J. Shapiro

Governing Sustainable Development
Partnership, protest and power at the world summit
Carl Death

Insuring Security
Biopolitics, security and risk
Luis Lobo-Guerrero

Foucault and International Relations
New critical engagements
Edited by Nicholas J. Kiersey and Doug Stokes

International Relations and Non-Western Thought
Imperialism, colonialism and investigations of global modernity
Edited by Robbie Shilliam

Autobiographical International Relations
I, IR
Edited by Naeem Inayatullah

This ground-breaking account of IR from the perspective of autobiography is a necessary first step in re-imagining the public / private divide that governs so much of modern intellectual life. A critical, coherent and holistic understanding of the discipline is impossible without this book which challenges us to reflect on how our seemingly dispassionate intellectual labours are shaped by personal, private, and often unacknowledged narratives.
        Debbie Lisle, Queens University Belfast, Ireland

Inayatullah's volume brings together a wonderfully diverse group of scholars to consider the role of the self in the writing of academic international relations. It is critical reading for anyone concerned with how the 'stories' of international politics are formed and told.
        Elizabeth Dauphinee, York University, Canada

Autobiographical International Relations illuminates our understandings of global politics. By bringing out the all too often ignored factors that shape an author's research, the contributors to this volume all reveal – in highly insightful ways - how the issues that drive them are intrinsically linked to the same political and cultural factors that lie at the heart of international relations.
        Roland Bleiker, Professor of International Relations,
        University of Queensland, Australia

This is one of the best books I have read during my academic career in IR. It is engaging, powerful, courageous, humorous and insightful. The autobiographical stories presented here by various IR scholars from all over the world reveal international politics in a way it is rarely thought of. The writers explore their personal experiences and in this process shed a new and unique light on concepts such as "Communism", "the Military," "Third World," and "Immigration." These stories help us connect with the writers and see ourselves within them. A wonderful read for everyone who wants to think about how politics actually works in the ordinary individual level.
        Oded Löwenheim, Senior Lecturer, Dept. of International
        Relations, The Hebrew University of Jerusalem, Israel

A strikingly original and provocative collection that reveals and suggests a vital role for personal narrative in International Relations. Vivid accounts of mundane moments and extraordinary experiences in life histories and career trajectories presage new approaches that challenge the very 'how' and 'why' of the field.
        Mike Pearson, Professor of Performance Studies,
        Aberystwyth University, Wales

Autobiographical International Relations

I, IR

Edited by
Naeem Inayatullah

Routledge
Taylor & Francis Group
LONDON AND NEW YORK

First published 2011
by Routledge
2 Park Square, Milton Park, Abingdon, Oxon, OX14 4RN

Simultaneously published in the USA and Canada
by Routledge
711 Third Avenue, New York, NY 10017

*Routledge is an imprint of the Taylor & Francis Group,
an informa business*

© 2011 Editorial and Selected matter, Naeem Inayatullah; individual chapters, the contributors

The right of Naeem Inayatullah to be identified as editor of this work has been asserted by him in accordance with the Copyright, Designs and Patent Act 1988.

Typeset in Times New Roman by Taylor & Francis Books

All rights reserved. No part of this book may be reprinted or reproduced or utilised in any form or by any electronic, mechanical, or other means, now known or hereafter invented, including photocopying and recording, or in any information storage or retrieval system, without permission in writing from the publishers.

British Library Cataloguing in Publication Data
A catalogue record for this book is available from the British Library

Library of Congress Cataloging in Publication Data
Autobiographical international relations : I, IR / edited by Naeem Inayatullah.
  p. cm. – (Interventions)
Includes bibliographical references and index.
1. International relations. 2. International relations specialists.
I. Inayatullah, Naeem.
JZ1305.A82 2010
327.092′2–dc22   2010021854

ISBN 13: 978-0-415-78142-8 (hbk)
ISBN 13: 978-0-415-78143-5 (pbk)
ISBN 13: 978-0-203-83722-1 (ebk)

For SYK

I've said before that every craftsman
searches for what's not there
to practice his craft.
A builder looks for the rotten hole
where the roof caved in. A water-carrier
picks the empty pot. A carpenter
stops at the house with no door.
Workers rush toward some hint
of emptiness, which they then
start to fill. Their hope, though,
is for emptiness, so don't think
you must avoid it. It contains
what you need!
Dear soul, if you were not friends
with the vast nothing inside,
why would you always be casting your net
into it, and waiting so patiently?

Rumi (1991: 106)

Contents

List of contributors	xi
Acknowledgments	xiv
Falling and flying: an introduction NAEEM INAYATULLAH	1
1 **Accidental scholarship and the myth of objectivity** STEPHEN CHAN	13
2 **Objects among objects** JENNY EDKINS	19
3 **Stammers between silence and speech** NARENDRAN KUMARAKULASINGAM	31
4 **Scenes of obscenity: the meaning of America under epistemic and military violence** KHADIJA F. EL ALAOUI	41
5 **I, the double soldier: an autobiographic case-study on the pitfalls of dual citizenship** RAINER HÜLSSE	56
6 **Weakness leaving my body: an essay on the interpersonal relations of international politics** JACOB L. STUMP	65
7 **Waiting for the revolution: a foreigner's narrative** ALINA SAJED	78
8 **Am I not that? at the feet of elders** SARA-MARIA SORENTINO	93

x Contents

9 Listening for the elsewhere and the not-yet: academic
   labor as a matter of ethical witness   103
   LORI AMY

10 To realize you're creolized: white flight, black
    culture, hybridity   118
    JOEL DINERSTEIN

11 Goodbye nostalgia! in memory of a country that
    never existed as such   136
    WANDA VRASTI

12 Shaping walls: moving through Lanka's forts   152
    NETHRA SAMARAWICKREMA

13 Three stories: a way of being in the world   161
    PATRICK THADDEUS JACKSON

14 G(r)azing the fields of IR: romping buffaloes,
    festive villagers   173
    QUỲNH PHẠM AND HIMADEEP MUPPIDI

15 The sound of conversation   187
    SORAYYA KHAN

    Cosmography recapitulates biography: an epilogue   196
    PETER MANDAVILLE

    Index   204

Contributors

Lori Amy is Associate Professor of Writing and Linguistics at Georgia Southern University. Her first book, *The Wars We Inherit* (Temple 2010) explores how military structures, as institutions of public, cultural violence, imbue society with physical, verbal, emotional, and sexual aggression.

Stephen Chan, OBE, is Professor of International Relations at the School of Oriental and African Studies in London, and the 2010 ISA Eminent Scholar in Global Development.

Joel Dinerstein is Associate Professor of English at Tulane University and director of the American Studies program. He is the author of an award-winning study of Jazz and industrialization, *Swinging the Machine: Modernity, Technology, and African-American Culture Between the World Wars* (University of Massachusetts Press 2003).

Jenny Edkins is Professor of International Politics at Aberystwyth University. Her books include: *Displaced, Missing, Disappeared* (Cornell, forthcoming), *Trauma and the Memory of Politics* (Cambridge 2003), *Whose Hunger? Concepts of Famine, Practices of Aid* (Minnesota 2000, re-issued in paperback 2008), and *Poststructuralism and International Politics* (Lynne Reinner 1999). She is co-editor with Maja Zehfuss of *Global Politics: A New Introduction* (Routledge 2008) and with Nick Vaughan-Williams of *Critical Theorists in International Relations* (Routledge 2009).

Khadija F. El Alaoui is Mellon Postdoctoral Fellow in Peace and Justice Studies in the American Culture Program at Vassar College, NY. Her writing focuses on the mutations of colonialism, especially within the current context of US–Arab encounters.

Rainer Hülsse, the former military cyclist, is now Lecturer in International Relations at the University of Munich, Germany. He is doing research on the role of metaphors in international politics, on money-laundering and investment promotion. On weekends, he participates in mountain bike races.

Naeem Inayatullah is Associate Professor of Politics at Ithaca College. With David Blaney, he is the author of *Savage Economics* (Routledge 2010), *International Relations and the Problem of Difference* (Routledge 2004), and with Robin Riley, editor of *Interrogating Imperialism* (Palgrave 2006).

Patrick Thaddeus Jackson is Associate Professor of International Relations and Director of General Education at American University. His most recent book is *The Conduct of Inquiry in International Relations* (Routledge 2010). He blogs at www.duckofminerva.com.

Sorayya Khan is the author of *Five Queen's Road* (Penguin India 2009) and *Noor* (Penguin India, 2003). She is the recipient of a Fulbright award, a Malahat Review Novella Prize, and a Constance Saltonstall Foundation Artist Grant. Her fiction has appeared in several literary reviews and anthologies.

Narendran Kumarakulasingam currently teaches International Relations at American University. He is interested in studying violence and contemporary forms of colonialism in international relations.

Peter Mandaville is Associate Professor of Government and Islamic Studies and Founding Director of the Center for Global Studies at George Mason University. He is the author of the books *Global Political Islam* (Routledge 2007) and *Transnational Muslim Politics: Reimagining the Umma* (Routledge 2003).

Himadeep Muppidi is Associate Professor of Political Science on the Betty Goff Cook Cartwright Chair in International Studies at Vassar College. He is the author of *The Colonial Signs of International Relations* (Columbia/Hurst 2010) and *The Politics of the Global* (University of Minnesota Press 2004).

Quỳnh N. Phạm is a senior majoring in Political Science at Vassar College. She will join the doctoral program in Political Science at the University of Minnesota in Fall 2010.

Alina Sajed has been an Assistant Professor of IR at the University of Hong Kong since September 2010. Two of her articles are forthcoming with *Citizenship Studies* and *Review of International Studies*. Routledge has agreed to publish her manuscript entitled *Transgressing International Relations: Postcolonial Encounters in the Maghreb*.

Nethra Samarawickrema has a BA in Politics from Ithaca College and will begin her MA in Social Anthropology at Dalhousie University. She is currently gathering oral histories in the Galle Fort on how generations of Muslim women have used its colonial architecture to express their agency.

Sara-Maria Sorentino graduated with a Bachelor of Arts in Politics from Ithaca in 2008. She has since been employed in the childcare field and is currently studying Dagomba drumming. She can be contacted at smsorentino@gmail.com.

Jacob L. Stump is Assistant Professor of Political Science at Shepherd University. His research and writing focus on the relationship between American national identity and interpersonal security conduct. He can be reached at jacoblstump@gmail.com.

Wanda Vrasti is a Post-Doctoral Fellow at the Humboldt University in Berlin. Her research uses critical and ethnographic lenses to discuss tourism, memory, affect, and immaterial work. She is working on a book project from her dissertation on "The Self as Enterprise: The Case of Volunteer Tourism." Her previous work has been published in *Millennium* and *Politics and Culture*.

Acknowledgments

I was thrilled to work with these 17 authors. I dropped everything when I received their drafts, savored their stories, and could not help but respond immediately. They tolerated my often heavy-handed interventions and they endured my illusive guidelines. I want to acknowledge their openness, generosity, and fearlessness. I am eager to continue this venture, in part, because that would allow us to include a number of colleagues whose participation was vital but who, for various reasons, could not be included in this volume. They are Xavier Guillaume, Jesse Crane-Seeber, Sidharth Mallavarapu, Chip Gagnon, and Arlene Tickner. I am grateful to Jenny Edkins and Nick Vaughan-Williams for including our volume in their *Interventions* series and to Craig Fowlie for his critical acumen and savoir-faire. Four anonymous reviewers offered insight, direction, and encouragement that I found uplifting. Roland Bleiker, Elizabeth Dauphinee, and Oded Lowenheim are engaged in similar endeavors. I thank them for their path blazing and their firm assurance. Along the way, Stephen Chan, Meili Steele, Lori Amy, Minnie Bruce Pratt, Zillah Eisenstein, and Sorayya Khan have inspired me to pursue this kind of work. I wish to make a special mention of Kiran Pervez who played a key role in organizing, sustaining, and enriching our collective but whose film making muse called her to a different path. I am very grateful to Rod Beers, Jim Best, James Davie, Ben Hogben, Karen Johnson, Kelly Merritt, Cheryl Neville, Ellen Shank, Laurie Wasik, Lynda Walters, Lynn Tordella, and especially Gail Belokur for their essential logistical support that they always delivered with kindness. Sorayya, Kamal, and Shahid fill my every breath with joyful humor and precious affection.

Falling and flying
An introduction[1]

Naeem Inayatullah

> The way of love is not a subtle argument. The door there is devastation. Birds make great sky-circles of their freedom. How do they learn it? They fall, and falling, they are given wings.
>
> Rumi (1995: 243)

Autobiographical International Relations began for me as, what Rumi might call, a falling without wings. Following the 2001 US bombing campaign against Afghanistan, people in my hometown of Ithaca started searching for experts on Afghanistan. They had suddenly acquired a thirst for information on the Afghan people and their landscape. Bombing begets pedagogy, we might say. I found myself naively stepping into this lack, first, by filling the role of "expert." I accepted nearly two-dozen speaking engagements in October and November of 2001. I also then wrote my first autobiographical essay (Inayatullah 2003a). Despite voraciously reading on Afghanistan, and despite the absence of any Afghanistan specialists in a town that contains three institutions of higher learning, I could not convince myself of my specialist status. But I did find claims to authorize my speaking voice: Louis Dupree and Nancy Hatch Dupree, two of the world's most knowledgeable people on Afghanistan, were my teachers; I was raised in the city of Peshawar; and I had twice visited Afghanistan in 1972 and 1973. Close enough, no?

Even prior to the bombing, I had been edging towards the cliff of autobiography – having been enticed there by the confessional political writing of Minnie Bruce Pratt, moved there by the graceful historical fiction of Sorayya Khan, and gently pushed there by my colleague Zillah Eisenstein who urged that I take some risks with my writing persona. But it was the bombing itself that triggered my jump and my fall. In my essay, I hoped to convey a simple idea, that there is *something there*: something real and intangible that the soon to be saturated media coverage would not provide. Afghanistan was not for me an abstract bombing zone. Its astounding mountains and rivers and its magnificent people were materializations of a profoundly important history and spirit. In my not altogether un-romantic view, Afghans had a quality I had not seen elsewhere, a quality without which I felt the world could not thrive, and a quality that I badly needed but which, I sensed, had eluded me my whole life. I began to call this quality *warm indifference*, a way of life that seems unconcerned about the West, modernity, and capitalism but nevertheless sustains a sense of hospitality to external values. Prior to writing the essay, I had not sensed my need for Afghanistan. What I had earlier was anger and rage at those perpetrating the bombing.

As I formulated the essay, I felt the need to make myself the target of my words. I wanted to show rather than tell, I wanted to exhibit a process of discovery, rather than steer towards a conclusion. In an elliptical and roundabout fashion, I illustrated how *I* diminished Afghan culture by placing it lower on the developmental scale, how *my* prejudice came to be challenged, and how this challenge forced a re-assessment, not just of my view of Afghanistan, but of my life altogether. My fervent need to convey something about Afghanistan forced me beyond my professional training towards what I hoped would be a more persuasive form of communication.

In 2002, my friend and colleague Meili Steele helped me craft the essay and then gave me ample time to present it at the fourth annual conference on the "The Future of Cultural Memory." I was surprised by the positive response I received from the audience. One colleague said, "I don't know what else you work on but you *must* continue this work." Initially, I was puzzled, annoyed, and angered by these reactions. I was puzzled by my inability to grasp what made autobiography so engaging, and I was annoyed at my suspicion that some form of orientalist exoticism was at work in my audience. (A noted scholar on autobiography commented, "Your life is so interesting." Aren't all lives interesting? I asked myself.)[2] And, I was slightly angered that after working on classical political economy and international relations theory for decades, it was my life and not my work that garnered attention. These irritations remain with me.

The circulation of my Afghanistan essay led to requests for more such writing – by Christine Sylvester and by Stephan Senders.[3] Having stepped off the cliff, and still falling, I seemed to have been lifted and given flight by unexpected sources. As I continued to harbor my suspicions, I also wondered if this form might not enable something. But I am getting ahead of myself because, as is always the case, my tale is thoroughly embedded within a collective story.

Cut to the lobby of a Montreal hotel during the 2004 International Studies Association conference: four or five of us converse intensely – off-panel, of course. As the conversation about our lives, journeys, and ideas spirals and then rockets, we note what is obvious to any conference participant: off-panel conversations are fascinating and enthralling whereas the formal presentations too often are not. We all seem struck that the life trajectories of our co-conversationalists are far more remarkable and more complex than what our theories can permit or carry. We wonder how we can exploit these contrasts between on- and off-panels sites and between on- and off-theory talking. We start planning.

Our first formal engagement was a roundtable at the 2005 ISA in Hawaii. There, indeed, the off-panel energy became infused within the formal space of the panel. The presentations were closer to stories, confessions, and autobiographies, and the audience responded with tales of their own. Confession begets confession and story begets story, we might say. Relative to a traditional panel, this seemed a free for all. And yet, no one left, no one leafed through their bulky program. Eyes, ears, whole bodies seemed present. We couldn't tell what it was, but it wasn't the usual. Excitement seemed mingled with suspicion, and desire mixed with fear. Not everyone's cup of tea, no doubt, but we picked up new members and mostly consolidated our resolve. For the 2006 ISA in San Diego, we offered two panels. These brought together more interlocutors, more energy, and more conversation.

Still, fear of falling and fear of flying abounded. At least three members wrote flat chronological accounts that seemed oddly devoid of life. In each case, I already knew something about their absorbing lives. Nor did their writing on other projects display an absence of vitality. I interpreted their unenthusiastic efforts as extended misgivings about their participation and about the project itself. They seemed to be saying, "Look, I am not sure I am ready to uncover things – my class or family origins – things, that I have so successfully covered up." One member finally admitted that writing in this manner might hurt intimates and that delivering such pain was not in the cards. A few worried that writing about their lives would play into the unwritten rule whereby "foreigners" are pushed to write about their home countries rather than to theorize about the world at large. Others wrote fine drafts but hesitated to share them with our collective. One person considered writing a draft only on the condition of anonymity, and another produced an excellent draft but only after I had promised that we could make cuts or move to anonymity if too much was revealed. One of our founding members astutely finessed the problem by continually deferring a submission past the deadline – five years later! Our collective sensibility had not yet gelled.

Frustrated with our inability to produce results beyond panels, I was ready to let go and admit that the project was too difficult. We presented nothing at the ISA 2007 in Chicago, but this produced a surprise. Many asked us about the status of the project and then complained about its absence. This project neither lives nor dies, I thought. Nevertheless, revitalized by concerns about the project's fate and hoping that the goal of a collective volume might galvanize us, Kiran Pervez and I made one more push. The lure of a tangible result seemed to produce momentum.

Shortly after the Chicago ISA, Jenny Edkins and Maja Zehfuss turned my/our falling into flying by inviting me to present two autobiographical essays as part of the BISA Poststructural Politics Group Workshop, titled *Dividing Practices: Race, Class, Religion and Global Economic Inequality*, at the University of Aberystwyth. There, I was bowled over by Jenny's colleagues who seemed very much at home with the kind of project I imagine we are engaging. One of them, Mike Pearson, was kind enough to give me his book *In Comes I: Performance, Memory and Landscape* (2006). In his astonishing work, I found words, concepts, and a posture that I felt came closest to conceptualizing our venture. Pearson's presentation of "chorography" and "mystory" seem especially apropos.

The word "chorography" was in fashion in the seventeenth century and has recently been retrieved by geographers. In contrast to "geography" – which deals with the earth in general – "chorography" refers to the practice of describing particular regions. It is Pearson's awareness of chorographic writing that calls our attention. He argues that, "Chorographic writing creates complex and unexpected relations from and within the landscape of the autobiographical subject, through processes analogous to non-linear, hypertextual linkage." Pearson quotes theorist Gregory L. Ulmer on the central principle of chorography: "do not choose between the different meanings of key terms, but compose by using all the meanings." Pearson adds, "The accent is on creativity, leading to new forms of research and new kinds of text, from the author's specific position in the time and space of culture. Citing Ulmer, he claims that the "chorographer, then, writes with paradigms, not arguments" (Pearson 2006: 9).

Pearson's second concept, "mystory," gets still closer to our concerns. Mystory combines "three kinds of discourse: personal, popular and expert." The expert's discourse, of course, is ubiquitous in IR. Nor, thankfully, is IR bereft of the popular – thanks to recent engagements.[4] Still, the popular and the personal have mostly been excised in order to produce the expert. For many of us, this project responds to that severing. In addition, mystory, "blurs the boundary between critical and creative writing, autobiography and cultural history, one text and the next: the author is located within an intertextual network of cultural references." In such writing the author "combines individual reflection with archival enquiry: drawing upon accumulated experiences." "Pattern is favoured over argument," says Pearson for the "creation of signature style that may be as much poetic as informational." In mystory:

> the author identifies with the object of study, acknowledging affiliations and bias, and this drives the research: whilst conventional academic practice is clearly present, it is infused with personal observations and sources of lay knowledge. The method is emotional, self-reflexive and revelatory. A life-story is mapped onto the discourse, and memory and desire are active agencies: the anecdote may be as significant as the historical fact.
>
> (Pearson 2006: 10)

"Chorography" and especially "mystory" helped me to understand that, what in my essays seemed like narrative meanderings between world events, synoptic analysis, and autobiographical anecdotes, were actually intuited systematic juxtapositions. Pearson seemed to be saying, "look, there is a form to all this and here it is." However, he also emphasizes the creation of a "signature style" that emerges from authors' needs. In producing that style, Pearson's form – chorography and mystory – are useful as a kind of compass. But it is just as important to put away the compass and allow the writing to wander. I sent our group a prompt that featured Pearson's concepts. But I also asked them to disregard him once they started writing.

Soon the essay drafts started to appear and we began to read them. By the time of 2009 ISA in New York, six of us presented essays in a panel titled "Autobiography as a Source for Exploring the Past and Anticipating the Future." There was standing room only. The presentations were crisp and engaging, and the audience response was highly enthusiastic. It seemed at last the timing was right. We had produced work that seemed to inspire others.

A proper motivation?

Why does IR need a volume such as this one? Academic writing supposes a precarious fiction. It assumes the simultaneous absence and presence of the writer within the writing. The writer presents herself/himself as absent, as distant, and as indifferent to the writing and ideas. The ideas are believed to speak for themselves while the writer serves as a vehicle for their expression. The author's absence qualifies him or her as "objective" and "scientific." This fictive distance, as we all know, dominates academic prose. And yet the reader always uncovers the presence of a particular person in the writing. As readers, we suspect that the writing emerges from a point of view, a gender, a class, a race, a nationality, a cultural heritage, a historical specificity, and a biography.

This simultaneous absence and presence of the writer provides both a problem and an opportunity. Of course, fictive distancing has all the advantages that science itself offers, namely, a kind of precision that helps us to distinguish between less and more accurate perceptions of the world. The argument on behalf of fictive distancing proceeds as follows: with personal disengagement, with an apprehension of the world from a purported neutral and objective stance, we can remove our personal biases from our descriptions and theorizations. The wager in fictive distancing is that it gets us greater precision, accuracy, and insight into the workings of natural and social processes.

The central problem of fictive distancing is that the supposed scientist only pretends to be absent. The personal biases that objectivity was meant to eliminate are merely hidden within and behind the science. Crucially, the scientist falsely assumes that the issues she/he addresses do not already constitute the scientist and are not already working themselves through the scientist's life. As scientists, we seem to exist in a space beyond the world and therefore are not somehow part of the world we study. This fiction can be counter-productive, if not dangerous. The critique of fictive distancing avers that such distancing, rather than giving us greater precision, accuracy, and insight, serves instead to blinker and distort actual world processes. The presumably absent scientist and the seemingly objective world he/she describes both derive from hidden commitments that often distort description and skew analysis. In addition, for many of us, fictive distancing disconnects our work from our daily life. It produces writing that often seems formal, abstruse, and lacking in practical purpose. Academic practice begets alienation, we might say.

These are not novel claims. Even in IR, post-colonialisms, post-modernisms, and feminisms have engaged in such commentary for the better part of three decades. And yet, we have seen few examples of alternative writing forms in IR.

It is time to engage in a form that retrieves the "I" and explicitly demonstrates its presence both within the world and within academic writing. Authors in this volume highlight their motives, their desires, and their wounds. By connecting their theoretical/practical engagements with their needs and wounds, and by working within the overlap between theory, history, culture, and autobiography, these essays aim to increase the clarity, urgency, and meaningfulness of scholarly work.

These essays are *autobiographical*, but focused on the academic aspect of authors' lives. Specifically, they are set within the domain of international relations/global politics. They are *theoretical*, but geared to demonstrate that theoretical decisions emerge from theorists' needs and wounds. Theoretical precision, rather than being explicitly deduced, is instead immanent to the autobiographical and the historical/cultural narrative each author portrays. And, these essays are framed in *historical/cultural* terms, but seek to bind together theory, history, culture, and the personal into a differentiated and vibrant whole. Our goal is to move the field of International Relations towards greater candidness about how personal narratives influence theoretical articulations.

A proper introduction?

A "proper" introduction invites the reader into the contents by describing and critiquing similar work. A set of mapping exercises helps the reader locate the issues and another set of critiquing moves explains why those other gateways remain inadequate. Such an introduction delivers readers to the current gate through which they are invited to enter the book as a matter of course. The normal introduction has the virtue of orientating readers and giving them firm, predictable guidance.

This introduction, however, makes only minimal gestures towards such an orientation because I remain convinced that a standard introduction would breach the spirit and character of our project.[5] *First*, the aim of this volume is not to establish an alternative theoretical framework. Not theoretical displacement, but rather summoning an additional form of writing is what we have in mind. These essays are engaged in a style of writing, thinking, and speaking that can give supplementary depth, urgency, and clarity to authors' preferred theoretical postures. Our essayists borrow from, among others, Foucault, Lacan, Derrida, Nandy, Fanon, Trinh T. Minh-ha, Zizek, Sarah Ahmed, Freire, and Butler, and they gesture towards post-modernisms, post-colonialisms, and feminisms. These signals are, however, muted in favor of describing and circling crucial autobiographical and world events. Authors highlight their struggle in illuminating things that seem just beyond their sight.[6]

Second, the sense of urgency envisioned in these otherwise calmly composed essays, bypasses the usual motions of establishing a project. Mostly we sidestep the question, "Why is this a better way to do things?" Instead of excavating this space, we occupy and cultivate it.[7] The essays speak to the reader directly, as if to say, "See how you, dear reader, and I, the writer, are working together to make this reading and writing a meaningful experience?" In this way, the self-conscious presence of the writing subject contravenes the usual fictive distance between reader and writer.

This breach of fictive distancing, however, does not transform these essays into fiction. Rather, we might say that these acts of writing are both scientific and trans-scientific. They are scientific because the essays present concrete, vivid, and impassioned details that invite us to understand and reconsider the world. They are trans-scientific because the essays disregard the rule of providing a definitive and explicit message. Their authors seem unconcerned, I might say, to present themselves as choice making agents. Nor do they demarcate social structures. What we get instead is something akin to pure processes. Agents and structures, after all, are convenient fictions through which we cut into a life that is manifold, continuous, and overwhelming in its complexity. Science aims at a mystic's goal – to explain and understand life's fullness. However, as scientists, we exclude the mystic's tools – poetry, dance, music, and meditative contemplation. These authors blur this boundary as they move towards a kind of artistic science with their writing. In the process they disclose themselves and their writing bares itself. I find myself feeling neither shame nor pride in their exposure. What we get instead is what I assume many of us actually desire from our reading – a substantive look at life/lives in process. Seamlessly, we are shown the mundane and the dramatic, the empirical and the theoretical, the structures and the processes that constitute and change humans. In sum, these essays place both the writer and reader within a dynamic flow.

Self-indulgence

The allegation of self-indulgence has obstinately dogged this project. Even some of those with the most international recognition and, interestingly, with the most commitment to the project, have felt "indulgent" in writing and presenting their essays. It is easy to understand the charge: we dread that our exposure will bring shame and embarrassment. Worse, we fear our revelations will mark us for having indulged in navel gazing and for having showcased our vanity. I will admit that my initial forays into this form left me with similar feelings. There are surely good reasons for this fear, and I can think of two. Without precise attention to the form, such essays come out either at the pole of "triumphalism" or the pole of "self-abnegation." It becomes difficult to write about one's self/selves where the balance between a triumphant-self and a defeated-self is so precarious, and when the fall from the tightrope seems a long drop into deep darkness. Nevertheless, overcoming this fear is merely a matter of courage and multiple drafts.

More telling is our secret belief, for this is what I think it is, that at the center of our self we find not world historical processes but rather an essence. When we ontologize ourselves, as most of us are likely to do at some point, we bask in the brilliance/dullness of our uniqueness. I am not saying that we are not in some way each unique individuals. Indeed, our desire to find and commune with others is founded in relative difference. Rather, I am suggesting that our uniqueness lies only in the *particular* bundle of mundane and ubiquitous cultural and historical forces that compose us. The more I am involved in this project, the less patience I find for the conceit of self-indulgence. As these essays make clear, exposure and disclosure of the self/selves, rather than locating some idiosyncratic "n of 1" or some *sui generis* entity, instead uncovers events, histories, cultures, and worlds. Fear of autobiographical writing may be calmed when we entertain the possibility that rather than being indulgent, we are actually not indulgent enough. The deeper secret we hide from ourselves is that, in the end, there is little to our claim of uniqueness or our presumed self-indulgence. Excavate the self and what do we find? Not ontologized and essentialized indulgence, but the differentiated dynamism of whole worlds. Scientists and mystics, I want to believe, can both harbor this claim.

Writing from the edge of articulation

We can hypothesize that no matter how and what we compose, writing emerges from our needs and wounds. The differences in form – from objectified, professionalized, jargon-filled, expert analyses of the type that fills our journals and conferences, to the autobiographical essays in this volume, to a still more confessional journaling – are no doubt important. This is because form shapes content. Yet, given my hypothesis, these differing forms all track around a need, a trauma, a wound. Writing orbits what cannot be said, and it struggles to express what we cannot articulate. Two forces shape this struggle: what we aim to produce in the work and what the writing writes back to us. Both are common experiences, and we are satisfied when in the course of writing we begin to uncover the motivating intuition through which we proceed to our goal. When I wrote my essay on Afghanistan, I needed to say and thereby understand that, yes, there is indeed something significant there. But, there was more. There is always something more, something unexpected, something surprising that writes back to us.

What my Afghanistan essay unexpectedly revealed to me was that, as the child of two Punjabi farming families searching for cosmopolitan effeteness, I had a complicated and contradictory relationship with those who we thought of as the "barbarous" Pushtoons. When I was not yet five years old, a village of Pushtoons – the developmental objects of my father's job as a professional modernizer – saved our family from an armed robbery. And who knows from what else. My childhood encounter with those four armed and masked men that night produced a fear in me that has not left. Nor, however, has the conundrum of why the Pushtoons in the neighboring village came so swiftly to our aid. Their hospitality, their "warm indifference" to our family would later continually confound my own professional trajectory as an aspiring modernizer. In college, I would imbibe Parsonian structural functionalism and then the stage theories of classical- and neo-Marxism. The armed robbery and the Pushtoon response was, however, a hard stone, an invisible impossible kernel, that interrupted my embrace of Pushtoons as lesser beings.

I had written the essay to show the contemporary significance of Afghans/Pushtoons, but I received more than I bargained for. The writing confronted me with the contradictory nature of my being. In retrospect, it may not be too much to say that all my professional work emerges from this trauma, this wound, this need to work out where I stand on the issue of greater and lesser beings, on the value of hierarchy and inequality.

The essays in this volume may be read within this same frame. These authors are working out something central to their being and becoming – their traumas, wounds, needs for which they do and do not have words. They are working out things that are as important to their own lives as they are, quite possibly, to the life of the planet. They are doing so in a form, theoretically informed autobiography, with which they fall and through which they fly.

A bit of guidance for undergraduates

Too often I feel heartbroken by students at my college who seem to occupy their resource rich seats because they were unable either to say "no" to their parents' wishes or because they don't know how to say "yes" to something that better quenches their desire. When I am frustrated, I am tempted to blame them for their alienation from our course materials, from my instruction as their teacher, from the deeper satisfactions of academic life, from a fuller involvement in mindful living, and from their better selves. I catch myself, though, by remembering that they and we are all victims of a larger malaise. Together, as students and teachers, we are enmeshed in a structure of alienation. I want to believe that a volume such as this one can, in a small manner, address and reduce our disaffection. How? By showing, first, that there is a way of speaking about international relations and, more generally, about social theory, that is sophisticated, subtle, attuned to complexity, but largely jargon free. To the degree that these essays present social theoretical knowledge without alienating prose, they can move students and teachers towards engaged and precise learning.

Second, and as important, students will note that most of these authors are practicing professional teachers. But here, rather than expressing their mastery their teachers *expose* their struggles: to the complexity of the world and their own frailty in the face of it; to the nearly paralyzing ethical dilemmas and their own complicity in both oppression and resistance; to finding and articulating language adequate to speak of their scars and wounds; to an inability to confidently assert how to go on with life; and to a fruitless effort in obtaining wisdom by means of their specialization. These professional teachers will seem very much like humans, perhaps even like kindred spirits.

Third, it may be striking to students that humans as real as those portrayed in these essays would turn to theory, history, and academic study in order to make sense of their own lives. Of course, there are other realms that help us make meaning – aesthetics, spirituality, and kinesthetics, to name a few. Nevertheless, students may be inspired to learn that academic inquiry too has a place in meaning making. And, finally, students may be heartened that in these essays, the tattered, stretched, and nearly broken effort authors make in order to articulate something, remains as close to silence as it does to speech. Students may witness that alienation from one's own life is not their lot alone.[8] In these ways, these essays create an implicit solidarity with their readers. In sum, the transparency of life-processes and of life-struggles displayed in these essays may invite students to walk through a wall of disaffection and into the realm of work that may not feel like work.

Coda

In those years when a part of my responsibilities included regular work with students writing masters theses and doctoral dissertations, I was more or less happy to work with anyone willing to have me on their committee. But there was one issue on which I acted as the "gate-keeper." No matter the topic or the student, I asked for a written response to this question: "What does the topic of your study mean to you as a person?" I lost a few students who simply refused my insistence on the connection between the micro and macro, the autobiographical and the international. Those who stayed almost always stumbled in their reply. But once the students rediscovered their motivation and personal connection, whatever writer's block they were experiencing quickly dissolved. I did not ask that their response to my probing become part of their dissertation, but only that the students locate it in their consciousness.

Once we cultivate an autobiographical awareness, the work of that awareness is mostly done. So, also, with these essays. These authors may never again write in this form. I hope they will, but they needn't. The *possibility* of the autobiographical sensibility, an awareness that gets us to think, write, and live in a particular manner, may well be enough. Beware though: after falling you may wish only to fly.

Notes

1 Between my first and final drafts, this introduction become a collective enterprise. I selected from the suggestions and insights of David Blaney, Evgenia Ilieva, Himadeep Muppidi, and Manu Samnotra, Narendran Kumarakulasingam, Xavier Guillaume, Nethra Samarawickrema, Sarah Roe Tubbs, Zillah Eisenstein, Oded Lowenheim, Sorayya Khan, and Keith Brown. To lesser and greater degrees, they share the responsibility with me.
2 But consider this counter-interpretation by Himadeep Muppidi: "Maybe in listening to you, they allowed themselves to mourn with you. And they were grateful for that. So it was not about you but what your words made possible for others in a difficult time, a collective ritual." (Personal correspondence.)
3 See (Inayatullah 2003b) and (Inayatullah 2007).
4 See for example, Weldes (2003) and Franklin (2005).
5 Nevertheless, I offer the following as a gesture to those who might require a more professional introduction: In IR, one volume (Kruzel and Rosenau 1989) resembles ours. However, three characteristics – focus, form, and tone – differentiate our volume from the Kruzel and Rosenau book. Three works that do the most to move IR towards our concerns are Brigg and Bleiker (2010), Lowenheim (2010), and Dauphinee (2010). Each moves the field of IR towards considering the place of the "I" and the significance of "autoethnography." The articles by Brigg and Bleiker and by Lowenheim are rich in citations and provide thorough literature reviews. Other noteworthy efforts that partially overlap with the concerns of our volume include Doty (2004) and Dauphinee (2007). All the projects above compliment the aims of this volume. Each in its own way carves out a gateway within the walls of "fictive distancing." The authors above devote themselves to the actual construction of the gate(s) through which they invite in other scholars towards autobiography. Our volume, in contrast, assumes that gate, walks through it, and cultivates the fields beyond the wall. Within IR, important feminists' efforts have moved the above scholars to construct the gateways to autobiography/autoethnography. These include Tickner (2006), Zalewski (2006), and Weldon (2006). See also Cohn (1987). Further afield, feminists and historians joined to produce a special issue of the journal *Gender and History*, titled "Autobiography and Biography" (1990). Looking beyond IR, we can find the following: In the field of history, many famous historians are turning to autobiographies. Their books are not retrospective codas to their lifetime achievements. Rather, they consider how actual experience of producing history framed their lives as historians and humans. Similarly, in sociology, for almost two decades, scholars have been debating what they call "autoethnography" as well as generating autoethnographic works. Indeed, the journal *Qualitative Inquiry* is a home to authoethnographic writing. And, of course, in anthropology, autoethnographic themes have been central in the field's effort to decolonize itself.
6 If, in the process of adding a form of writing to their repertoire, the theoretical proclivities of the reader or writer somehow shift, then we can regard this as a secondary and somewhat unintended effect.
7 For the proper excavation see Lowenheim (2010) and Brigg and Bleiker (2010).
8 Consider Narendran Kumarakulasingam's comment on this sentence: "This is what is at stake in our project right? The heart of it. We all know that the excising

of the personal and the popular from the expert (to go back to Pearson) has a cost. And it is this."

References

Bland Lucy and Angela V. John (1990) *Gender and History*, "Autobiography and Biography," special issue, 2: 1.

Brigg, Morgan and Roland Bleiker (forthcoming 2010) "Autoethnographic International Relations: Exploring the Self as a Source of Knowledge," *Review of International Studies*.

Cohn, Carol (1987) "Sex and Death in the Rational World of Defense Intellectuals," *Signs* 12, 4: 687–718.

Dauphinee, Elizabeth (2007) *The Ethics of Researching War: Looking for Bosnia*, Manchester: Manchester University Press, 2007.

——(forthcoming 2010) "The Ethics of Autobiography," *Review of International Studies*.

Doty, Roxanne Lynn (2004) "Maladies of Our Souls: Identity and Voice in the Writing of Academic International Relations," *Cambridge Review of International Affairs* 17, 2: 377–92.

Franklin, Marianne (2005) *Resounding International Relations: On Music, Culture and Politics*, New York: Palgrave.

Inayatullah, Naeem (2003a) "Something There: Love, War, and Basketball in Afghanistan," *Intertexts*, 7, 2: 143–56.

——(2003b) "Present Dangers," *Borderlands eJournal* 2, 2, available at: www.borderlands.net.au/vol2no2_2003/inayatullah_dangers.htm (accessed July 1, 2010).

——(2007) "Circuits of Conversion: Auto-ethnographic Encounters with Money," in Senders, S. and Truitt, A. (eds.), *Money: Ethnographic Encounters*, New York: Berg.

Jalal al-Din Rumi, Maulana, "One-handed basket weaving: poems on the theme of work", translated by Coleman Barks (1991) Athens, GA: MAYPOP.

Kruzel, Joseph and James Rosenau (1989) *Journey Through World Politics: Autobiographical Reflections of Thirty-four Academic Travelers*, Lexington, MA: Lexington Books.

Lowenheim, Oded (forthcoming 2010) "The I in IR: An Autoethnographic Account," *Review of International Studies*.

Pearson, Mike (2006) *In Comes I: Performance, Memory and Landscape*, Exeter: University of Exeter Press.

Tickner, J. Ann (2006) "Feminism meets International Relations: Some Methodological Issues," in Ackerly, B.A., Stern, M., and True, J. (eds.), *Feminist Methodologies for International Relations*, Cambridge: Cambridge University Press.

Weldes, Jutta (2003) *To Seek Out New Worlds: Exploring Links Between Science Fiction and World Politics*, New York: Palgrave.

Weldon, S. Laurel (2006) "Inclusion and Understanding: a collective methodology for feminist International Relations," in Ackerly, B.A., Stern, M., and True, J. (eds.), *Feminist Methodologies for International Relations*, Cambridge: Cambridge University Press.

Zalewski, Marysia (2006) "Distracted reflections on the production, narration, and refusal of feminist knowledge in international relations," in Ackerly, B.A., Stern, M., and True, J. (eds.), *Feminist Methodologies for International Relations*, Cambridge: Cambridge University Press.

1 Accidental scholarship and the myth of objectivity

Stephen Chan

When, in spring 2007, I was sent an email informing me that the Mountains of the Moon University sought a new Vice-Chancellor (or President), I was nostalgic for weeks. I didn't even know the Mountains of the Moon had a university. As it turned out, it was a young, small, private institution, but one that had already attracted a great deal of official Irish and Austrian aid; and its entire computer stock had been a gift from Liverpool Hope University in the UK. The civil war in the mountains had died down, and now was the time to begin building a bright new campus on land donated by the municipality. It would be an eco-campus and it would be full of optimism. I set about applying for the post and became, I think, the front runner – but I came to realize that nostalgia was not the best credential for a university being built on hope for the future.

The mountains are actually called the Ruwenzori Mountains – they were given the Moon tag by Victorian explorers – and they sit on the equator, on the borders of Uganda and the Democratic Republic of Congo. There is even a derelict ski lift on Mt Marguerita, a snow-covered peak in the heart of Africa. The current Ugandan president, Museveni, had mobilized his young soldiers in those mountains. It is said they were blessed by the magic light of the area. It is said that, during Amin's retreat from the advancing Tanzanian forces, his soldiers ate elephants in place of normal rations – and that the elephant nation had assembled and had marched in a long refugee column over the Mountains of the Moon to safety.

When Amin fell and the reconstruction of Uganda began, all the senior institutions and ministries were assigned to senior advisers and trainers. Two years on, part of the most junior (and derelict) of the ministries – Social Development and Culture – was thrust into my hands for its reconstruction. I was barely 33 but, even then, had become a veteran of Africa's woes and triumphs. Among many others, the Ugandan adventure was in between my early participation in the transition of Zimbabwe from Rhodesian rule to independence, and my somewhat later efforts to help ministerial and parliamentary development in post-Dergue Eritrea and Ethiopia. Somehow, looking back, all those major projects were something of a failure. Zimbabwe has slid into a catastrophic melt-down, Eritrea and Ethiopia went to war with each other, and Uganda has also begun its flirtation with authoritarian rule under the surface colours of democracy.

But the Ugandan adventure was enough at the time to convince me that the lies and deceits, false hopes and vacuous promises I had been required to spin as an international civil servant were not worth the moral asking price. Not that Uganda was a disaster to me – it was a triumph in many ways – but that the magic light got to me too, and I realized that when I came down from those mountains I could never be the same again. So I undertook to become an academic. Accidentally, there was a visiting fellowship at Oxford on offer and, after that, a lectureship at the University of Zambia. I wanted to write about the perfidies of international life, and about moral asking prices. When I left Uganda, I flew to Nairobi, took my first hot bath for quite some time, and resigned.

There was something else about asking prices too. I had seen my share of the effects of war in Zimbabwe, and would later see much more in Eritrea; there was something qualitatively different about Uganda. It wasn't that people were prepared to die while fighting – it was that so many of the ministerial officers with whom I was working had lived in dread of being "picked," that is led off to execution by Amin. Without having fought him or having the ability to fight for their own lives. This helpless dread was still a blanket over all of them, and I used to think about it when my academic colleagues, some time later, lectured on (and on) about moral choices, cosmopolitan values, and emancipatory theory. It's a pretty armchair discipline, this I had chosen to join. But innocent and naïve enough. And the spires of Oxford, the (then) beautiful bougainvillea-strewn campus of the University of Zambia, the green hill-top campus of Kent, even the incomplete and patchy landscaping at Nottingham Trent, and the jumbled oasis of Bloomsbury in the heart of London – they have all made the quarter of a century since I left official international life tolerable. And, even though I soon came to combine Deaning with scholarly production, I always found enough time to maintain several private practices – advising African governments, running philanthropic projects, defending asylum seekers in court, and playing the public intellectual within the unending greed of the media for talking heads and sound-bites (within a carefully calibrated hierarchy of who gets what slots on which programmes). And a fair swag of non-academic writing too. I think that my restlessness, my razor-cutting of my time, have the same roots as my ambivalence towards the value of academic work.

And to be fair to academic life, I would probably have felt this way no matter which profession I pursued. I was the first-born son of refugee parents and grew up in story-book poverty and, upon being sent to school without any English language (in the robust and physical company of young New Zealanders), learnt English in two weeks flat. From a very early age there was a need to over-achieve to compensate being a minority of one – and to rebel, to be tolerant in the face of racism (but remember), and to protest against almost everything else. When 1968 and 1969 coincided with my first years at university, I was the natural student leader and, even in New Zealand, protest marches had a habit of "engagement" with the police. When the prime minister libelled me, and got away with it because of parliamentary immunity, I left the country in 1976 and have lived in Britain or Africa ever since. There have been 19 changes of address in that time.

But New Zealand was also an impossibly beautiful place in which to grow up. The beach in the film, *The Piano*, was where I used to body-surf in my late teenage years and, aged 20, I made an "easy ride" to all the locations that later featured in *Lord of the Rings: Return of the King*, revelling in the sparseness and beauty of it all – and writing a lot of bad poetry about it, about politics, but mostly about the typical loves and laments of almost every young man. That was, however, the basic problem. You could do anything in New Zealand. By the time I had completed my MA, I had also been the national student president, a veteran of countless protests, a much published poet and playwright, a publisher and newspaper editor. These things mean little outside a small environment where, in fact, a few people must do much to service a small population that demands, all the same, the amenities and performances of a normal Western life. But it meant a culture shock when hitting England – with its work-to-rules, job demarcations, and professional jealousies.

I became most unpopular in the Commonwealth Secretariat, with its still large contingent of Britishers and, anyway, I got a lot of things wrong. When I sent up a note, as the Tanzanians were preparing to invade Amin's Uganda, stressing that the Tanzanians could not win – Amin had far more firepower – I mentioned not a word about morale, motivation, discipline, and officership. When the Rhodesian forces stormed the Zimbabwean rear base of Chimoio, I sent to the London representatives of the guerrillas an impossibly naïve and simplistic defensive system for the future. I learnt very quickly that book learning is one thing (I had completed a second MA at King's in War Studies) but, when you have no experience of blood and death, shut the fuck up.

And that is the key ambivalence. Should academics talk and write on a basis so textually bound and so ontologically naïve? What is produced means much to ongoing Western and, to an increasing degree, globalized debate on liberty – even if that meaning is terrifyingly mediated by the spin-doctors of those who rule (who take the trouble to learn multiple vocabularies of discourse) – and means very little to those who are impoverished and oppressed, and who die without literacy, but who might have died anyway making a futile last stand before the camel-riding militias come to slaughter their families. But that is the key difference in experiences: Horkheimer and Adorno, in their determination that the concentration camps should never be repeated, reflected the determination of a generation that had survived and *who could make record* of all they had undergone and all that had, throughout the future, to be avoided. As academics we depend on the record, the text; in the case of Others without text, we impute text to them or, in recording their oral histories, commit all manner of epistemological impositions (from our own texts) or impose ontological assumptions (based on our own experience) upon them. Hayden White's proposition of a *telos* in our writing is not so much applicable to ourselves – for the simple reason that we interrogate writing, its contexts and meanings, and compare contrasting projects of *telos*. Upon the Third World we impose our own *telos* of concern, but are unable to test our project against actually lived suffering and sorrow.

Coming into academia basically meant leaving one set of lies for another.

Why then spend a quarter century within academia? Why take the bother to become successful within it? It may have had something to do with an infant imprinting. There are photographs of me, very small, being taken by my parents to Albert Park in Auckland, New Zealand, and posed across the road from the imitation gothic tower that marked the university. They never plucked up the nerve to enter the campus. But they were determined that I would. But I was avaricious. When I finally did enter the campus to begin my studies I didn't want to read every book in the library, I wanted to own the Vice-Chancellor's office and its amazing blue New Zealand wool carpet. I wanted to run the university. Dr Colin Maiden, the Vice-Chancellor, wisely took my measure and seconded me to every committee possible; nurtured my participation, indeed tutored me – while advising my student political rivals on how to out-manoeuvre me. It was a wonderful and transparent (he never made a secret of it) upbringing in procedures and treacheries. I have suffered very few knives in my back because of Colin's tuition. And he gave me things to run. My first seven figure turnover was a responsibility within the university in 1971 or 72. I was 22, learning fast. But I think what I learnt most of all was that universities provide a platform for being a public intellectual. And that is how I have used them ever since coming down from the Mountains of the Moon.

In a way, going to the Vice-Chancellorship of the Mountains of the Moon University would have closed a lovely circle. It would also have meant – since I believe in poetic logics – the need to leave academia afterwards. But the offer came at precisely the time when the project of being a public intellectual was finally breaking through in terms of the hierarchies within the British media and their audiences. You have to learn various discourses and presentational forms of discourse. Even a sound-bite can be discursive. The spin-doctors know this. It can be learnt – even by academics. But you have to know what you're talking about – what you mean. You can't be an intellectual without being an academic. This may not be true of French society, but it is of English society and its snobberies. And its trans-Atlantic links. You need the academic research because so much of what academics have done, being courtiers and advising US administrations, is simply wrong. And, in England, there simply isn't an intellectual society outside the universities which is not corrupted by its own jealousies, professional tricks and rivalries, and myriad cliques. Academic life is like that too, but learning multiple discourses need not mean multiple immersions in different vexations. And snobberies: you need an acceptable base, academic standing. In Britain, at least in England, the class society has not disappeared – but it has certainly become more complexly variegated.

In some ways I pass as exotica, a curiosity. At least, unlike New Zealand, it's not because I'm Chinese. But there are different sorts of conformity. I remember at a recent formal function in the Lord Mayor of London's Mansion House, arriving in my "smoking," long hair combed back and pinned by an Alice band, and being seized by friendly hands for introduction to someone or another: "This is Stephen. He may *look* like an orchestra conductor, *but* ... " Ah, I thought, at last, an acceptable style for public consumption. I've been mistaken twice for Kent Nagano anyway, and I think it was a fair enough compliment by way of confusion.

This is to tell a story against myself, but also against the seductions of glamour on the peripheries of London society. There are thin and fragile lines. Sometimes it doesn't matter *what* you say. You get recognized because you are seen *saying* it. The trick is to get people *remembering* what you say, why it was said, and why it should continue to be said, and by more people. This is a lot of very hard work. And what I am saying is the same as I have said throughout the entire quarter century of academic life – in each one of 27 books and over 100 articles (yes, even in the cheap and nasty "quickies" I've churned out) – that the West (and the Western discipline of International Relations) does not understand the "international," and that a common ethics of globalization and global cooperation will always be impossible without understanding. And that means not only deeper studies of Other philosophies, cultures, religions, and languages, it also means the struggle towards a perhaps wordless empathetic engagement with the traumatized, oppressed, and hungry. It means, at least in part, a struggle away from the text and intertextual discourse. It means what Christine Sylvester first called for. She meant an empathetic engagement among women. I mean the same thing among all people. It means that International Relations scholars have got to put down Horkheimer and Adorno and spend time in the modern killing fields.

I was approached recently to advise a youngish financier. He works in Africa, raising the capital African magnates require for their projects. He's quite good at putting together the multiple millions, even billions required. He's lived some years in Mozambique, Angola, and Eritrea. He wears superb suits. He's a Masters graduate of the London Business School (the closest we have to a Harvard MBA), speaks fluent Portuguese and French as well as English, was a Captain in the British army sent out to train the Mozambican forces and transferred, at the age of 27, to a Brigadier's rank in the Mozambican forces themselves – and has a pan-African address book that took my breath away. And he knows more about the continent than most Africanist scholars I've met. It struck me, as I sent him politely on his way, that the "other side" are doing what we as scholars do not do, grudgingly do or, because of difficulties of funding, irregularly do. He may not have been much good at empathy (except with his very rich colleagues) but, by God, was he *engaged*. Oh, and he knew a few things about blood and death too. I want that sort of engagement, *with* empathy, on the part of all my academic colleagues. Then I would like them all to speak in the languages, if not of the world, then of the various forms of public media. Then, when everybody is doing what I am doing, and I am happily redundant, I shall go to the Mountains of the Moon, having redeemed my asking price, and never come back.

2 Objects among objects

Jenny Edkins

> I came into the world imbued with the will to find a meaning in things, my spirit filled with the desire to attain to the source of the world, and then I found that I was an object in the midst of other objects.
>
> (Franz Fanon, *Black Skin, White Masks*: 109)

When she died in 1989 at the age of 101, my grandmother left few possessions. She had lived since she was in her sixties in a room in my parents' various houses, so there wasn't much space for personal property. Her most treasured objects were in a small black wooden box, and most prized among them were a few photographs. Black and white, of course, and most of them formal portraits or wedding photographs mounted on thick card. Encouraged by her granddaughter she had written the names of those featured in the main family portrait: Lizzie, Father, Annie, John, Martha, Mother, and Mary. In my conversations with her, the photographs would often be shown as we talked about her childhood, her three mile walk over the moors to school, the times when she was sent to the pub to haul her father from his drinking and bring him home, and her work as a young girl in the Lancashire cotton mills. After her mother died, at the age of 48, the family moved to the seaside town of Lytham St Anne's. Mary also died relatively young, nursed by my grandmother through a long illness, and Martha died in childbirth. Annie married a Catholic, and bore four surviving children, one of whom is my godmother and still lives in Lytham where I was born, with her children and grandchildren. The only one of my grandmother's siblings I met was Uncle John, who lived in the Lancashire textile town of Accrington with his daughter Cicely until his death.

I never met either of my grandfathers. I have no memories of them, only photographs. The pictures of my maternal grandfather, Richard Smith, were among the most precious of the photographs carried by my grandmother through all the 30-odd years she lived with my parents, my brother, and me. As well as two portraits of Dick, as she called him, one full-face and one in semi profile, there was a photograph of him in a hospital bed in a field hospital at the front in the First World War. She also had his army papers. He served in the Lancashire Fusiliers for one year and 103 days, and was with the

British Expeditionary Force from 13 March to 20 October 1917. His papers show that he was discharged on 8 June 1918 no longer fit for war service. He had been gassed in the trenches, and never fully recovered. He came home of course, and he and my grandmother were married in 1920. By 1925 he was dead. During that period the family moved backward and forward between the industrial and shipping town of Salford, where Dick had worked before the war as a cotton packer, and Diggle, a village in Saddleworth on the Yorkshire moors a short distance away from the smoke of the city, which he could no longer tolerate. My mother was born in 1922 in Diggle, and she was just two and a half when her father died. My grandmother was not entitled to a war widow's pension – the couple had waited until after his discharge before they married. She moved back to Lytham, to live with her father in Holmfield Road, and took work where she could find it, mostly as a chambermaid in local hotels, I think. This type of work suited her circumstances, though not her sharp intellect. With a child to raise, she turned down opportunities for more responsibility in favour of being able to look after her daughter, and, eventually, her sister Annie's sons and daughters too.

Many of us these days have far more than a few treasured photographs. Behind me as I write is a large wooden trunk, much larger than my grandmother's box, full of unsorted family snapshots. Elsewhere in the house are several albums. Drawers in a filing cabinet are full of the overflow from the trunk, and on my hard drive hundreds more images are stored. If they had to rescue something in a house fire, most people would choose the family photographs, such is their value and importance. In my case that would be difficult: I could hardly gather up the whole trunk-full. I have been meaning for years to have a clear-out. But the reason I haven't done this is not just lack of time or motivation. I haven't put any photographs in albums since my father died, suddenly, 20-odd years ago. It seemed to me that if I looked at the photographs of him, I would somehow lose my memories of him as a physical, moving, solid being. And I wanted above all to retain those as long as I could.

What is most precious, and what is most lost when someone dies, is their physical presence: the smell of them, their flesh, the hairs on their arms, the look in their eyes. Even if – or, maybe, perhaps, especially if – the relationship was fraught and difficult. And it is hard that things – objects, furniture, jewelry, clothes, places – remain, mocking us with their indestructibility when compared with the frailty of flesh. I remember my father one time when he visited us – maybe even the last time – bringing a large suitcase up our narrow, winding stairs. I reached down to take the suitcase from him, and he was grateful. The stretch of his arm as he handed the suitcase to me, the look in his eyes – a touch of shame at his own weakness, and gratitude, even a pride in me – I still remember these. Another time I remember the huge strength of his concern – and the hug he gave me – as I was leaving for the hospital, in the advanced stages of labour with my second son. I remember thinking, "If you don't let me go soon, your grandson will be born *here* in this hallway."

A photograph is a strange thing, particularly a photograph of a person. On the one hand it is an object among other objects – to use Franz Fanon's phrase – and it circulates, changes hands, is reproduced, enlarged, cropped, captioned, displayed, filed in an album. On the other hand, it is very intimate, almost painfully so. If it is a portrait, and if the eyes look at the camera, then we have potentially the same feeling of intimacy of contact as when we meet someone's eyes face-to-face. They are looking at us as if we were the person in front of them – or the person behind the camera, the one taking the photograph. The illusion is amplified if, as I have done from time to time with old portraits where the negatives are long since lost, we take a photograph of the photograph. Looking through the lens as you focus carefully, it feels almost as though you are facing the original subject in person, there before you, summoned up like a ghost.

My father died on 1 February 1985. His time of death was recorded as 7.30 pm, I learned later, but he died in hospital, having suffered a massive heart attack. So I imagine that he had been subjected to several attempts at resuscitation. He began to feel ill at around 4.30 in the afternoon, on a visit to the supermarket in Henleaze. My mother spent time driving him (slowly, very slowly) from their house in Westbury-on-Trym to see the doctor in Shirehampton. They returned home, having seen or not seen the doctor, I don't know, but not having had any help. My father felt terrible – he didn't know whether to sit up or lie down, or what to do. He got rapidly worse, and they finally called the ambulance. My mother didn't go with him, though I think he was still conscious then. She remained in the house to look after my grandmother. Eventually she called a neighbour to granny-sit and followed the ambulance down to the Bristol Royal Infirmary, but she didn't see my father alive again I don't think. I was telephoned by my brother at about 7.45 pm. I remember most of all the conviction that I was in the wrong place: I had to go to Bristol. Nothing else mattered. I bundled my sons into their car seats (they were two and three years old and fast asleep) and we drove to Bristol at once – a two and a half hour journey. It's strange, the impact of a death. I must have been totally self-absorbed, because when we got to Bristol and my eldest son woke and asked eagerly "Where's Grandad?" I couldn't think what to say. I hadn't expected that question.

In my own mind, trying to think through the shock during the course of that long journey, three things became perfectly clear. Decisions that had been forming, to do with my future academic work, where we should live, and my own political activism, suddenly clarified themselves. It was not a question of being brought up short and making time to consider important issues generally put to one side – though there must surely have been some sense that priorities had changed – rather it was just that there was no longer any need to doubt. What I should do became plain, all by itself. There really wasn't a process of deciding. That was what was so striking about it. There is no slow motion version I can give, indeed there is no narrative time at all. I wanted to travel to Bristol "instantly". I mention the two and a half hours the journey must have taken, reminding myself perhaps that time did indeed elapse, but I suppose that in some sense I did transport myself from one place to the other in an instant, my body catching up with where my intention already was. And maybe the process of deciding took "time" – but it appeared to me to have been instantaneous.

My father's death confirmed me in my political convictions. The period 1984–85 was the time of the miner's strike, Prime Minister Margaret Thatcher's successful attempt to break the back of organized Trades Unionism in the UK once and for all and clear the way for privatization, de-regulation, and the move away from the welfare state. It was also a time of intensified Cold War antagonisms and a real concern about the possibility of nuclear war with a sharp escalation in the arms race. Cruise missiles were being installed in Europe, despite grassroots opposition. Greenham Common Women's Peace Camp had been established, and nuclear convoys were being tracked by protestors. The Ecology Party (later re-named the Green Party) had fielded 100 candidates in the 1983 General Election, including one in my own constituency, St Albans, and I had been active in the campaign. I was beginning to find my own way politically: prompted by the arrival of my two sons, politics suddenly seemed more important, activism a must.

My father had been an active supporter of the Liberal Party – and as a child I had delivered election leaflets with him – but I wasn't drawn in that direction. My own activism had been motivated in part by the recognition of the Green Party as my political home. I was sympathetic to its anti-nuclear, almost pacifist, stance. Economically it was left wing, and yet there was more: a belief in the local, the face-to-face, alongside a concern for the global, and a commitment to ecology – a deep ecology, involving an attitude and comportment towards the world as whole. And it confirmed me in my desire to escape Thatcherism. By then we had been contemplating for a while a move to Wales – to Aberystwyth in particular – as a way of leaving behind the sterile and heartless environment England seemed to be becoming under Thatcher. There was no such thing, she proclaimed, as "society": individual effort and ambition should be allowed free rein. Looking after each other was to encourage dependency, and social welfare was an invitation to the profligate poor to abnegate any sense of self-responsibility. Neo-liberal market economics was all. The state was to be "rolled back" – except of course that a strong state was essential in certain circumstances: the Falklands War being the prime example. Socialism, unionism, nationalized industry, these were "the enemy within". In contrast, Wales was still, it seemed to us, based on different, what we thought of as more "civilized" values of community and commitment. Culture, public service, and community responsibilities were still taken seriously. People in Wales did not move every few years, following their careers; families remained in the same broad locality for generations. The sense of reciprocity and the need to compromise that went with a more settled commitment to place made for a different approach to life. And poetry, literature, and art remained more central than money or possessions.

It also confirmed me in my decision to take a second undergraduate degree, a degree in the social sciences with the Open University. As a teenager trying, as I thought at that stage in my life was necessary, to find my place in the world, the only thing I knew was that I wanted to find "the source of the world", to use Fanon's words again. I had no idea how to go about it. As to what I was going to "do", what I was going to "be", I knew nothing of the possibilities of an academic life, and nothing about the options of studying sociology or politics. I knew, so I thought, that I didn't want to be a teacher like my parents: I could not see myself standing up in front of a class. The closest I could get to studying something that would feed my intellectual curiosity at that point seemed to be the natural sciences. To find the source of the world meant to engage with the big questions about life, the universe, and everything – and the natural sciences, as I had been taught them, certainly did that. By then, my choices were fairly limited anyway. My qualifications led neatly to degrees in mathematics or physics; I had been persuaded against studying English and history alongside physics at advanced level at school. It wouldn't fit the timetable, for one thing. For another, it didn't make sense in terms of university entrance requirements. My feeling that a broader, interdisciplinary approach would be more what I was interested in was not supported by the school. In the all-girls school I attended, it was taken for granted that a girl who could do science and maths should follow that track. It was also obvious to the school that anyone capable of it should be aiming for a place at Oxbridge, not at one of what were then the "new" universities like Sussex or Keele, where disciplinary boundaries were no longer sacrosanct and exploration and innovation were encouraged. And of course, it was good for the school's recruitment to be able to boast of the number of girls it sent on to Oxford and Cambridge. I did not have the self-confidence to make a stand on my own against these views, and there was no-one I could turn to with the experience to support me – and of course, to be regarded as capable of getting a place at a prestigious university was flattering too. So, bowing to the inevitable, I applied to Oxford to read for a physics degree.

I had a wonderful time at Oxford. I punted on the river Cherwell, partied, and latterly, and rather briefly, spent ten weeks in my final year studying in the libraries in preparation for my examinations. But almost as soon as I had started at St Anne's, I realized my mistake: physics was not for me. We were spending our time re-working the physics I had already been taught, and whereas my physics mistress at school had taken us through the subject by following the sense of curiosity and adventure generated by the puzzles posed by trying to grasp the world, at college we focused in our first year on the detailed mathematical expression of the solutions that had been posited. My friends were historians, philosophers, political theorists – that was what I should have been doing. They were the ones encountering interesting new ideas and challenging debates. And my other enthusiasm, first fostered by a perceptive English teacher at school and many years as a season ticket holder at the Bristol Old Vic, was in drama. At St Anne's, two of us set up a drama group in college and built a stage, and I played a series of parts in theatrical productions put on elsewhere. A change of course from physics to philosophy, politics, and economics, or even to psychology and philosophy, was not countenanced by the college authorities: what I wanted to do was too difficult a move to make within the time span of my three-year grant, and there was not the tutorial support necessary. I had to continue and complete my physics degree, which I did. I attended sessions on the history of science in a basement room filled with astrolabes, and incomprehensibly dense lectures on the philosophy of science by Rom Harré. I took copious notes in a mathematical language I can no longer understand in lectures on nuclear physics and solid state electronics.

In my final year, quite unexpectedly, I re-captured the interest in the subject that I thought I had lost. Suddenly we were no longer putting the mathematical underpinnings to ideas to which we had been introduced before, but rather reaching the boundaries of knowledge in nuclear, particle, and high energy physics. And what became apparent was the way in which knowledge was not what it was all about. No longer were we looking to find out what was happening in some world of which we were objective observers – objects looking at objects. Rather, we were attempting to think up pictures or models that would help us imagine what might be going on – and more than one picture seemed to be necessary. The world was not fathomable in one image. And, indeed, the world was not fathomable, full stop. It was not "out there", waiting to be "discovered": we were part of it and our observations as scientists changed the world we were observing. This was heady and exciting stuff, and my tutorial sessions in the eighteenth century rooms of Christchurch College were purposeful and invigorating. The insights from that time continue to inform my theoretical orientation now, in a way that studying philosophy and politics in a very traditional context would never have done.

It was many years later that I had the opportunity to make the change of course I had tried to make at Oxford. My eldest son had just been born, and I had been made redundant from my job shortly before his arrival. After several fruitless attempts to find a similar job elsewhere, I finally began to look at the possibility of returning to study. The Open University proved the ideal institution for this move. It admits anyone and everyone – no questions asked, no qualifications required – that's one part of what "Open" means. Its teaching is through course units sent out in the post, with complementary television broadcasts and radio programmes, monthly tutorial meetings held on Saturdays, and summer schools. It prides itself on being open in other ways too – to ideas of all kinds and to a range of teaching methods. It was the only option available logistically, since with young children there was no way I could get to any of the local universities, but it turned out that it could not have been more suited to what I wanted to do. I began with a foundation course in the social sciences – and immediately it was like coming home intellectually. This was where I had wanted to be. The teaching of Stuart Hall in particular was an absolute inspiration. Encountering Marxism for the first time was extraordinary: why had I not come across this before? Conversations suddenly made sense for the first time. It was amazing. And at that point I knew that I would like to carry on – to do research. I went to see a university counsellor about it at one of the summer schools. I told him what I was thinking, and, bless him, his response was "I don't see why not."

At the time of my father's death, this was in the future, though: I registered for my first Open University course in March 1985. We stayed in Bristol for a fortnight or so after his death, dealing with the bureaucracy, organizing the funeral, and trying to support my mother and explain what had happened to the children. The funeral service was well attended: my father's work as a head teacher hugely supportive of his students and staff and innovative in his approach was widely respected. But then came the bombshell. During one of the many quiet conversations that took place over those weeks, my mother mentioned, almost in passing, two things, both to me totally astonishing, that threw into turmoil the memories I thought I had of my small, contented, "normal" childhood. She told me that my father had been married before: my mother was his second wife. And she told me that his father – my grandfather – had disappeared, walked out on his wife and child, when my father was in his teens. None of this had I ever so much as suspected. I knew, or so I thought, that both my grandfathers were dead. Now it turned out that no one knew whether my father's father was alive or dead. I knew that my parents were very much in love, and their wedding photograph showed my mother looking young and beautiful in a dashing 1940s hat and dark dress. They had been married in a Registry Office, but of course it had never occurred to me that that was because as a divorcee my father couldn't remarry in a church. I had thought that it was just his beliefs – his atheism – that led them to avoid a church wedding. And I had arranged that my own wedding would be in a Registry Office too.

Nothing my father said on that occasion, or indeed any other, led me to suspect that he had more experience of marriage as an institution than I thought. Whole areas of my childhood, and whole undercurrents of the shame and secrecy that divorce entailed in those days, had been hidden from me – or, rather, not so much hidden, since I never thought that anything was mysterious or concealed, but just not known about. Children are logical beings, and they opt for the straightforward: they do not question what seems obvious. My mother's quiet sessions in the bedroom sorting pennies into sections of a small blue cash box to try to stretch the weekly housekeeping were not just because my father's pay as a head teacher was low, but that he had to send regular payments to his ex-wife; my father's locked metal box kept under the bed wasn't just because he was well-organized and tidy: this was where the documents relating to the divorce and the maintenance payments were kept; his lack of a university education was not through choice, but because his father had refused to support him; their move to Bristol from Lytham when my father got his first teaching job was not just a preference for the West Country over the North, where they were both from, but in part to escape contact with his former wife; and an absence in my childhood world of my parents entertaining friends and family and visiting relations in Lytham was not just because they were both only children: the reticence and diffidence it reflected could be traced in part to their situation.

This is how, eventually, I came to have a photograph of my paternal grandfather. Faced with the news that no one knew what had become of him, I set out to find out. There was a blind spot in my childhood – in my sense of self – and I wanted to fill it in. My grandfather could not be allowed to just disappear. My father had made no attempt to trace him: he had been a violent husband, and my father's young life had been spent protecting his mother from that violence. But I needed to know more. How could I understand my father and his all too violent concern for me if I did not know more of his father? It was not difficult to trace him, the missing grandfather. Absurd in a way, since we seem to spend all our lives trying to piece together traces of people we are close to in the hope of finding out who they – and we – are. Searches of the Register of Deaths in Somerset House showed that he had died when I was 12. I managed to trace more of the family history – motivated now by all the questions I had failed to ask as a child, I combed the records for all branches of the family, on my mother's side as well, but in particular I traced those who had registered my grandfather's death. It turned out that he had gone back to his relations from Worcestershire, by then living in Birmingham. Finally, I tracked down the current phone number of a second cousin, who confirmed that he had known my grandfather in his later years, and who sent me a copy of a family photograph. There was more – hints of a bigamous relationship and further children. I was offered the phone number of another cousin who would be able to tell me more. But there my curiosity ended. I'm not sure why. Maybe my seemingly endless trawling through the records was a little too disembodied: I could face the intellectual challenge of piecing together the fragments of family history from the archives. What I couldn't face was the prospect of an actual, physical encounter. I visited my grandfather's grave in Birmingham, and left flowers, alongside flowers left by someone else: I was not the only visitor to his grave. And I filed the photograph. I'm not sure it meant that much to me in the end. I wonder now why I had never asked before – at home, as a child – to see his photograph. Of course, there was no such photograph, but I do wonder what would have been the outcome had I asked the question and been told the answer, before my father's death.

Family photographs are brutally torn from their context and displayed for all to gaze on when tragedy strikes. When someone is missing, or when they are the victim of a crime, a family snapshot will be reproduced in newspapers or on missing person posters – or, in the case of children missing in the United States in the past, on milk cartons. If the disappearance is part of a larger scale catastrophe – the collapse of the World Trade Center in New York in 2001, or the Asian tsunami of 2004, for example – the images will be displayed alongside those of other people's missing friends and relations. When large-scale disappearances are orchestrated by a tyrannical regime, blown-up pictures of those abducted and tortured are held aloft by people protesting against the disappearances in demonstrations and marches.

Often genocidal regimes will document their practices, strangely enough, by photographing those they incarcerate or kill as part of the bureaucracy of genocide. Such was the case in Pol Pot's Cambodia and in Nazi Germany for example. Even in liberal democracies, the mug shot has its function in recording suspects and criminals as well as controlling populations and their movements more generally through ID cards, passports, and other documents. And when photography first became available it provided a means for administrators to record the features of different groups of people (the poor or the deviant, for example), a technique soon taken up by anthropologists and travellers keen to capture the images of exotic peoples.

I am working at the moment on a book entitled *Missing Persons*. I thought I was working on a book about the portrait photograph, but the motif of the missing kept returning to haunt and distort that book. It was only belatedly that it occurred to me that I had a personal reason for my interest in this area, albeit in a very attenuated way. Most of those "missing" whose stories I examine or will examine in the book are heartbreaking and traumatic in a way my own most definitely is not: I look at the missing in New York after September 11, and in London in the aftermath of the July 2005 bombings, and in Argentina. The first two are difficult enough, but in the case of the missing in Argentina (and other countries in Latin America), not only were people "disappeared", but this happened in a context of fear, denial, and silencing that made the suffering of those searching for relatives much worse. It is only now, some 20 years later, that many of the most difficult stories are beginning to emerge: stories for example of the children of the missing who were seized by those who had abducted their parents and adopted by families connected to or involved in the military regimes. It is only now that some of them have discovered their "origins" and been re-united with their surviving blood relatives.

There is another way, of course, of thinking about our abiding interest in what I have just described as the heartbreaking and the traumatic. Our conversations, as well as our newspapers and news broadcasts, are full of tales of dreadful or even devastating events that happen to others. As I have argued in my other writing, events we call traumatic provide an opening for us to pry open the systems of oppression and depersonalization that we live under – that we produce and reproduce for ourselves of course: no-one else is there to take responsibility. It is probably a mistake to highlight the dramatic and the overwhelming, though: trauma is not absent from everyday exploitation. It is perhaps at the everyday level that it is most amenable to challenge, and at this level that finding a different way is most important. One of the most interesting aspects of the aftermath of the bombings in London a couple of years ago was the way in which people helped each other. While regulations prevented the emergency services from attending the scene of the events until it could be confirmed that there was no further danger of explosions or risk of biological or chemical contamination, the people on the trains, and the train drivers, stayed with the injured, talking to them and helping where they could. We are encouraged to leave response to the emergency services, and accused of "rubber-necking" when we don't, but it seems that the capacity to respond – person-to-person – remains.

It has taken a long time, surprisingly enough, for me to realize that an abiding concern in all my research from the start has been the question of the instrumentalization or commodification of life. And it has taken perceptive friends to point this out to me. In my doctoral thesis, this concern with the instrumentalization of life was expressed through the term "technologization". In my discussion of famine, I argued that technical solutions to famine missed the point: to adopt a technical solution was to conceal the way that famines often arise through deliberate actions or inactions of people who are aware of what this will lead to. Famines are not so much a failure of a social or economic system, but rather its product – in some sense, they are a sign of its success. They are in large part the outcome of a system that enables the private ownership of the means of subsistence; people starve because they are dispossessed of the earth, if you like, not because of some natural calamity. And in a large part the aid that is offered to famine "victims" compounds the error: people are treated as what philosopher Giorgio Agamben has aptly called "bare life". Their lives are "saved", but nothing is done to enable them to re-instate the way of life that was theirs before exploitation or brute force deprived them of it. They have no voice in the way in which they are helped; they are assumed to be helpless and apolitical. We judge what is best for them.

A similar approach is found in the treatment today of "victims" of what we call terrorist attacks. There is no doubt of course that as far as those who carry out the attacks are concerned, for the most part at least, it does not matter who precisely is injured or killed in the attack. More often than not it does not even matter what nationality, religious affiliation, or class the victims might belong to. This disregard for the particularities of personhood is repeated by the authorities who deal with the aftermath of such attacks. We find, for example, to return to the London bombings, that many if not all victims were treated as potential perpetrators – assumed guilty until proven innocent – and relatives and friends were deliberately kept in the dark about the fate of those missing for days on end despite the obvious distress this caused. In New York, victims of the Trade Center attacks were co-opted into the Bush administration's campaign of vengeance and retribution against Afghanistan, and later Iraq. Their consent, or the consent of their families to this use of their names – to their invocation as heroes who sacrificed their lives for the nation in the newly declared war on terror – was not sought. They were treated not as persons with diverse political views but as lives lost, lives belonging to the nation-state.

Treatment of persons in this way – as objects – makes me angry, and motivates me to examine the system of social and political relations of which this treatment is a part. I am angry on behalf of my grandmother, whose life was constrained by her treatment – and that of her husband – as objects to be disposed of or used. I am angry on behalf of my father, whose childhood and later life were restrained by the way in which he was unable to admit to who he was. But both of them tried to find another way, and to some degree they both succeeded. My grandmother made a life for herself that had its own integrity and purpose. She didn't give up on her commitment to my grandfather, and she adapted, and flourished, in whatever situation she found herself. She didn't compromise on her strength or her independence. My father devoted himself to his students. He once described his work with children with what these days are called learning difficulties as an attempt to discover, as one might with a machine, what had gone wrong and hence how to put it right. But his work belied this approach. Throughout my childhood, his pupils would call him at home to seek help – they would come round to the house, and he would go to them. He insisted that the system be adaptable, and fought against regulations that prevented him from doing what he thought would be best for each person. And every Christmas, he would carefully choose and wrap individual presents for each of his staff. His funeral was testament to the regard in which he was held – as a person.

It is no longer my aim, as it once was, to seek the origin of the world. The desire that motivates my work now is a desire to contest the way in which people become objects among other objects. At the end of *Black Skin, White Masks*, Fanon (1986: 231) remarks that he wants:

> only this: That the tool never possess the man. That the enslavement of man by man cease forever. That is, of one by another ... Why not the quite simple attempt to touch the other, to feel the other, to explain the other to myself?

In Marx's analysis of alienation, Foucault's description of disciplinary practices and technologization and Derrida's call for a justice beyond the law, a justice answerable to the absolutely other, we find a series of ways of approaching this question. In my work at the moment I am approaching it through an analysis of the way in which "personhood" as such is missing in today's politics. For me injustice lies in the objectification of human lives – the treatment of people by each other as nothing more than identical figures in a population that is to be administered or made secure, a treatment sometimes so rule-bound and heartless that it has no space for exceptions, for difference, for concessions, for understanding and, importantly, for the acknowledgement of the impossibility of ever fully understanding.

It is this impossibility of full understanding that is perhaps most important here. As my friend and co-author Véronique Pin-Fat often reminds me, the person as such must and always does remain missing. In the process of attempting to write this account of how my intellectual pursuits might relate to my life more broadly – to draw back some of the veils that we normally, as academics, draw over such things – something has changed. Prompted by Naeem Inayatullah, my extraordinary editor, to delve more and more into aspects that I wanted to move past quickly, I have come to understand my own motivations and limitations more closely. However, I still do not in any sense fully grasp what I am about, or who I am; in any case, as my student Marie Suetsugu relates in her doctoral thesis – itself an attempt to transgress the boundaries between the academic and the personal – in telling an autobiographical story we are necessarily concealing as well as revealing. In the Lacanian sense I suppose, the veils do not conceal anything but the fact that behind the veils there is nothing: the person is missing. As I write this, it seems that a more modest motivation than that I identified just now is appropriate: not the desire to somehow achieve a world where the tool never possesses the man, but rather what Fanon describes, maybe somewhat disingenuously, as the "quite simple attempt" on an everyday level, to make time for the endeavour to attend to and to open to the "other" – and the other within the self – alongside an appreciation, and a willing assumption, of the impossibility of ever succeeding. The anger dissipates, to give place to, or, more appropriately perhaps, to give birth to, a more tempered and more careful sensibility.

A few days ago, my mother showed me a letter, written to her by my father shortly after my brother had been born. My brother was premature, and initially not expected to survive. The letter was touching, full of my father's love for his wife and his six year old daughter – he was looking after me alone, presumably for the first time, and had just tucked me up in bed – and hope for his new son. He spoke of his plans for the future, for the move back to Bristol from Darlington that the family was about to make, how sometimes he felt he wanted to push things on, while at others he thought he should let them take their course. He wondered how things would turn out.

The letter showed me a father I had hardly known: reflective, emotional, full of feeling. It also showed him as an intellectual: I remembered the books, few in number, but challenging and wide-ranging, on his shelves. He had been too diffident to parade his intellect at home. I am my father's daughter, nothing more, despite any feeling of having made my own route in the world. And, possibly, hopefully, I am my father's daughter in other ways too. That's how things have turned out, in one small area at least.

References

Fanon, Frantz (1986) *Black Skin, White Masks*, translated by Charles Lam Markman, London: Pluto.

3 Stammers between silence and speech[1]

Narendran Kumarakulasingam

> The enemy of silence is speech, but there can be no speech without words, and there can be no words without meanings – so it follows, inexorably, in the manner of syllogisms, that when we try to speak of events of which we do not know the meaning, we must lose ourselves in the silence that lies in the gap between words and the world. This is a silence that is proof against any conceivable act of scorn or courage; it lies beyond defiance – for what means have we to defy the mere absence of meaning?
>
> (Amitav Ghosh, *The Shadow Lines*: 214)

This piece is late. By almost two years. Ostensibly I have been busy, but that is not the real reason. Rather, I am hesitant. I am afraid. I am wary. I am suspicious. I am not entirely sure of the object of my fears, suspicions, wariness, and hesitancy. I am not sure why it is that these conditions afflict me. But they are there, willing me not to write. So great is their force that sometimes I liken finishing this piece to a giant exorcism.

The doubts and fears that make it difficult to write this piece are very different from those that accompany the kind of writing that I am trained to do as an acolyte in the discipline of International Relations (IR), and of contemporary American social science. *Those* doubts concern whether I am sufficiently and faithfully reproducing a certain genre, a certain plotline. A genre that goes beyond which particular methods or theoretical frameworks I use. *Those* doubts center on how well I am constructing the problem, whether I have consulted the appropriate literature, and of course, whether I have been rigorous enough in my methods. I have until now had a sense of dissatisfaction about the ways in which I have proceeded with that endeavor. It seemed to be a rather mechanical task: find problem, contort problem into a paradox that then begs for a particular theoretical approach, set up three schools of thought as literature review, introduce particular framework, apply methods, predictably solve problem.

Part of my fear comes from having to write without this map. I have no control. There is no predictability. There are no rules on what I should do. There are no signposts indicating how to proceed. And most importantly, no safe separation between object and subject. I turn to the editor who refuses to provide the comfort of guidelines, except for a "helpful" suggestion about word length.

Let me be clear. I am not clear about the precise reasons for embarking on this journey, or its destination. Fear, hesitancy, suspicion, wariness, and now resentment are the cargo onboard. The only life jacket aboard, and this is what allows me to cut the moorings, is this thought: if I am a social being, then there must other ships carrying similar cargo. And if there are other ships at sea, then my burdens are not my burdens alone, but shared. Moreover, while I may not be clear as to where I am heading, I already know that I cannot remain at port any longer. I cannot ignore the stormy waters of the deep sea anymore. The shallowness of the sailors at port alternatively infuriates and bores me. These sailors do not speak of being battered by stormy waves not of their making. They do not speak of uncharted, deep waters. They do not speak of the possibilities of dangerous currents and eddies. To them, the possibility of distant dangerous seas does not exist. If it does, it is not something to be acknowledged.

The words, concepts, and theories of disciplinary IR are inadequate for my purposes. They map the shallow waters around port but cannot and refuse to acknowledge deeper waters. Yet, these words are the ones readily at my disposal. The long, hard years of apprenticeship seem to have ironically paid off. Even as I recognize the inadequacy of much of this language that I have mastered, I realize that I don't have an alternative that can even provide a glimpse of the stormy waters, let alone navigate them. I fear that my writing in this essay will be no more than stammers. Stammers that do not add up.

Fighting history

The first time I ever fought in the school yard, I lost before I could even put up my fists. I was in the second grade and the year was 1981. Cricket was the game of choice and there was always 15 minutes before school started that could not be, and never were, wasted. One of my classmates hit the ball very far away and I went to get it. Someone standing in the vicinity got to it first. Jayantha was in another class in second grade and we were on the swim team together. Our mothers knew each other from the PTA. I put my hand out expecting him to hand me the rubber ball that we had pooled money to purchase from the old woman just beyond the school gate who satisfied our demands for sweets, gum, raw mangoes, marbles, and sometimes rubber balls. J didn't toss me the ball. He picked it up, and deliberately threw it as far as he could in the opposite direction and taunted, "Para Demala" (glossed as low class, outsider Tamil. The venom of course I can only hint at). I stood there. A part of me knew that this was sufficient provocation for me to bunch my fists. But I didn't, for another part of me knew that it was futile. I had already lost when he uttered those words because there was no symmetrical comeback available to me. His words had the power of official Sri Lankanist history and archaeology behind them. His words made me an outsider, a usurper; they made him a son of the soil. The power of this history made me an outsider within my home. My fists were no match for this history. At that time, I was unaware that some Tamils had challenged the Jayanthas of Sri Lanka with their own version of history. Historically speaking, they said, Sri Lanka was a colonial concoction. The north and east of the island had been, and therefore was, Tamil territory. And, in order to be home, they would go on to expel the Muslims. For the Sinhalese to be home, the Tamils had to be made homeless. For the Tamils to be home, the Muslims had to be made homeless. Madness! How did we Sinhalese and Tamils become so proficient in this bloody language of history that demands that the other be made homeless in order for the self to be home?

My second school yard fight was much more physically serious but again had to do with my ethnicity. I was in my teens. The venue was again the same playground, although this time the incident occurred at the opposite end of it. Playing at the opposite end meant that we could use the trees that surrounded one part of the ground as a wicket for our daily cricket games. This time the fight occurred during intermission and my antagonist was Silva. Not only was Silva younger, but he was also far below me in the hierarchy that was the school tennis team. The ball was batted towards where Silva was and I went to chase it. As I went to get it, Silva picked up the ball and threw it away from me instead of to me. I gave him a piece of my mind. I do not remember what I said, but I do remember being very surprised at the reaction it evoked: he started crying and ran off. I was a little puzzled but didn't think much of it. A few overs later, he returned, accompanied by his brother, a year older than me, and a number of his brother's friends. My heart sank as I saw them. I recognized some of them as school toughs who had forged a reputation by virtue of their physically intimidating other groups of boys in school. Moreover, some of them, it was rumored, had connections to the Sri Lankan military and to underworld characters. I had no possible exit and I was bracing for the worst when my classmates came to my defense. Pillai stood out on account of his being a lot bigger and stronger than others in our grade, and on the basis of his prowess on the rugby field somehow got into a physical altercation with someone from the other side at the edges of the confrontation. In pummeling his opponent, he not only violated hierarchies of age and ethnicity, but also pierced the veil of fear that was so central to the power of school toughs. It was unheard of for boys in younger grades to stand up to those in older grades. Not only that, but his actions did not conform to the script of the Tamil who was supposed to know his place. Next thing we knew, there were three or four of the toughs wailing at him. Unable to bear this any longer, Anandan, whose melodious voice often entertained us, picked up a bat and hammered one of the assailants. The bell had already rung. Soon we were separated by a school teacher. He was well known for his dislike of Tamil students and he disliked our class in particular. It was certainly not our lucky day. It was Sunil, a young teacher, who was unpopular with many students. We used to ridicule him behind his back for his extra-curricular interest in one of the married, younger Tamil teachers who taught us. An interest that was as uncomfortable to her, as it was entertaining to us. We were witnesses to his discomfort and failure with regard to Ms. Ganesh. He asked us some peremptory questions and then promptly slapped Pillai. We were admonished for the altercation. Our antagonists went off without questioning.

Given what was to follow, getting slapped for a fight we didn't start was a piece of cake. Soon, word was sent around to our class, saying that we had better be prepared for what was coming. Rumor had it that one of our antagonists had broken his back and had been taken to hospital. Over the course of the day, students kept walking to and fro, outside of our classroom reminding us that our safety was guaranteed only until the end of the school day. The incident had spread like wildfire and we were subsequently summoned to the vice-principal's office. He let us know that the school didn't tolerate either fisticuffs or communalism within its walls. He was from another generation, a generation to whom what was happening all around was alien and unfathomable. An institution in the school, he was known for his fair play, sense of dedication, and he embodied the best that the school had to offer: civic virtue, unbending loyalty to the school, gentleness, and self-sacrifice. Yet, it was clear from the way he dealt with us, that he understood that he was fighting a losing battle. He spoke in a tired voice and told us that there was no place for "this sort of thing" within school walls. He was an anomaly, a rapidly disappearing species, a product of an Anglicized secular culture that was unable to respond effectively to the rise of what he would have called communalism or sectionalism. For him, the problem was not so much the bloody language of history that was being "spoken" by our adolescent bodies. Instead, the problem was our allegiance to what he would have called "communal" identities. For him we were, and should be, "Sri Lankans," not "Sinhalese" and "Tamils." It is a wonder that he could think of Sri Lanka as if it were a tabula rasa that could be inhabited by proper Sri Lankans once Sinhalese, Tamils, and others forgot their identities, memories, and histories.

The rest of that day passed in a blur. Classes were dismissed early. Our teachers were worried for our safety, and concerned that the issue would spiral. Even though no one spoke of it, everyone knew that they were worried that the fight might escalate into a larger assault on Tamils. No one spoke of the massive attacks on Tamils that had occurred three years before that in 1983 – but we were all acutely conscious of it. We were told to leave school ten minutes before the end of the day, so that we could get home safely. The next few days were unbearable. We lived in fear of imminent physical assault every time we came to school. In order to minimize the chances of being attacked, we came to school well before classes began and left either before school ended or later in the evening.

The tension ended when Pillai, my friend who had stood up for me, decided that the status quo was unbearable. Through some mutual acquaintances,

Pillai had offered an olive branch and an apology. The hierarchy was restored, albeit, not exactly the way it had been. Pillai was now considered a friend of sorts by our erstwhile antagonists. They grudgingly admired his standing up to them. What had happened was considered forgotten. Many of them ignored us. A few even acknowledged us. Somehow the distance between us and them had lessened, even if only a little. Later, they would even try to recruit Pillai to go with them when a huge fight with boys from another school would arise. The language of history, it is worth remembering, is not all powerful. It can be and is subverted and deflected by other "languages" such as those of adolescent masculinity and (misplaced) school pride.

Talking violence

In 2005, I was at the annual international studies conference in an island paradise presenting what amounted to a first cut of field research. I had spent ten months in another island paradise trying to understand how people coped with and remembered a momentous "ethnic riot" that had occurred there in July 1983. The conference panel was held in a hotel meeting room. The room was small and the audience smaller. But it was still too large for me. How was I to tell them that what I had found in the field did not make sense; that I had not found any meaningful patterns in the data about who had been attacked or who had been the attackers; that all I had found out was that people had had to jump over neighbors' walls and run for their lives with nothing but the clothes on their backs. They had to hide under a neighbor's bed knowing that their home next door and everything else they worked all their life for, was being burned to the ground. Hoping that no one would find them. That they can still smell the smoke. That people did not want to talk about it. "What is there to tell?" they would ask, more to themselves than to me. And how could I blame them when I had no answer to the question they would invariably ask me: "Why do you want to know?"

All I had gathered in the field was loss, uncertainty, fear, and silence. All of this augmented by my inability to listen, to understand that this was the story. Seduced by theory, I failed to acknowledge, understand, the shattering reality that is mass violence. Yet somewhere deep within myself, despite my seduction by master theory, I must have known. For, I have been and remain tentative about probing the depths of those dark days when certainty was shattered and reality was nothing more than a contingency.

How could I tell an audience that seemingly expected problem, theory, argument, and significance, that I did not know anymore what the problem was? But the issue was not the audience, it was my own expectations. I too wanted to narrate *the* Story. All I had was a jumble of many stories that did not come together. I suppose I could have written a story. I could have stilled the senselessness and the strangeness of what I had encountered and somehow mastered it with concept, theory, and prose. After all that is what my tribe does, and this was just another step in a long initiation ceremony.

Yet, somehow an undercurrent of senselessness had insinuated itself. Become a part of me.

I knew that I was in trouble. But I had no way out. What I was saying, was not what I wanted to say. And what I wanted to say was not what I was saying. I wanted to do both and neither. It did not make for a listener-friendly presentation. But things got worse. The discussant for some reason didn't play by the rules. Clearly a heretic. There was no theoretical critique. No questions about methods, about literature, about findings. Instead, he grilled me about why I was doing what I was doing. Somehow, I don't remember how, but the conversation took a dangerous turn. Now the questions were about what I remembered. What had happened to me? We were on biographical terrain. Had I not learned the disciplinary acumen to head off the line of the questioning onto safer ground? Or did I simply not resist? The safe distance between subject and object was collapsing. Or, was it that I was now the object?

The room was hot and the back of my neck was wet with sweat. Words failed me. I tried to provide "context." The kind that comes in a book under a chapter called historical background. That alchemy that controls difference and disorder so that the familiar plotline can be rehearsed once again. But my interrogator and audience were not satisfied. They wanted more. My fumbling attempts at providing context were not good enough. I tried desperately to think a theory that would explain it. Something. Anything to cover the hole that was all there was. Didn't they understand? Or did they? I never had the courage to find out what people thought of that moment, of the kind that we work so assiduously to avoid in our encounters.

But it is not frustration alone that lingers from that encounter, in that other island paradise. It is a vague sense of shame. I surmise that my fumbling, lack of memory, my silence says all. The audience is astute. My shame at being rendered into an object is compounded by the response that it must have evoked in the subject, pity. A knowing pity. The color of my skin, my name, and now my confession that I had been there when it happened must have made sense. Ahhh, they must have thought, he was victimized by communal violence and so he studies it.

Pity. That look of concern and knowing. Pity, a truly pitiful gesture indeed. A chasm wider and deeper than any ocean. A response that maintains the hierarchy between the pitier and the pitied and safety of the former.

Today, I would have blurted, argued, hectored, screamed: "Violence fractures theory ... It bends, distorts, breaks ... your/my theory." And even that would be insufficient, for even while saying it, I realize I am defeated. It is not a theoretical argument. It is a scream to the insufficiency of language, to the arrogance of social science, to the pity of the deaf and the blind. It is reality slipping loose of the deadly embrace of theory. Reality screaming in a voice that comes out of my throat, but is barely recognizable to me. "I cannot explain it. I can only respond to it. You cannot understand it or even acknowledge it." Screams that are revelatory to some. But perhaps nothing more than incoherence to you. And in our failed encounter, we faithfully reproduce the autism that is much of our academic encounters.

But that day in paradise, while I was victim, while I was object, I was also the master. I was complicit in the arrogance of trying to master violence. In trying to tame reality. In thinking that the strokes of my keyboard and the words of my mouth could and would somehow perform that sleight of hand through which Idea/Theory/Concept subsumes world, and domesticates it. Or tries.

Encountering terror

In 2004, Sri Lanka was in the midst of a cease fire between the government and the Liberation Tigers of Tamil Eelam. After more than 20 years of a most uncivil war, people in Colombo were able to go about their daily lives without the fear of military checkpoints, suicide bombings, and police search operations. Many hailed the reemergence of peace in the country and optimistically looked forward towards the future. However, peace appeared not to have made it to Batticaloa, situated on the east coast of Sri Lanka, about 175 miles or so from Colombo. News of assassinations, a volatile split within the LTTE, and abductions of children suggested another reality, one far from the one I was used to as I did my fieldwork.

In May, a fellow researcher asked me if I was interested in joining her and a few other people in a trip to Batticaloa. They were interested, she said, in finding for themselves what the situation was like in Batticaloa. As news of the proposed trip spread among other researchers and civil society activists, it was clear that a few opposed the plan. "Do you want yours to be another voyeuristic trip?" one asked. Another voyeuristic trip into the war zone to gawk at fearful faces, pockmarked buildings. Was I to become one of those people? The consumer-tourist-academic-NGOers who parley such trips into little more than career stepping stones. Just another interesting object, like a shiny marble to a child, holding one's fancy until something more interesting came up.

The purpose of the trip, I was told, was to find out what was happening in Batticaloa and to register solidarity with the silent. To say to our fellow citizens in Batticaloa that the prospect of peace had not seduced us into forgetting them. I was ambivalent about my participation. On the one hand, I was curious to see what was going on in Batticaloa with my own eyes. I thought that going there would provide me with clarity about events there. About who exactly was killing whom and why. On the other hand, I could not easily dismiss the concerns of those who brought up the critique of voyeurism and careerism. Moreover, another part of me was uneasy. I had no idea about the motivations of those going. What was I getting into, I wondered.

As we traveled in a van towards Batticaloa, I got to know some of the other people and I was drawn by their energy, commitment, and experiences. I was especially conscious of a sense of resoluteness among some of them, a resoluteness that I certainly did not possess. There was S, who was driven out of her home in the north overnight and was now officially a displaced person. She was told to get out as there as was no place for a Muslim in the Tamil homeland. A Tamil homeland for which the liberators were fighting because the Sinhala homeland could not be home to Tamils. What a world! Making the other homeless seems to be a sine qua non for the self to be home in the world. If S had been exiled because she was prevented from being home, M was self-exiled after being seen as a traitor to the cause of Tamil liberation. Brought up in the heyday of Tamil nationalist politics, she like many others had begun questioning the increasingly arbitrarily violent nature of the quest for liberating the homeland. Despite, or perhaps because of their exile, both S and M exuded a firm resolve in solidarity with those in the midst of the war zone that was Batticaloa.

Our arrival in Batticaloa coincided with the news of yet another assassination – this one of a journalist, who I would later learn was distantly related to me. No one knew exactly which group had perpetrated the killing, but rumor had it that it had been carried out by those who had liberated themselves from the liberators just a little while ago. The rumor was that he had been killed on account of being critical of Tamil paramilitary groups allied with the government. My unease turned to fear when we were in Batticaloa. It was not that there was complete chaos in Batticaloa. Instead it was rather quiet. I got the feeling that there was an unseen eye watching our every movement. What multiplied my fear was the realization that I did not know who the watching eye was. Was it the State? Was it those who sought liberation from the State? Or was it those who sought liberation from those who sought liberation from the State? Or was it those who had formally sought liberation from the state but now were part of the State?

Batticaloa was at war but there were no clearly discernible combatants or sides. There had been and continued to be abductions, assassinations, and disappearances. Yet no one knew who precisely was behind what. Moreover, no one wanted to know, for doing so would have meant jeopardizing oneself and one's family. No one was sure who to trust in that sinister atmosphere and surviving entailed seeing, hearing, and speaking nothing. We ourselves would experience a momentary sense of utter panic when we saw unmarked vehicles pull up to the entrance of where we were lodging late one night. Were we going to be abducted? some of us wondered. After a sleepless night, we learned the next morning that some men had come around asking our hosts who we were and what we were doing in the area. Luckily for us, our hosts had reassured the men that we were a university group engaged in some university work.

Our group would write of the visit that the East was occupied:

> Occupation buys your willingness to live under the most difficult conditions: Occupation is about consenting to violence. Occupation allows one to be spoken for and spoken to. Occupation means one does not hear or

talk about the violent death of a friend, the trauma of a brother/father/mother ... Occupation means: "we do not know who killed X. We do not ask. It is not our concern."

(Collective for Batticaloa, 2004)

All true but there is more. In the heart of the homeland, the nation, the state, the liberators, the forces of law and order, the terrorists, they all cannibalize its children; tear parents from their offspring, brutalize brothers and sisters and sunder all social connectivity. In the name of security, a soldier burns a cigarette butt on a woman's breasts as his younger brother watches wide-eyed. In the name of the nation, a mother is calmly told that a mother's love is an unwelcome interloper in the cultivation of the love for the motherland. Yesterday's child combatant, today's temporarily liberated, tomorrow's abductee sits in silence suspended between camp and home, abduction and liberation, motherland and mother. There is only empty space between her silence and ours. We have nothing to offer. "Please take me out," a child pleads. Promises and evasions are all we can offer. How to tell her that she is today's "wretched of the earth." Not counted. Not acknowledged. Not remembered. Just avoided, or if we are lucky, never encountered. A (hopefully) momentary irritation in our otherwise busy lives, as we rush to feed family, buy homes, build careers, get tenure, and soullessly tame violence with the alchemy that is theory/method/epistemology.

The east was occupied for sure. That I knew. What I didn't know was that I too would be occupied. After the trip, our group tried to meet a few times, but it was clear that not everyone's heart was in it. I found myself wanting to avoid the people with whom I had toured the east. We never spoke of what really had happened to us. Never acknowledged it. Never talked about it. Through my silence, my atomization, I had become part of the occupation of the east. I had become a part of the silencing of fear and terror. The east was no longer there. It is here, there, everywhere. Even as I spoke of critical IR, of violence, of terror, of fear, I occupied the east. I had become the occupier. The master. Taming reality through high (but critical mind you) theory. Taming fear, terror, uncertainty, violence even as they lodge themselves in my veins. Afraid to acknowledge that I was afraid. Afraid to acknowledge that I was object. Unwilling to acknowledge that I was trying to be master Subject.

Concluding remarks

There is no heroic ending, although I am aware that our dominant cultural sensibility demands one. Perhaps the fear, suspicion, wariness, and hesitation I encountered at the beginning of this essay were the traces of terror. Perhaps they were pointing to what I know. That words/representation cannot faithfully convey reality. That to be faithful to the other, one has to sometimes fracture and bend syntax and sentence. Logic and grammar. Perhaps I was afraid of admitting that much of what passes for our lives is but a moment in a larger circuit of things. A circuit that we know exists but are unwilling to acknowledge. Most of all, I was afraid that what I would write here would not make sense, not even to the reader in me who demands coherence, concordance between reality and theory, between world and word, and compliance.

Note

1 Many thanks to Naeem Inayatullah, Himadeep Muppidi, Reina Neufeldt, and Kiran Pervez for their generous comments and support.

References

Ghosh, Amitav (1988) *The Shadow Lines*, New York: Houghton Mifflin.
Collective for Batticaloa (2004) "Also In Our Name," Sri Lanka Democracy Forum, available at: www.lankademocracy.org/documents/batticollective.html (accessed 24 June 2010).

4 Scenes of obscenity

The meaning of America under epistemic and military violence

Khadija F. El Alaoui

> Gathering hope, she looked for anything that she remembered from her village, those odds and ends that lay trapped between house and street. And as she sought those things out, she lost what she already had.
>
> (Latife Tekin, *Dear Shameless Death*: 84)

Hollywood cinema was a familiar presence in 1980s Moroccan households even prior to the widespread phenomenon of satellite dishes. As a middle-school teenager, I was sometimes allowed to join the evening viewing of American TV series and films. While I avidly followed series such as *Dallas* (1978–91), wherein I happily slid into a fantasy trip to beautiful, wealthy, and white USA, it was the movies, especially war films, that unveiled an obscene script.

Blacks die first

Watching French dubbed Hollywood movies in my family's living room was never a silent affair: first, whoever had mastery of French had to intermittently throw out some translations for those who didn't know the language. Second, we gradually joined my father in what he seemed to consider the fun exercise of anticipating the movie's script once the main characters were introduced. The joy in the exercise, I think, was due to the epistemic predictability involved in the anticipation: a typical scene in our living room would be that once the "good team" that comprised whites (one of whom was always a star actor) and non-whites was introduced, one of us would comment upon seeing the black actor on the good team side by saying: "The black will go [die] first!" None of us paid serious attention to the fate of the bad guys, whose identity varied according to the film genre. In the war films we watched, the enemy were largely faceless and storyless Vietnamese. Their elimination was always a question of the film's length. Sometimes we wagered on how soon the black character on the good guys' side would exit the narrative. We noticed that Hollywood scripts could not cast blacks in what they imagine as heroism and goodness for more than a few minutes of their feature-length films. We saw that these scripts could not plot a happy-ending without the death of blacks! I am sure that my family and I quickly noticed the trope of "kill-the-black-first" because we carry the memory of "burn-and-kill-brown-Moroccans-and-Algerians-first" so that white France could reach its happy ending.

Today, trying to think from an American-culture student vantage point, I think that our bodies knew all too well what it was to live in a world/narrative scripted by whites/Westerners: since black characters were constantly sacrificed, they must not have been involved in the process of telling the story. So I always kept in the back of my mind the observation that Hollywood movies killed the black male character – usually in the very first encounter on their rescue mission. Yet, in the act of watching, I also read the murder and mutilation of the black body as a powerful signifier that inflected the film's space with a sense of "threat," that is, a threat that promises to entertain, create suspense, generate meaning, but a threat that would never, could never, touch the disturbing predictability of the story line and the sacred invincibility of the white star actor.

Later when I became a student of English literature, a field that also encompassed American literature and history, there was no classroom where I could introduce and deepen the observations made in our family living room. In fact, the American-survey and American-literature classes largely focused on the stories of the Pilgrims and the ideals and ideas of the transcendentalist intellectuals of the nineteenth century. My query about the automatic sacrifice of the black body became irrelevant since the classroom experience negated its very existence. The US largely appeared as the land of Buffalo Bill's self-reliance and hard work, the Horatio Alger myth, and whites ... The classroom reproduced a US that was more the academic version of *Dallas* and *Little House on the Prairie* (1974–83).

This particular US appeared as if it were totally disconnected from the questions and ambivalences I carried with me about Europe, especially about France and French people. For instance, I was neither at ease with the automatic envy and resentment I felt towards the French, nor with the shame that inundated me when my family members, who could not speak or act French, encountered Europeans! My malaise, I think, came from the contradiction embedded in the attitude of so many grown-ups of my community. On the one hand, they spoke of French violence, its open contempt for our ways of lives, and how it relentlessly corroded our habits, sensibilities, and religious ways in a fashion that was beyond our control. On the other hand, they exhibited a deferential pose towards so many of France's stories, including the idea that French education is the surest road toward acquiring knowledge of Western thought and science, hence material development and progress.

At some point, I also internalized this resentful and deferential attitude towards Western Europe in general and France in particular. Today, I wonder whether my grandmother's recognition of this particular "structure of feeling" (Raymond Williams's expression) explains her frequent remark: "these times demand hypocrisy!" My grandmother never bought the civilizing mission of the French – to whom she referred as *Nsara* (Christians). Even though she saw them as unscrupulous colonizers and nothing else, she did not offer an alternative to our ambivalence. Or was hypocrisy itself the alternative, since at least it has the merit of not taking Europe's civilizing mission too seriously? Indeed, my grandmother's repetitive observation about our hypocrisy articulated what seemed, even for her, an inescapable predicament that called for a particular kind of conversation. Ashis Nandy also pertinently asks:

> Does the hypocrisy of cultures on closer scrutiny turn out to be a contradiction in the human condition itself? For that matter, is a hypocrite only a cheat? Or is he someone who reaffirms the basic human values in a world hostile to such values, while himself succumbing to worldly temptations? Is a hypocrite an unwilling critic of everyday life whose personal failure signals a larger cultural crisis?
>
> (1988: 83–84)

While conversations in our living rooms routinely reflected on how to encounter what we called the disasters of colonialism and Westernization, the talks interestingly did not consider looking into the role of the educational system in producing and normalizing allegiances to the very disruptive forces people sought to resist. If there were still caravans of goods and knowledge crisscrossing Africa, the Arabian Peninsula, and South Asia, we might have got wind of Ali Shari'ati's warning against turning modern education into a self-defeating project that produces generations "talking with other people's tongues and walking with other people's feet" (1986: 63). Yet, despite the limitations of the conversations I grew up listening to, I enjoyed and learned from the passionate debates and the convivial battles against modernity. I enjoyed them, I should say, until I started my four-year university studies as a major in English literature in Casablanca. So what happened in those years? Were my feet and tongue put up for amputation and replacement by something else? One thing I noticed from the very beginning was that our study of US and English modern cultures and literatures was totally divorced from our tongue, feelings, and experiences outside the classroom. For instance, one of the unwritten rules was the non-use of (Moroccan) Arabic in classes and during meetings with professors, who certainly spoke the forbidden language in the streets but not in their offices. At that time I complied wholeheartedly and thought this was the natural order of studies.

However, by disregarding the ambivalent feelings coursing under our skin, the classroom exacted and normalized the obliteration of our bodies. It sped up the process of diluting the memory of our accents and the accents of our memory. Years later, from the vantage point of 2003, I came to think of these classroom experiences as floating beyond the gravity of my culture's stories and memories and dashing into another planet. The mission was about hunting and stocking up information, be it about the Pilgrims, the transcendentalists, or the Victorian Age. I zealously collected information like the peddlers who walked up and down my neighborhood asking for old bread and piling it up in their carts. Unlike the peddlers, who sold or bartered the given-away bread to farmers, I could hold onto my pile. In fact, I checked (almost fondled) my notes every evening and early morning, especially the precious pieces that I stocked as deposited by their owners – no wonder I was able to produce long quotes from memory in classroom exams. My strategy, like most of my classmates', was to trade the painstakingly accumulated information for good grades – this business, I should note, was safe for I could never lose my capital unless, maybe, I stopped believing in the civilizing mission. The good grades would reward us with higher classes that would provide more complex information, and once we become affluent in a particular kind of information, we are called educated. I guess the endgame is to land in the Moroccan middle class, exhibit some affinity with Western Europeans, look around and find that the majority of people speak and live differently, and, maybe, to stay the course, write a book on either identity crisis or the urgent need to reform and modernize.

It is for good reason that the poet Mahmoud Darwish writes, in his immensely popular poem "Identity Card" (1964), that in his village his grandfather teaches him pride and dignity before teaching him how to read books. What kind of literacy did I acquire, if the home and neighborhood's conversations that used to make so much sense to me appeared gradually unintelligible? From where came these ridiculous, new habits of expecting conversations to clearly state the problem, focus on the problem, and fix the problem through referencing some Western names? From where came the arrogant, new conviction that the talks in the classroom were opening my eyes and broadening my horizons even as I became deaf and blind to so much happening around me, all of which I conveniently dismissed as a waste of time? What did I think time was (about)? Years later, I could certainly understand, but fortunately, feel outraged by the tales of Western travelers. For instance, Freya Stark writes about her acceptance of her guide's invitation, whom she calls "my Afghan," to look at a group of women celebrating a wedding in Makalla, Yemen. She writes: "I slipped in through a fold and found myself in chaos of women packed in hot and dense twilight, and as far removed from anything to do with modern education as it is possible" (1945: 38). For Stark and an army of Western writers who suffer the blindfold modern education bestows on its ardent believers, anyone who fails to sit and converse their ways becomes chaos, probably even a waste, tout court. The last thought that could have come to my mind was that the Casablanca English classroom obscenely participated in the very epistemic erasure that dismissed our stories and normalized our dispensability. Yet, another site, this time the streets, would give me a glimpse of our role in the script: not dissimilar to Hollywood's script for the black body...

The glaring script: browns are expendable

Another rescue mission. This time: Fall 1990. In the beginning of that school year, Casablanca and, I sense, the largest part of the Arab World, were full of premonitions about the US's swift moves to reverse Saddam Hussein's invasion of Kuwait on its own terms. The US, along with France and Britain – both of which have a long history of crimes against humanity still fresh in our collective memory – were hatching the familiar scenario of saving the browns (this time Saudis and Kuwaitis) from the browns (Iraqis) for the sake of world order and civilization. In fact, this time not only my family but the majority of Arabs and so many third worlders could easily anticipate who would die: obviously those announced to be under "the rule of the jungle,"[1] besides the thousands of "good" Arabs, who would be sacrificed in Bush Senior's mission of saving the damsel Kuwait in distress.

In my immediate world, the US President's declarations, the November troop build-up, and the UN/US's deadline for attacking Iraq pounded out upon us the familiar tune of Western epistemic and military violence, which we have been stomaching for five hundred years. Even though the protests I joined did not necessarily invoke that history, our bodies knew where we were that day – we were where powerlessness is. We were an irrelevant mass of protestors because we invested too much credibility in the stories emanating from Western Europe despite their being predicated on the relentless maintenance of our very irrelevance and powerlessness. And yet we did not protest against our credulity, long-enough credulity. The protests I participated in or heard about did not seek to seriously reactivate the possible, albeit difficult, ways of widening the scope of our interlocutors beyond the Western imperialists. We generally trod the very conversational path mapped by the West, wherein they appointed themselves and turned their space to a kind of supreme call center. Accordingly, even in the apogee of our anger and indignation we dialed the US, France, and Britain, appealed to them expecting explications for their actions (for instance, we pointed out how they were ignoring at that time the more than 23 year old Israeli occupation of Palestinian territories and yet instantly screamed foul for the Iraqi invasion of Kuwait). We thought they were the only possible justice dispenser. Yet if, as is obviously the case, most Arab countries are controlled by police states and the Western liberal democracies do not care a whit about our screaming their double standards, then what's the point of that kind of protest?

In the real world, the protocols of neocolonial order were being executed to the letter. After President Bush declared war on Iraq, King Hassan II announced his joining Bush's coalition against Iraq and commanded his subjects to "remember their place" by ritually banning any form of protest against the war. The translations of these violent decrees into the messiness of the everyday life of the majority of us in Casablanca, who were among other things seething with resentment at the hasty war option, was that our state was at the service of powers that have the horrible urge to destroy Iraq.

Recalling his conversation after the Gulf War with a group he identifies as Egyptian Islamists, journalist Chris Hedges writes:

> They saw the Persian Gulf War for what it was, a use of force by a country that consumed 25 percent of the world's petrol to protect its access to cheap oil. The message that was sent to them was this: We have everything and if you try to take it away from us we will kill you. It was a message I couldn't dispute.
>
> (2003: 148)

If the Arab states were supporting that message, as I think they were, what kind of politics is this? It seems to me to be suicidal, but then our very education, our captivity in the historical mode that prescribes the West's present as our future is also suicidal. One might object by pointing out the weakness of Morocco and other US Arab allies, such as Egypt. But then we have an inspiring model in Shahrazad, who kept postponing her death by telling endless stories to the cruel King, Shahrayar. Recall that Shahrazad not only forestalled her death but also cured the king of his habit of killing.

However, already in the fall of 1990, a storyless King Hassan II, acting fully on behalf of the super-power, commanded us to bow before the US's self-appointed right to impose with military might its exclusive knowledge of what's good for the world. Our collective memory that suffers what Shari'ati calls "the intimidating monster of the West which both butts and bewitches" perfectly understood what was going on (1986: 47). George W.H. Bush's enunciation to help save the good Arabs from the bad Arabs, and the native rulers' move to brandish the *chicotte* at any sign of disagreement, re-enacts the colonial hierarchical chain of command. We are again commanded to dissimulate our feelings in public places and act as if we don't know, don't understand, and don't feel. Nothing new here. The West's epistemic privilege has been sitting for more than five centuries on this dissimulation, whose doomed extermination under the crushing weight of universalism has been celebrated in so many of the books we avidly memorized in Casablanca.

While the US was spurring the technologies of modern violence to mobilize its population's political imaginary in tune with missions that seek to erase "the rule of jungle" and implement the "new world order" via/starring George W.H. Bush, Colin Powell, and Norman Schwartzkopf, neither my family nor I could indulge in the "fun exercise" of anticipating the dead. Yet, I still made a mental note of Colin Powell's participation, whose presence made me rethink whether color can predict the script.[2] Interestingly, Hollywood itself signaled a kind of a change in the role of blacks in the movies. For instance, David O. Russell's *Three Kings* (1999) sends three GIs and their leader (played, typically, by star George Clooney) in the mission of stealing Kuwaiti bullion (back?) from the Iraqis and incidentally involves them in the business of rescuing a group of Shia rebels. Again following the iconic scene of Hollywood war films, the US platoon/team invades a whole nation, destroys thousands of lives and suffers the loss of only one or two of its members. This time, however, contrary to the familiar trope of "minorities" dying first, Clooney and his team, made up of three inexperienced reservists, lose white Conrad (Spike Jones), cast as a racist, but good-hearted redneck, and not black Chief Elgin (Ice Cube). The third remaining GI Troy Barlow (Mark Whalberg) is tortured and later seriously wounded; while Chief's body, similar to his leader's, does not even come close to getting scratched! Clearly both Washington and Hollywood were treading a somewhat different path that demanded we rethink our colorful childhood living-room theories.

The US war on Iraq "ended" on February 28, 1991. The Mutla Ridge massacre (the highway of death), the heavy bombing of Baghdad, and the unspeakable damage and destruction visited on Iraq were all drowned out by the celebrations in several American cities of the US's perceived swift victory and the widely played video of the beating of black motorist Rodney King by four white Los Angeles police officers. In the fictional world of *Three Kings*, the historical beating of black (Rodney) King is watched by Ice Cube's character in an Iraqi bunker. Interestingly, even as his body language is allowed to show its dismay with the scene, he can not push his understandable reaction into making what I'd call a global beating analysis, which would demand the articulation of the obvious connections between the violence of empire at home and abroad. Such connections would inevitably implicate him as an agent of empire who enlisted in the war in order to enjoy a paid "vacation" from his daily life in Detroit, scripted as dull. Why not read, then, the beating of Rodney King as the LA police officers' similarly having fun in breaking up the monotony of their daily lives by playing imperialists with their batons in their very district? After all their commander-in-chief declared the "bombing of Iraq back to the Middle Ages," surely in addition to the already-forgotten invasion of Panama on December 20, 1989, as having "exorcised the ghosts of Vietnam." What ghosts were the police officers putting to rest when they jumped on the black body of Rodney King?

W.E.B. Du Bois, Langston Hughes, and Malcolm X, among many other African Americans, recognized that the racial politics of beating and murdering non-whites abroad were inextricable from the beating and murdering of black and other colored bodies at home. They also witnessed and suffered the cultural and psychological pathologies that the global beating and murdering, whose common denominator was unmistakably the color line, produces in the beater-nation, in which the three men uneasily lived. Du Bois, for instance, wonders what the effects could be on a nation that passionately believes that "whiteness is the ownership of the earth forever and ever, Amen!"(Du Bois 1972: 30) Du Bois's own conclusions after decades of observing "white folks" is:

> I know their thoughts and they know that I know. This knowledge makes them now embarrassed, now furious! They deny my right to live and be and call me misbirth! My word is to them mere bitterness and my

soul, pessimism. And yet as they preach and strut and shout and threaten, crouching as they clutch at rags of facts and fancies to hide their nakedness, they go twisting, flying by my tired eyes and I see them ever stripped, – ugly, human.

(1972: 29)

Langston Hughes writes in "Columbia," about the US's elaborate, neurotic act – or probably habit, if one recalls genocide, slavery, apartheid, and lynching – of killing "little brown fellows" abroad and yelling rape when they resisted (2001: 230–31). Malcolm X in his inimitable style says: "The white man has perpetrated upon himself, as well as upon the black man, so gigantic a fraud that he has put himself into a crack. ... The white man seems tone deaf to the total orchestration of humanity" (1999: 184, 291).

My own little experience of the US in its films, on the one hand, in its actions towards Palestine and Israel and its management of the Gulf War, on the other hand, made me aware of the contradictions, the fraud, and the ugliness. Yet, the Casablanca classroom was insistent on ignoring what was happening in the world and in us. During the destruction of Iraq I studiously immersed myself in preparing for my DEUG (diplôme d'études universitaires générales) that sucked me back into the Pilgrims and *Great Gatsby*. I was seriously studying about the notion of "city upon a hill" in both pilgrim's thought and novels at the turn of the twentieth century. Imagine!

Now I cannot help but imagine, in a different way, what would have happened, if the US sent to the Arab and Muslim World more of Muhammed Ali, who famously said "I ain't got no quarrel with them Viet Cong ... They never called me nigger," and less of Ice Cube, who rejects the epithet of "sand-nigger" but approves "camel-jockeys" and "towel-heads." More of Tupac Amaru Shakur who willed us the impossible: roses growing from the concrete of power's violence and life with dignity despite "an American culture plagued with nights" of racism and white supremacy (1999: 3). Less of Michael Jackson, whose impressive artistic energy willed another impossibility, which, however, a hundred years of ideological production and economic gains turned to a possibility: butchering one's body and bleaching one's skin to look white! I can't but feel the urgency in Mohammed Ali's daring truth and Tupac's daring imagination. I imagine: what if my professors and we students decided during the Gulf War to turn the required texts into bedtime reading and used the English-lesson classroom to read Jalal Al-i Ahmad's *Occidentosis*, Ali Shari'ati's *What is to be Done,* Walter Rodney's *Grounding with my Brothers,* Franz Fanon's *The Wretched of the Earth,* Abdelrahmane Munif's *Cities of Salt* ... ? We wouldn't have allowed studies (American or whatever) to be channeled towards diploma or towards social mobility only but mainly towards theorizing what our memories carried and our bodies already saw on screens and in streets. Our bodies knew what Fanon succinctly articulated with regard to Europe: "When I search for Man in the technique and the style of Europe, I see only a succession of negations of man, and an avalanche of murders ... " (1990: 252).

Yet, I did my BA in Casablanca, Morocco: I could read, write, and could discuss a little bit of post-modernism, I definitely joined the number that would demonstrate the increasing literacy in the Arab world. The question this number does not ask, however, is what did I learn to read and valorize? For sure not the memories of butcheries and erased ways of life, not my lived experience, not what I discussed with my parents and friends and felt full of emotions and dreams about. More important, whom was I drilled to engage as my main interlocutors whenever I engaged in some academic practice? Certainly not my family and community, not the Arab poets, the revolutionary Iranian thinkers, or the black anticolonial intellectuals. "The collective white man's history," Malcolm X writes "has left the non-white peoples no alternative ... but to draw closer to each other" (1999: 291). Why did the education system in Morocco miss this urgent alternative? Is it because out of a generous consideration such a move would reveal the immorality, arrogance, and guilt of cultures we taught ourselves to be impressed by? Or is it the crudity of power relations? In any case, it is certainly not an envious position to be caught flirting with the rapist! By dismissing or ignoring the other conversational routes, we succumbed to the perverse temptation of hiding the truth from ourselves.

Malcolm X, whose eyes are on both the colonizer and the colonized, adds:

> This pattern, this "system" that the white man created, of teaching Negroes to hide the truth from him behind a façade of grinning, "yessir-bossing," foot-shuffling and head-scratching – that system has done the American white man more harm than an invading army would do to him. Why do I say this? Because all this has steadily helped this American white man to build up, deep in his psyche, absolute conviction that he *is* "superior."
> (1999: 279–80)

I admit that I had no idea that the knowledge I acquired about the US from home and the streets in Casablanca could be of any help to the arrogant US, whose abuse in the continuing Gulf War period displays a multi-colored face. I was walking in the opposite direction. With the tempting US filling my head, I turned my growing doubt about the US designs into self-doubt: I, probably grinning and head-scratching, thought it wiser to learn more about the US from Europe!

Indeed, in a typical move of getting close to the very source from which our self-appointed interlocutors spoke to the world, I packed and journeyed to Dresden, Germany to do an MA in American and German studies. Certainly, the US I encountered in the German classroom was multi-faceted, we discussed its myths, symbols, creeds, and national character. We delved in its racial, ethnic, gender relations and studied its international relations. Yet, I couldn't ignore a growing sense of revolt, not so much because

I regretted the curriculum's disinterest in US militarism and neoliberalism, but because of the silence about the colossal cultural work servicing US imperialism in the name of universal values and global burdens.

I should add here that I had my own personal story with regard to neoliberalism's invasion of Morocco in the beginning of 1980s. As a child then I learned a very important lesson: when violence occurs (Moroccan military intervention to kill the protestors in Casablanca), many versions erupt to account for and remember what happened. The version of the rulers is as loud and as true as the guns they wield (King Hassan II spoke of Khumeini's traces and leaflets); the versions of the ruled are whispered and never-ending like their troubles and dreams (oppression, unemployment, the IMF structural adjustment programs, the rise in the price of staple food, the incompatibility between secularization, Westernization, and certain habits grounded in religious life, the ongoing crimes of the state, life without dignity …). But as I said, this story was irrelevant as far as American studies were concerned, after all economy did not become an important factor until a decade later when Bill Clinton ran his 1992 presidential campaign with the slogan "it's the economy, stupid!" Too bad for those who suffered this stupidity for centuries …

I sat in classrooms feeling eaten by something I could not name, for, being within the American Studies department in a German university, US imperialism or at least the darker sides of its international or domestic relations was always a matter of the past. Yet, there I sat translating, as part of American Studies course requirements, dozens of US news articles from English to German and vice-versa, some of which dovetailed glaringly with the colonial discourse, as analyzed in Edward Said's *Orientalism* (1978). I recall that I had to force myself to concentrate on showing the professors my mastery of both languages, instead of letting loose my growing frustration with the news content which, for instance, unembarrassedly equated my culture(s) and religion(s) with violence and terrorism. After all, I kept telling myself, it was just an exercise in acquiring the skills to easily move between two languages! But what about my simultaneous move between at least two worlds, wherein my translational act stabbed a world with languages, cultures, and ways of being that are fundamental to my being? The easier I moved between European languages and their analytical concepts, the more acute became my feeling of treason and humiliation. Unfortunately, I was not able to pursue the ethical charges of those sentiments even as I was fascinated by the amount of knowledge and theory I was accumulating. I was learning to articulate my critique of US foreign policy. I must admit that what I was saying at that time was not far from what I debated with my friends in Casablanca cafés, or shouted in its streets, to no avail, so far.

In fact, what is presented as the US's burdensome responsibilities, fraught with all kinds of conflicting interests in the American Studies classroom, beckons me to an entry from which I can maneuver my critical moves. Yet all this attention to US mistakes and the perception of the US in the world leave the universalized story untouched; namely the US's entitlement to capitalize on modernity's biggest fraud of locating superior being and acting in the world within a particular space with all the privileges and rights this accrues to the few and the horrors it forcibly entails for the rest of humanity. One has only to recall the whole framework of knowledge through which we decipher those blunders and the "world's" perceptions of the US to remain suspicious that the grand story, far from being vitiated, is still alive and killing.

No wonder that in the long decade I spent in Dresden, countless are the instances where my German interlocutors shared with me their viscerality towards what they perceived as Iran's suppression of freedom of speech, Islam's call to violence, Palestinians' suicide bombing, Saddam Hussein's butcheries, Saudis' extravagant way of life, Moroccans' swindling European tourists, and so on. While I do not contest the relevancy of these reactions, it is certainly odd, to say the least, that not once was I asked how it feels to live in a world that has no historical shame towards what it did and still does to people like me in the so-called third world. Or how it feels to live in a space that, instead of interacting with me in a way that centers its negation of non-whites and its avalanche of murders, wherever these happened, shamelessly lectures me by means of the very imperialistic mode of thoughts that has produced and legitimated my dispensability in the first place! Again I cannot help but imagine the world that could be if moral outrage flew not only when the "other" is appraised but also towards their knowledge and violence. But then, if what Malcolm X describes as the invading army that has erected innumerable bases of white supremacy in the Western psyche were to contemplate withdrawing, what should their eyes suddenly see?

By the time the US invaded Iraq in March 2003, what I still considered systems of knowledge became more what Assia Djebar describes, with reference to French records of its invasion of Algiers in July 1830, as "scribblomania" to "form a pyramid to hide the initial violence from view" (1993: 44–45). Djebar asks: "What is the significance behind the urge of so many fighting men to relive in print this month of July 1830? Did their writings allow them to savor the seducer's triumph, the rapist's intoxication?"(1993: 45). Djebar finds out that there was another paradoxical reason for the pyramid of writing: to escape the confinement of conscience. She writes: "The accounts of this past invasion reveal *a contrario* an identical nature: invaders who imagine they are taking the Impregnable City [Algiers], but also wander aimlessly in the undergrowth of their disquiet" (1993: 45). The US's triumphant capture of Baghdad in April 2003 was duly prepared for and followed by "scribblomania" and "filmomania" that dwarfed the French discursive monuments to their conquests and rapes.

Beirut, a beginning?

In 2006, again I packed and enthusiastically accepted an American Studies teaching position at the American University of Beirut. In that space, which is dissimilar to the rest of the country in so many ways, it didn't take my Lebanese and Palestinian students long to make the seminar less about the *texts* and more about *contexts*, that is, the position(s) from which Arab-speaking students encounter the US texts in an environment still constituted by colonialism and violence. The questions that haunted us were: What does it mean to read texts, theoretically progressive as they may be, when one's humanity is still put in question, one's body can be degraded, and one's future squandered – with impunity? How does it feel to deal with texts announcing (post)modernity's goodies – such as democracy, human rights, and development – while life is being threatened by high-tech weaponry and bombs, which will inevitably inflict deaths on hundreds of thousands of people? How is it possible to read the texts in any hermeneutic fashion while so many familiar brown bodies are being terminated (targeted and slaughtered)?

In a sense, my teaching experience at AUB had to focus on what happened when our memory and these questions encounter US textbooks in the cozy space of a classroom. What's the meaning of America to our bodies? How could I invite the students to look at and delve into the complexity of America: an America that shows us one face and produces us as a single story? Why, despite death's shadows, are the students and I, to expand one of Mahmoud Darwish's central metaphors, expected to ignore the rifle that stands between our eyes and the US, whose firing bullets shoot at the very dialogical bridges we are homing in on traversing? Franz Fanon pertinently remarks:

> There are many people in Martinique who at the age of twenty or thirty begin to steep themselves in Montesquieu or Claudel for the sole purpose of being able to quote them. That is because, through their knowledge of these writers, they expect their color to be forgotten.
>
> (1967: 193).

I wonder what are we learning to forget by quoting Huntington and Warhol?

Within the particularity of the AUB classroom, I obviously had no interest in putting the students under the spell of forgetting their bodies and memories. On the contrary I was thinking hard of how to break away from it. Just this simple insistence allowed the articulation of a different relationship with temporality. I could clearly hear that many students with an Arab background moved in a different fashion between pasts, presents, and futures. For instance, 1948 is a fresh wound and so many other things; yet, while 2006 (the time of the seminar) allowed more students to access education and be globally connected, the pains became all the more acute because the conditions of the present so commonly written as "advanced" (excellent education and intellectual skills) de-valorized the stories around the festering wounds. A Palestinian student pointed out that the *Nakba* started with the Napoleonic invasion of Egypt in 1798 and the US's long history of racism and genocidal practices within what is today called its national territory anticipated the terms of the encounter with difference without. Where to go with this?

I became convinced about the need to practice (American) Studies with ears that hearken to Fanon's final prayer, which is also his last sentence in *Black Skin White Masks*: "O my body, make of me always a man who questions!" (1967: 232). Our bodies and collective memory, holders of other possible knowledge routes, can show us the way. Even if the routes have been announced to be antique and useless by the map of modern knowledge, we can consider walking and traveling them again! Even if the modern categories of knowledge have successfully partitioned the past, we can shift the gaze from those who conquered and divided to the very partitions themselves. We might begin to retrieve some traces of Caravans that transgress the normalized map of the international order. Sneaking back to these paths, we might begin to mess up the partitions' definitive character (see Ghosh, 1994: 339–42). English can be a practical means to engage in inspiring conversations with our Iranian, Turkish, and Indian neighbors! We can engage defiant voices, such as Abdelrahman Munif, Malcolm X, Ali Shari'ati, and Ashis Nandy in conversations that, without collapsing these thinkers' historical and cultural specificities, might give us important tales about ourselves, what we can want and do and where to go …

I went to Vassar College, NY, wondering whether the conversations I had in Lebanon were possible in the context of a US classroom. I know that sometimes I didn't know where to start when anything I'd say would be politely heard as one point of view (lost) among many others. Sometimes I would feel so choked up when I responded to some students' frequent references to US occupation of Iraq as "that invasion was a mistake!" Did I appear to my students like the hysterical, chaotic Arab, African, Muslim women they encountered in *National Geographic* and other sources of learning or did some of what I had to say touch something?

Today, I am sure if I could sit at the feet of my grandmother and tell her all that I think and feel, she'd say:

> daughter, these people you've been talking about seem to me to be inhabited by a Jinni of supremacy they fabricated themselves. Either they should be working hard on dis-inviting it, or they should spill rivers of blood as a sacrifice to appease it. Can you and those who see it, and not many can see a Jinn, call it out, lock it in a bottle and throw it in the ocean?

Then she would add, with a smile: "But don't make this a lifetime priority: it might end up inhabiting you as well!"

Notes

1 Here is what President George W.H. Bush announced to Congress in Fall 1990:

> We stand today at a unique and extraordinary moment. … Out of these troubled times … a new world order can emerge. … Today, that new world

order is struggling to be born, a world quite different from the one we have known, a world where the rule of law supplants the rule of the jungle, a world in which nations recognize the shared responsibility for freedom and justice, a world where the strong respect the weak.

(in Dumbrell 1997: 163)

2 Significantly, Colin Powell was fluent in the imperialist tradition he was serving. Here is what he wrote in the aftermath of the official ending of the war and Saddam Hussein's eventual crushing of the rebellion in March 1991:

President Bush's rhetoric urging the Iraqis to overthrow Saddam, however, may have given encouragement to the rebels. But our practical intention was to leave Baghdad enough power to survive as a threat to an Iran that remained bitterly hostile toward the United States. Nevertheless, we could not ignore the worsening plight of the rebellious Kurds. ... Jack Galvin, operating out of Mons, Belgium, as our European commander, had long-distance control over our forces in this region [Iraq]. One Sunday afternoon, with me in Washington and Jack in Belgium, each with a map in front of us, we sketched out a "security zone," a sector around Kurdish cities in Iraq that Saddam's troops would not be allowed to enter. I felt like one of those British diplomats in the 1920s carving out nations like Jordan and Iraq on a tablecloth at a gentleman's club. I called Galvin, in his trans-European role, "Charlemagne," and I told him that now he was truly a kingdom maker.

(Powell 1996: 516–17)

References

Al-i Ahmad, J. (1984) *Occidentosis: A Plague From the West*, translated by R. Campbell, Berkeley, CA: Mizan Press.
Djebar, A. (1993) *Fantasia: An Algerian Cavalcade*, translated by D.S. Blair, Portsmouth, NH: Heinemann.
DuBois, W.E.B. (1972) *Darkwater: Voices from Within the Veil*, New York: Schocken.
Dumbrell, J. (1997) *American Foreign Policy: Carter to Clinton*, New York: St. Martin's Press.
Fanon, F. (1967) *Black Skin White Masks*, translated by C.L. Markman, New York: Grove Press.
——(1990) *The Wretched of the Earth*, translated by C. Farrington, London: Penguin.
Ghosh, A. (1994) *In An Antique Land: History in the Guise of a Traveler's Tale*, New York: Vintage.
Hedges, C. (2003) *War is a Force that Gives Us Meaning*, New York: Anchor Books.
Hughes, L. (2001) "Columbia," *The Collected Works of Langston Hughes, Volume 1: The Poems: 1921–1940*, Columbia: University of Missouri Press.
Malcolm X (1999) *The Autobiography of Malcolm X as Told to Alex Haley*, New York: Ballantine.
Munif, A. (1989) *Cities of Salt*, translated by P. Theroux, New York: Vintage.
Nandy, A. (1988) *The Intimate Enemy: Loss and Recovery of Self under Colonialism*, New Delhi: Oxford University Press.
Powell, C. (1996) *My American Journey*, New York: Ballantine.
Rodney, W. (1975) *The Grounding with My Brothers*, London: Bogle-L'Ouverture.
Shakur, T.A. (1999) *The Rose that Grew from Concrete*, New York: Pocket Books.

Shari'ati, Ali (1986) *What is to be Done: The Enlightened Thinkers and an Islamic Renaissance*, edited and annotated by F. Rajaee, Houston, TX: The Institute for Research and Islamic Studies.

Stark, F. (1945) *The Southern Gates of Arabia: A Journey in the Hadhramaut*, London: Penguin.

Tekin, Latife (2001) *Dear Shameless Death*, translated by Saliha Paker and Mel Kenne, New York: Marion Boyars.

Three Kings, (1999) [film] directed by David O. Russell, USA: Warner Brothers.

5 I, the double soldier
An autobiographic case-study on the pitfalls of dual citizenship

Rainer Hülsse

What is comedy but tragedy plus time?

(Allen 1989)

When I ask my students why they are interested in international politics, most of them begin telling about their past. Many have traveled extensively before going to college, some have worked in development projects in Africa, while others have served in military missions in Kosovo or Afghanistan. Somehow such foreign experiences have raised their interest in the international. And the same holds true for me as well. At some stage in my biography, international politics has made more of an impact on my life than I would have liked. In retrospect, at least, this experience seems to be what some of us would call the "cause" of my becoming a student of International Relations (IR). And probably, it also goes some way into explaining my foremost research interest: the social construction of reality, especially the making of identity and difference.

Yet, if I tell my story here, I do so less to explain where my IR comes from, but more to illustrate a point that is very dear to me: international politics is not just a series of big events, important "men" and crucial decisions (as we often teach our students), but it is also an important shaper of our lives. Accordingly, the IR I favor studies the impact of international politics on the everyday lives of ordinary people like myself. Therefore, the following is foremost a case-study in international politics' influence on biographies. Indeed, many people have stories to tell in which the international has made a much greater impact on their lives than in my case – and often an infinitely more painful one. However, as I am particularly familiar with my own case, this is probably where I should begin.

In July 1989, barely two months after I had graduated from high-school in a small town in the south of Germany, I became a soldier in the Swiss army. Until then, I had never lived in Switzerland, I barely spoke the rather peculiar German dialect spoken there and did not know anyone in Switzerland except some family. Yet due to a Swiss mother, I carried a Swiss passport in addition to my German one. And when I was 18, this passport for the first time seemed to be of real value. Both Germany and Switzerland have conscription armies, but the length of the compulsory military service varies considerably. While young men in Germany had to serve 15 months back then, the basic military training in Switzerland, the so-called *Rekrutenschule,* lasted only four months.

My friends were stunned when they heard me considering going to the Swiss army. Most of them were conscientious objectors about to take up their civilian service in hospitals, nursing homes, or houses for disabled people. And they reminded me of the fact that I, too, had always taken pacifist positions in our discussions. How could I betray my normative principles just to save a couple of months? I tried to justify my decision with reference to the legal situation. At the time, Switzerland was among the few remaining countries in Europe without an alternative civilian service. It was only three years later, in 1992, that a referendum decided to establish a civilian service for conscientious objectors. But in 1989, conscientious objectors in Switzerland still went to prison. And my conscience was too pragmatic for jail.

Just forget about your Swiss passport then, my friends suggested, and do your civilian service in Germany instead. Yet, my friends had underestimated the complexities of dual citizenship. I had inquired with the Swiss authorities about how they would handle my case assuming that I would do my civilian service in Germany. This, they told me, would have no influence on my military duties in Switzerland. As there was no civilian service in Switzerland, they would have to treat my German civilian service as if it had never taken place. Should I ever take residence in Switzerland, I would still be recruited into the Swiss army. Military service in Germany, however, would be accepted as a substitute for Swiss military service. This meant that I could not avoid going to the military if I ever wanted to move to Switzerland. As I had planned to go to university in Zürich, and preferred four months in the military over 15 months, I eventually became a Swiss soldier and moved into the barracks of the garrison town of Drognens in the Swiss canton of Fribourg.

I loved sports and the outdoors, and also had a taste for the curious, so I applied for the Swiss army's bicycle division. A number of countries, including the United States, had installed bicycle troops in the late nineteenth century, but Switzerland was the only country where they were still operative in the late twentieth century (and even in Switzerland they were dissolved in 2003). The bicycle division was regarded as an elite troop, of key importance for defending the country. It could cover far greater distances than the normal infantryman, but without making as much noise as motorized troops. A high ranking officer of the Swiss cyclist troops describes the advantages: "We are fast! We can leave within ten minutes after an alarm, because we simply take our bikes and off we go ... Our soundlessness! A cycling platoon can march into a village without the enemy taking notice" (Leuenberger 2000).[1] I knew that the military cyclist's life had a reputation for being particularly tough and physically very demanding. Yet I did not consider this a disadvantage.

On the contrary: I was looking for a challenge and the bicycle troop promised a great adventure. If I was to go to the army, I wanted the "real thing." So at the physical entry examination I covered more distance than anyone else in the Swiss army's traditional 12 minute run and was accepted.

Yet, this feeling would not last very long. In fact, it had vanished a short time after I had taken up my military training in the *Rekrutenschule*. While I did not mind the 200 km bike exercises on a one gear bike constructed in 1904 (though I could have done without carrying a gun on my back), I was disgusted by what was probably simply military routine. Suddenly I was to exercise and to march lock step, to share a room with 24 others, and to have my appearance inspected ad nauseam. I was deprived of regular sleep by surprise emergency exercises in the middle of the night and faced myriad other humiliations, all of which aimed at transforming individuals into soldiers. Discipline was the keyword, defined in the army's *Dienstrichtlinie* 205: "Discipline means the conscious integration into the whole and carrying out one's duty to the best of one's knowledge, without respect for personal desires or opinions" (quoted in Gubler 1993: 195).[2] So I learned to do away with my desires and opinions. Within a few days of my arrival, I had learned just how powerful structures can be. I clearly felt that there was no way out, that I was at the mercy of a totalitarian institution.

There was a brief moment of hope, when a couple of days later someone told me about the possibility of being exempted from military service for health reasons (which was, of course, a euphemism for mental disorders). So, about three weeks after my military training had started, I was put on a military truck and together with a number of other loonies, I was taken to a subterranean bunker that was a two hour drive from our barracks. There, I talked to a military psychiatrist who made me draw a picture of a tree and then decided that I was stable enough to carry a gun. I was declared "fit for service" and had to return to the barracks.

I arrived in time for the real combat training. As elite troops, we had to be ready to fight behind the lines, in territory occupied by the enemy. So I was taught not only how to use an assault rifle, but also how to handle the bayonet (though this seemed to be a rather old fashioned way of killing your enemy even in 1989). I was shown how to throw hand grenades (do not forget to yell "attention, a hand grenade" to warn those targeted) and advised in urban warfare. Some techniques of house to house fighting I remember to this very day, much to the entertainment of friends, who sometimes get me to leave parties through a second floor window. Moreover, I have proven expertise in shooting with a mobile rocket propelled grenade, a weapon operated by two soldiers and supposedly able to blow up a tank (military cyclists can cope with any enemy). And, I also enjoyed special training as an explosives expert. Should need arise, I could blow up bridges and destroy the enemy's infrastructure.

Yet, the individual combat training was only part of what was happening. I was also given a lesson in the forming of discipline and identity.

While individual identities were sidelined, group identities had to be formed, foremost the platoon's identity. And this was done in a very sophisticated way. If any member of our unit failed to comply with one of the innumerable rules, for example cleaning one's boots, one's rifle, one's anything, there followed a double punishment. First, there was individual punishment. The most popular method was to wake up the wrongdoer in the middle of the night and teach him proper behavior. I remember quite vividly how I once had to clean my gun for over an hour one night, simply because the evening before I was caught sitting instead of laying on my bed. In another instance I was given special training (exercising with my gas mask on at 3 am), because I had failed to store my gun correctly. These, I have to admit, were fairly effective means of securing compliance. Yet, the second form of punishment was even more effective, as it was collective: punishing the entire platoon for individual failures.[3] I recall one Saturday, when we were all waiting in the barrack yard to be sent off for a 24-hour holiday. Yet, because one of us had not greeted an officer correctly just before, we all had to wait until he got his dose of special training. And so the 24-hour holiday had shrunk to a 22-hour one. That guy did not have an easy standing on the train ride back home. From now on, any kind of behavior that would potentially be of harm to the group was ruled out by self-discipline: we were checking on each other prior to the official controls by the sergeants.

Who then, was our enemy? Curiously, it was to be found within rather than outside the Swiss army. The cyclist identity was constructed by constantly confirming to us how important we were and how much better than other parts of the troop. We were the elite; they just ordinary soldiers. We had bicycles; they had to walk. Interestingly, the medical corps ranked lowest in the unofficial troop hierarchy, as the medics did not carry guns and thus were unable to fight. Also, many of them were students and thus found to be predisposed towards cowardice. An even greater threat came from within our troop: the potentially bad impression we would make when leaving the barracks. On the rare occasions when we were allowed an evening off, our uniform, shave, haircut, and so on were controlled exhaustively. In fact, our appearance and behavior were said to be important for the country's security. As a former high ranking officer in the bicycle division explains: "There is still the danger that foreign observers – seeing Swiss soldiers' careless attire and casual appearance – could draw completely wrong conclusions as to the commitment and clout of our army" (Gubler 1993: 199).[4] This is how the soldiers' looks are securitized.

Where was I in all this? More than once I failed to comply and thus became subject to punishment. Yet, in this respect I was no different from anybody else. But I was different from the rest because I was German, both in the other recruits' view and in my self-perception. I did not speak the Swiss dialect properly and lacked the cultural knowledge others could draw upon concerning Swiss military training. My colleagues all had been raised in Switzerland and thus had friends and family who had already done their military service. In fact, belonging to a particular division is often a family tradition. Hence, the fathers and even grandfathers of many of my colleagues were military cyclists, too. Thus they knew pretty well what to expect. I, in contrast, had imagined the Swiss army to be largely similar to the German *Bundeswehr*. Of the latter I had heard a lot while I was in high-school. The military service in Germany was supposed to be boring, but none too strenuous. In many respects, it seemed like a normal job – including regular working hours and holidays. To my surprise, I soon found out that the military training in the Swiss army, and the elitist bicycle troop in particular, was much more ambitious. It reminded me of what I had heard about the training of US marines. Not that my colleagues did not suffer just because they were better prepared than I was, but at least they knew some survival strategies – such as using the free of charge military mail service to have all your family and friends send you huge packets of Swiss chocolate on an almost daily basis. I was pushed to the group's margins, because I was the only one not to receive such parcels. However, I also developed a technique to mitigate this effect: I volunteered to become the group's postman and was therefore in charge of handing out the parcels, as a result of which I became part of the ritual (and able to secure my share of sweets).

A lack of cultural knowledge was also the reason that I felt alienated by the military language used. For my fellow soldiers there was apparently nothing strange about going to the *KZ* when feeling sick. For me, *KZ* was the abbreviation of the Nazis' *Konzentrationslager* (concentration camps). For them, it simply was the short version of *Krankenzimmer* (sick room). Also, I seemed to be the only one shocked by the fact that a particular type of canned meat was commonly referred to as 'stamped jew' (*g'stampfter Jud'*).

However, it was in the second half of the *Rekrutenschule* when I felt my liminal position most strongly. Our unit had been displaced – on bicycles, of course – from the French speaking part of Switzerland to the German speaking part. I was now closer to home, though it turned out that it was a bit too close perhaps. As it happened, we were assigned the task of patrolling a stretch of the border between Switzerland and Germany. That stretch, we were told, was particularly difficult to control because of its hilly terrain and dense woods. Allegedly, many illegal immigrants from third world countries had crossed the border and entered Switzerland here. And we should help stopping them. So here I was, armed with my gun, hiding behind a barn only a few steps from the German border and watching out for refugees. I was never quite sure whether this was only meant to be an exercise or whether our commanders really thought that we would capture poor migrants. Fortunately, no one tried to cross the border while I was on patrol (not that I noticed, at least), except for the farmers who owned land on the other side and crossed the border without either them or anyone else taking much notice that there was a border. I was relieved when our division was moved elsewhere, even though the next phase of our military training meant that we were rehearsing combat situations – like stopping a "Czech tank" – at an artillery range at the Säntis, a mountain in the north-east of Switzerland from where one can see – weather conditions permitting – the German village where I grew up.

I thought about not going back to the barracks whenever we were given a day off. However, I was not brave enough to actually desert by taking refuge in Germany. Somehow I managed to hold out. And just a few days before the end of my *Rekrutenschule*, I was rewarded with a last strange experience. In the night of November 9 to 10, 1989, I was on guard in the barracks, by then already well acquainted with spending long hours in the cold looking out for potential dangers. After two hours of fighting against the sleep, my replacement came, quite excited as I noticed, and told me to tune in to the radio. And so I found out that the Berlin wall came down that night. Soldiers that had been trained for years not to let anyone escape were now unable to control the border anymore. Tens of thousands of people crossed the iron curtain and entered West Berlin. And I sat there in a Swiss casern and joked with my colleagues about how long it would take the East Germans to get from Berlin to the Swiss border, where we would certainly do a better job than our colleagues from the GDR. Our cycling division would definitely be able to prevent these East Germans from entering our beautiful country.

One day later, after 17 long weeks, I was discharged from the *Rekrutenschule*, free again. I went to the theater in Zürich the very same evening, to see a play Max Frisch (1989) had written in support of a political initiative for abolishing the Swiss army. Two weeks later a referendum was held, in which the initiative gained more votes than anyone had ever imagined. Thirty-five and a half percent of all voters had favored doing away with the army, an astonishing number given that until then many firmly believed in the saying that Switzerland does not have an army, but is one. To some extent this reconciled me with the country; after all I had discovered that I am not the only one in doubt about the use of this army. Yet, I did not want to wait until, in some distant future, a further 15 percent of the population would turn their back on the army and help dissolve it. I was realistic enough to see that this would not happen while I was still a soldier. Because, this is what I continued to be.

For the time being, I had only completed my basic military training, the *Rekrutenschule*. But in Switzerland this is just the beginning. Every soldier not only takes home his entire military gear, including rifle and ammunition, thus being ready to go to war anytime. He also returns to the barracks for three weeks every year until age 35, doing a so-called *Wiederholungskurs* (repetition course). Thus I was facing another 15 years as a part time soldier, spending most of my holidays in the years to come in a battle suit, cycling and shooting. This was a perspective that I found more than disturbing. Yet, it is not so easy to escape. If one refuses to attend the repetition courses, a prison sentence is the consequence. I was still too pragmatic to go that far. Instead, I chose a more convenient way out: leaving the country, which in this case was very much fleeing the country. Yet, I could not simply go, but had to ask my regional army commander for what is called *Auslandsurlaub* (holiday abroad). Once granted, I was allowed to store my military equipment in an armory and to move back to Germany. And this is what I did – and I have not returned to this very day.

In fact, I still am on *Auslandsurlaub*. This means that I am still a Swiss soldier; at least I was one until I turned 35 years, the age the normal soldier is demobilized (though I was never informed of my demobilization). The status of a holiday maker allowed me to stay away from the yearly repetition courses. However, it did not mean that I would no longer belong to the army. In fact, there are clear rules on how a soldier on leave for holiday ought to behave. And a soldier I still was, my official rank now being that of a cyclist. I was obliged to notify the Swiss embassy of my new address one month after taking residence abroad, just as I had to inform them of any change of residence thereafter. More importantly, a leaflet I was handed out when granted *Auslandsurlaub* specifies what I have to do in case of war: "In the case of a war mobilization of the Swiss Army all ... 'holiday makers abroad' have to return to Switzerland the fastest way" (Eidgenössisches Militärdepartement).[5]

There was no war mobilization, so I did not have to go back. And, as a small sign of civil disobedience, I never informed the Swiss embassy of my frequent changes of address in the following years, without any consequence (almost to my disappointment – could I have overestimated the accuracy of the Swiss authorities?). So it seemed as if I had pretty much escaped the Swiss army simply by not living in Switzerland anymore. Yet, there was a price to pay for that: I had to call off my plans to study in Zürich and went to university in Germany instead. As it happened, I enrolled for political science at the university of Konstanz, a German city located right at the Swiss border; in fact, the border runs right through the city, separating it from its Swiss twin Kreuzlingen. Affordable flats were very rare in Konstanz at the time and therefore many students lived in Switzerland, where rents were much lower. To do so, they had to apply for one of the temporary residence permits, which the Swiss authorities would grant every year. For obvious reasons, I could not move to Kreuzlingen and had to pay the higher rents of Konstanz instead. My military past made its impact felt. This situation was somewhat absurd, but at the end of the day little more than an annoyance. However, a few years later both the degree of absurdity and annoyance increased considerably.

After some time away, I returned to Konstanz to finish my university degree. In the meantime, the housing situation had become even worse than before. I simply could not find a place to stay. The only room I was offered happened to be in Kreuzlingen, that is on Swiss territory. With no alternative, I accepted. Obviously, I could not take residence there officially, as this would have meant that I had to return to the military cyclists for my repetition courses. Thus, I became an illegal inhabitant of the country of which I was a citizen, the country that only a few years ago I had defended against illegal immigrants. Every time I crossed the border to and from Germany, which I did almost every day to get to the university (by bicycle, of course), I was worried that somehow the Swiss customs officers would find out that the

German passport I showed to them was not my only one. Fortunately, they seemed not to have discovered my little secret.

However, let me return to the year 1989, as the story about my military career is not quite finished yet. The very day my request for "holiday abroad" was accepted, I left Switzerland. I traveled to Berlin to see what had happened in the "real world" while I was away, and then spend a couple of weeks at my parents' place to recover from my military training. I deeply regretted my "rational choice" to serve in the Swiss army. The only good thing about it seemed that I would now begin my studies, while all my friends had still more than a year of civilian service ahead of them. However, it soon turned out that I was terribly wrong. I was in the middle of skimming through the information brochures of different universities in order to make up my mind where and what to study, when one day in January 1990 I received a letter from the German military. The *Bundeswehr* informed me that as a German citizen living in Germany I would have to serve in the German military. And, as if to leave no room for misunderstanding, they named the place and time when my military service was to start. Only a few weeks later I should take up my military training in the nearby city of Pfullendorf.

Surprised, but not really worried, I responded that their letter must have been a mistake, as I had already served in the Swiss Army, proofs attached. But no, I was told. Switzerland had not signed the "Convention on the Reduction of Cases of Multiple Nationality and on Military Obligations in Cases of Multiple Nationality" of May 6, 1963. Nor did there exist a bilateral agreement between Germany and Switzerland on how to deal with the military duties of double citizens. Therefore, the 1930 Hague Convention applies, which stipulates that "a person having two or more nationalities may be regarded as its national by each of the States whose nationality he possesses" (*Convention on Certain Questions relating to the Conflict of Nationality Laws*, 1930: Article 3). Hence international law enabled Germany to treat me as if I was solely its citizen and consequently to disregard that I had already been doing a military service in Switzerland. Never before or since have I been affected as directly by international cooperation (or rather the lack thereof).

A couple of letter exchanges later (I had now taken a lawyer to support my case), the German authorities had not changed their point of view. Even the fact that it would be considered a criminal offence in Switzerland, namely treason, if I would serve in a foreign army, was rejected as not being Germany's business. Only in one regard did the German authorities offer me a concession: they would take into account the time I had already served in the Swiss army and reduce my military service in Germany accordingly. Thus, they changed my conscription order: instead of 15 months, I would now have to serve a mere 11 months!

I was worried, in fact shocked. I simply could not imagine starting yet another military career. Only, how would I get out? At first, an injury came to my help. Due to a broken ankle my conscription was postponed another three months. In the meantime, I had filed a petition for being recognized as a conscientious objector, arguing that my ethical principles would not allow me to carry a gun. Given my existing military record, this appeared not very convincing. Like all such requests by former soldiers, it was dealt with by a special committee, which had the reputation of giving candidates a very hard time. In disciplinary hearings they test the applicant's conscience, confronting him with scenarios like: What would you do if you see someone rape your girl-friend? Suppose you had a weapon, would you use it to stop the rape or would you simply stand aside and look, given that your conscience does not allow you to interfere? In my case, however, they did not seem very interested in proving that my argument was inconsistent and that therefore my conscience was only a pretext for my unwillingness to serve in the *Bundeswehr*. In fact, I was simply informed of the fact that the committee had accepted my request. It seemed as if the German authorities were glad they could avoid having a Swiss soldier serving in the *Bundeswehr*.

I was now an acknowledged conscientious objector. As such I would have to do the alternative civilian service. Some time later I took up my civilian service in a school for disabled children in Konstanz, located only a few steps from the Swiss border. Sometimes we would be playing the kids' favorite game – soldiers at war – and they admired me for how good I was at it.

Notes

1 Author's translation.
2 Author's translation.
3 This form of collective punishment and its effectiveness has also been described in Max Frisch's (1974) account of his experiences in the Swiss military.
4 Author's translation.
5 Author's translation.

References

Allen, Woody (dir.) (1989) *Crimes and Misdemeanors* [film].
Convention on Certain Questions relating to the Conflict of Nationality Laws (1930) The Hague, April 12.
Eidgenössisches Militärdepartement (without date): Weisungen für Auslandschweizer (Form 2.47).
Frisch, Max (1974) *Dienstbüchlein*, Frankfurt am Main: Suhrkamp.
Frisch, Max (1989) *Schweiz ohne Armee? Ein Palaver*, Zürich: Limmat.
Gubler, Robert (1993) *Schweizerische Militärradfahrer, 1891–1993*, Zürich: Verlag Neue Zürcher Zeitung.
Leuenberger, Jean-Pierre (2000) Interview in *Süddeutsche Zeitung Magazin*, April 20.

6 Weakness leaving my body

An essay on the interpersonal relations of international politics

Jacob L. Stump

> George A. never saw John Wayne on the sands of Iwo Jima.
> "The Sands of Iwo Jima," *Drive-By Truckers*

I've struggled with this chapter. Naren, my friend and colleague, encapsulates well what I mean.

> I am hesitant. I am afraid. I am wary. I am suspicious. I am not entirely sure of the object of my fears, suspicions, wariness, and hesitancy. I am not sure why it is that these conditions afflict me. But they are there, willing me not to write. So great is their force that sometimes I liken finishing this piece to a giant exorcism.
> (Kumarakulasingam, this volume)

This essay allows only a relatively small window on the course of my life. I focus on a particularly formative span of time where I moved through three institutional settings and constructions of self: 1) just as I graduated high school, 2) when I joined the United States Army, 3) and then when I left the military and went to the university. These episodes illustrate how practices of self crafting are historically contingent, flexible, and "built up" achievements (Blumer 1986).

Where does "my IR come from"? (Hulsse, this volume). Surely I cannot explain myself, but I can highlight some biographical and historical sources that, from my present vantage, seem to shed light on the various relations that make my "ways of world making" possible in the first place (Goodman 1978). This is not only a "giant exorcism," as Naren says, but an effort to be intellectually honest, because what I study and how I study and write are grounded in my biography and personal history. In that case, it may well be that the predominate "norms of scholarship do not require that researchers bare their souls, only their procedures" (Lofland and Lofland 1995: 13), but volumes like this one are challenging those norms and reconfiguring scholarship to include richer personal detail and reflection about the trajectory from which one's IR comes.

****

I joined the US Army as my junior year in high school neared its end. From the start of our class's senior year, my long time friend and I, who had already joined the Army, began training our bodies. We also rehearsed the stories that enabled us to make sense of our lives. During "Advanced P.E.," as the class was called, we imposed a disciplinary regime on ourselves that our Army recruiter encouraged and affirmed as "showing initiative." We ran a couple of miles around the track everyday and lifted weights, we talked about being soldiers and going to war and what it meant to have honor, be courageous, and to kill for the country. We affirmed each other. The recruiter's work and the high school class were enough to keep us moving toward a new sense of self and a new institutional setting.

Two weeks after I graduated, I was scheduled to leave for Basic Training. My dad drove me to the recruiter's office so that I could board a bus that would take me to a regional processing station in Knoxville, Tennessee. We pulled into the strip mall parking lot where the office was located and found a spot. Dad cut the engine. We sat there silently for a moment; our eyes straight ahead, looking out at a moderately crowded four lane road that traced through town. Suddenly, dad broke down and cried: "What will I do?"

Up until that day, for the 12 years since my mom died of breast cancer, it had just been my dad and me living together. He worked at a steel fabrication shop about 40 minutes away in a nearby town and I attended school in another town. Most every evening, unless I had some after school sports event that dad would attend in his dirty work clothes, he cooked supper and we ate together.

Technically skilled at interpreting blue prints, cutting details, and laying out steel designs to ensure they work in practice, dad never learned to read. He had severe dyslexia. Ever since I can remember, dad has been dependent on me or other family members to read and write for him. I clearly recall helping dad fill out paper work at the unemployment office, for instance, or describing what some bank statement read. Ironically, I read early as a child. Mom, who greatly enjoyed reading books, particularly the Holy Bible and Louis Lamoure westerns, read to me every night. After she died, I continued to read. Dad always encouraged the activity by paying for magazine subscriptions and buying me all the *Dragon Lance* and Stephen Koontz novels I consumed. He took me on special trips to a nearby mall bookstore, where I browsed the aisles as he looked at picture books of old steam engines and Second World War images. It pleased him to see me read; he said often "you have your mom's love of books."

Unable to read and with little institutional support for learning disabilities, dad dropped out of school when he was 12 years old. Under aged, he worked illegally at a saw mill near his house for 50 cents per hour. Sometimes, he now tells me laughingly, he made and distributed moonshine to supplement the family income.

He can vividly recall his stark poverty. I've heard stories about how he could see chickens roaming beneath his house through the cracks between the floor boards. During the winter, to keep the cold drafts out of the house and the heat inside, he used a combination of cardboard and newspaper insulation; blankets were sewn out of flour sacks and burlap sacks provided an extra layer to one's pants. The Great Depression precipitated these harsh conditions. In particular, all the valuable, virgin timber around the area had been cut less than 20 years before by the Hassinger Lumber Company (McGuinn 2008). After the saw mill closed in 1929, the largest natural resource was gone and so was the employer that extracted them. There was very little work and generally the people were very poor (Gable and Davis 1997). Also important for my dad's particular situation was that his father ("grandpa Ed" as I knew him) abandoned them during the Second World War. Ed left dad, his older sister Gladys and their mom, Dora (my "granny"), when he joined the US Navy, as a *single* male, to fight the Japanese in the Pacific Ocean.

When dad turned 18, like so many younger people around the Whitetop, Greencove, and Konnarock areas at the time, he went "up a country," which is a colloquial way of identifying some urban area like DC, Baltimore, or Richmond. Dad went to DC. He had saved 18 dollars and had a bag of clothes. This was the first time dad had left the mountains; he would not return for one year. Enabling him to make this move was a network of people (mostly single men, but also some married couples) originally from the mountains, that served as social and economic supports to get him (and so many others like him) started. Friends and relatives provided dad a place to stay those first few weeks until he established himself in the new environment. Connections in local steel shops were critical in helping him land a job and start learning a skilled trade. They offered transportation between home and the city. And they provided great drinking buddies. For ten years, between 1958 and 1968, dad lived, labored, and loved in around Washington, DC. Shortly after the riots that burned through DC, he left and moved closer to home.

I didn't know what to do or say at the sight of Dad crying; I was sort of stunned. I only saw my dad cry one other time and that was when mom died. "I have to go," I said as I pushed the car door open, stepped out, peeked in one last time and then slammed it shut.

****

The Army recruiter that I met in high school served me well. Recruiters from the various branches of the armed services were regularly in the cafeteria during the lunch periods. Sitting at a table together near the door, they were easily seen by entering students. Their uniform always stood out against the high school context. Surveying the crowd of students, they were a visible possibility waiting to be activated. Sometimes, near the end of lunch, one or two of them would circulate and mingle with the students. The particular Army recruiter that I approached had stopped by our table on a few occasions. He knew, as I'm sure I told him dozens of times, that I had hopes of going to Airborne school and then trying out for the Green Berets.[1] I was "fired up," he would say of me, which is exactly what recruiters like to see, I imagine. He functioned like a relay and just seemed to direct my energy.

The connections that enabled my path to the military are complex and difficult to discern. Significantly, however, Jack, my mom's brother, volunteered to fight in Vietnam. I never met him. But I grew up around and continue to communicate with a community of men in Konnarock who were close friends with Jack. As they still remark, there is a noticeable resemblance between Jack and me. These men were drafted during the Vietnam War and sent to fight for ideas they didn't even know about. Jack didn't survive. But I learned of my uncle's exploits through his war-time friends. In their eyes, and in mine, he was a warrior. Climbing nearby Straight Mountain with nothing but a knife and surviving for two, three, and four days at time. Jack swam in the same swimming hole that I did. As I knew him through the stories of his friends, Jack would jump from the highest reaches of the bridge and swim under water for long stretches. And, I recently learned from a friend of Jack's, he often listened to the "Ballad of the Green Berets," a patriotic song that hit number one on the Billboard Charts for five weeks in 1966. It was that year in December when a 19 year old Jack left to wage war in Vietnam. Nine months later he was "killed in action." In my later teen years especially, the stories about Jack played an important role in shaping my understanding of the military and what it meant to serve.

Those stories played alongside the old war movies that my father and I watched together when I was a kid. I remember on many occasions sitting with dad for a couple of hours as movies like *The Dirty Dozen*, *The Bridge on the River Kwai*, *Patton*, *Apocalypse Now*, *Rambo*, and *Platoon* played across the television screen. It was an activity that we shared, and something that undoubtedly shaped my understanding of war and soldiering. But the movies and the stories about Jack played out in my life in more concrete ways long before I ever joined the military. One of my favorite activities as a kid was to play war. Dad's large yard and the adjoining neighbors' empty fields were my stage: I built forts, spied, played combat with neighboring boys, camped alongside the creek bank, and fished. This memory was recently made concrete. Stuffed in my father's attic, my wife Rebecca found an old painted stick that I pretended to use as a rifle. It occurred to me, as I stood there looking at the piece of wood, this cultural artifact of my childhood helps me understand "who I was" and the views I once had toward war and the nation-state.

Either way, I was confident that I did not want to be in the infantry; but I did aim to get a "combat arms job." During war, this kind of job would position me along the "edge of the spear" and not in a "support" position, as it is commonly phrased.

I made this decision at the regional processing station in Knoxville. There, I was subjected to a *very* thorough physical exam that complemented the Armed Services Vocational Aptitude Battery that I had taken some time ago. The physical involved all the usual number of tests and inspections – vision, hearing, fluids, pressures, and so on. But the bodily surveillance and performances meant to decipher my health went even further, as one might expect in the military context. For instance, I recall standing naked, shoulder-to-shoulder with a group of maybe 15 other young men. Our eyes were fixed on the doctor standing before us; no one dared look around. With our hands behind our backs, we were instructed to slowly squat until our knees were resting on the floor; walk forward a few steps on our knees; then stand back up without using our hands for balance or to push off the floor. These two instruments enabled the military to get a better fix on my mental faculties and bodily condition. Was "Stump" worth the investment? I imagine some military bureaucrat might calculate. Apparently so.

After much discussion with the liaison assigned to me, I decided that a 12B ("twelve bravo"), or "combat engineer," was the way I wanted to go. Most appealing, perhaps, was that the job would involve carrying and implementing explosives for defensive and combat operations and it had a close correlation with a position on Special Forces A-Teams.[2]

When the opportunity presented itself, I insisted that I get an "airborne slot" in writing *before* I signed up, a technique my recruiter had instructed me to use. He told me to "hold out because they'll want you." This slot would ensure that after I completed Basic Training and Advanced Individual Training in Missouri I would be sent to Fort Benning, Georgia, where the Army trains soldiers to "jump from perfectly good airplanes."[3] The problem, my liaison told me, was that there were no slots available. What I thought would be a smooth operation was turning out to be more complicated. Off balance and angry at the turn of events, I basically said: "no, I won't be joining today. If you can get an airborne slot, call me." A few hours later I was back at home. My dad was happy; he was not keen on my decision to join in the first place. For me, however, *my* plans seemed to unravel just as I was trying to put them together. There was nothing more I could do.

To my surprise, the next morning my recruiter called and told me that there was a slot with "your name on it." I just had to go sign up, but it had to be soon. A short while later I was back in Knoxville. My recruiter had picked me up from home and drove us the four hours to the processing station. With an airborne slot in writing, I signed the contract with the Army. Along with a few other people who had just signed up, I was placed in a small, somber room lined with dark wood. This was in sharp contrast to the rest of the regional processing center's white, sterile, standardized hospital-feel. It gave the room a serious look that was emphasized further by an Army officer instructing the undisciplined group of "civilians" on the proper bodily postures, motions, and times to "stand at attention" and to "salute" the large American flag in the front and center of the room. After a bit of practice and correction, we performed a ritual oath in rough unison that formally inducted us into this living tradition of people sworn to defend the Constitution of the United States of America. The transformation of my body and sense of self was starting to ramp up and formalize as I entered the new institutional setting.

****

Four months of strictly disciplined physical and mental training in the Missouri Ozarks and the Georgia flatland had indelibly changed me. My life, time, space, and ethical conduct were, in a very concrete sense, being structured or over-coded on a daily basis by military rule and discipline. When and where I appeared and how I acted were authorized matters with very little room for debate; it was perhaps a "total institution" (Goffman 1961). I was no longer a "civilian," but had started mastering the basics of being a "soldier," which set me apart from the civilian world in important ways – from dress, physical appearance, and use of language, to orientation toward life. Additionally, I closely tied myself to the oft repeated claim that I was not simply a "soldier," or "leg," as the airborne instructors called those civilian and military that lacked the silver airborne wings. No, *I* felt a strong sense of pride: *I* was an "airborne combat engineer" that would soon be assigned to a light, combat ready unit at Fort Bragg, North Carolina.

Between Georgia and North Carolina, however, I returned home for the first time. The change in my conduct was especially evident in a nonmilitary context. Even without the angry and urgent commands of an instructor directing me, I woke early everyday and ran for an allotted time and performed the basic set of calisthenics that I had been trained to do over the past four months. Before my contact with the Army, I had never jogged; indeed, even today, there are no joggers in Konnarock. These changes were also visible to other people. My dad remarked that I had "a filthy mouth," "a mouth like a sailor," and he told me to "watch my mouth" around younger family members. I didn't have a saintly vocabulary before I left for the military, but since I had started the training process my use of profanity had become more striking, intense, and wide-ranging. Outside the military context this was troubling; inside that context, however, it was a commonplace feature of my everyday life.

This new, spicier vocabulary was accompanied with a newly refashioned body and sense of self. With closely cropped hair, I was cocky and assertive, physically stronger, more aggressive, visibly thicker and more toned than before I left. I was proud of how fast I could run four miles or rip out one hundred pushups and sit ups, and I told people as much; but only after I bedazzled them with stories from basic training and jump school. My uniform served to set me further apart and to amplify my presentation to the audience. A distinctive maroon beret, silver wings, and weapons qualifications medals on my puffed up chest, dress pants tucked into spit-shined leather Corcoran boots, all worked to affirm my sense of self and status in relation to those around me.

My symbolic arrangement also shaped others' response to me. People wanted to see me in uniform and they wanted photographs. I posed alone and together with family and friends. When I visited my high school, I recall well how teachers and administrative staff that had been indifferent towards me before responded with displays of respect and treated me as someone special. They introduced me proudly to their current class of students. This was a significant change. In four months, I had transformed myself from a student and sometime troublemaker to an honored guest and a lauded example. The meaning of who I was in relation to long time connections had changed in dramatic ways and the responses that flowed from those associations – taking my photograph and displaying me as an example to a high school class – worked to mutually affirm that construction of self.

****

The first year that I was in the military I was mostly deployed into the field for training exercises or to conduct humanitarian missions abroad.

One cool and wet spring morning in 1997, Charlie Company 37th Engineers (Combat) (Airborne) along with some other elements from Fort Bragg deployed from North Carolina to the Dominican Republic (DR). I loaded on to a C-130 Hercules at the adjacent Pope Air Force Base just as the sun was breaking the horizon and evaporating the morning fog. A few hours later, I stepped into the humid Caribbean heat. We landed at a DR airbase that had only two or three propeller planes and one helicopter – a point I remember well because it was the butt of so many jokes among my friends and me.

As I sit here today, I think this is *only* a joke from *our* perspective as US soldiers. I am confident that the DR soldiers that we saw around the base, but hardly interacted with, would not have found their national air force a joke. What was the function of that joke, I wonder? It aided us in making sense of our situation in a foreign land by affirming our national position relative to their weaker, limper version of our superior air force. The joke, like our deployment in general, seems to fit into the overall pattern of asymmetry that constitutes an "imperial encounter," to use Roxanne Doty's words (1996).

Either way, I was as surprised by the heat as I was by the historical, social, and economic contexts in which I was being temporarily inserted and utilized for strategic aims of which I was largely unaware. At the same time and on my part, I was ignorant of and unconcerned about United State foreign policy toward the DR and of the larger history of European involvement with that region of the world. As an 18-year-old, low ranking private, my daily mission centered on shuttling military personnel and resources in a HUMVEE between work sites and the HQ, maintaining and cleaning the vehicle, and doing various manual jobs like digging a foundation, laying cinder blocks, or pouring and smoothing concrete. As I understood our official mission, we were primarily there to build a hospital and a helipad and to extend a runway to handle larger aircraft, which was combined with some combat water training and an airborne operation with our foreign counterparts. Simple enough, I thought. The official mission didn't really involve interacting with people from the Dominican Republic apart from the candy that we were sometimes given to toss to kids that ran alongside as we maneuvered through the crowded neighborhood streets.

These small acts of diplomacy, however, were often set against an enforced separation. Our worksite, tools, and construction supplies were fenced off from the locals and guarded 24 hours a day by an armed member of the DR's military. There was very little commingling of local and US soldiers. What interactions there were centered around the work of US officers, noncommissioned officers (NCOs), and Spanish speaking enlisted members that could help translate the divide between local leaders and US Army personnel. I never even spoke to the guards that marked the line between us and them. We all just kind of watched each other and went about our business: the guards watching the locals and us, just as we watched the guards and the locals, and the locals watching all the soldiers (Dominican and American) because usually neither would be in their midst. We appeared every day of the week for a couple of months, mostly kept to ourselves as we built a clinic adjacent to a pristine baseball field that some big name Major League Baseball player had funded. Then we left.

I remember well the first day that we made it to the work site. The only people there, it seemed, were the crowds of poor people that probably couldn't leave if they wanted to, we soldiers, and one of the baseball player's agents. When we pulled up in our military vehicles, the agent walked over from the baseball field and gave each US soldier a T-shirt, a baseball hat, and a miniature wooden baseball bat. I wonder, now, if he knew we were scheduled to arrive. Regardless, it seemed surreal to me, so dreamlike, disconnected and out of place to have this fast talking, wheeling and dealing agent pass out Major League trinkets, especially against the backdrop of the manicured field with sharp white lines, red-orange mud, deeply potted roads, skinny bodies, and curious dark eyes.

On several occasions while at the work site, a few meters from the building that was taking shape, I sat at the top of a hill under a shade tree to eat my Meal Ready to Eat. The tree grew at the hill crest, giving me a view of either slope. But what always caught my attention was not the clinic. Rather, I could see thin tendrils of smoke drifting into the air, as cook fires burned among the rows of one-room, wood and tin shacks that stretched down into the valley below. That was the view that mesmerized me. The way the small houses were perched there, bending precariously with the contours of the hillside, hanging in poverty together. It was such a powerful sight. On the edge, they were so beautiful, so alive, so exotic, so scary, so sad, so infuriating, so confusing, so many things all at once. I could hear noises, loud speakers, radios, and shouts, and I could see kids playing and people going about their daily lives. Always at a distance, however; I never approached.

Usually on the weekends, when we were not scheduled to work or train, we interacted more with locals. People walked, rented motorcycles or cars, hired taxis, used road public transportation and official vehicles to get around to the popular resort areas of the island, which more often than not meant going to Boca Chica beach and joining the European tourists. Generally, we traveled in pairs or small groups – it was policy, but it was also the guys you lived and trained with on a daily basis, one's brother in arms – and, perhaps in the worst of these weekends, we acted as loose bands of young, loud, and pushy hooligans with ravenous appetites for food, drink, and sex. As I felt and am confident others felt similarly, our US military ID combined with an overly assured sense of self, was warrant enough to tread legal boundaries with little regard for consequences. On top of that, as the saying went for many of us (and this was long before the Las Vegas tourism bureau popularized it): "what happens on deployment stays on deployment." It was a quick throw away phrase used countless times during the course of the various weekends; said with a laugh to one's self and one's friends that justified any manner of conduct.

Near the end of the 37th's two months in the Dominican Republic, after a particularly intense weekend of drinking and partying in the Boca Chica area, our relations with the locals were becoming raw. Some rented scooters had been wrecked and not properly returned, outstanding bills had allegedly not been paid, too many drunken accidents and mishaps at bars and incidents between soldiers and locals fermented into a sharp point of interaction. Locals wanted us to leave, which was indicated clear enough to most of us by the gathering group of men and women raising their voices and boisterously making their presence felt. Laughter and our good time quickly turned into what I thought was a serious situation. A couple of alert sergeants acted quickly, loaded up the few soldiers in the area on a HUMVEE and exited the scene without incident.

On the same day that my wife found my childhood stick-gun stuffed in my dad's attic, I ran across a diary that I had kept while I was in the DR and some letters that I had mailed to my dad. Looking closely at them from my present vantage, I see how my encounter with the DR affirmed my *American* sense of self and how it called forth uncomfortable questions regarding "who I am" and "what are we doing there." My daily experience set in stark relief the high rhetoric of "freedom," "peace," "justice," "humanitarianism," and "security" that US soldiers often operate under, with the messy and tentative implementation of policies on the ground.

****

At some point, my relationship with the military changed. I don't know when, exactly, but it is a complex matter that I cannot claim to fully understand or describe.

While I was still in the Army, a number of events occurred. I was ordered to relocate to a different barracks a mile down the street and to move in with a man I did not know and who was in a different unit. We had little connection. This put social and physical distance between my closest friends and me. And it had a chain reaction. I no longer lived across the hallway, which meant that I was removed from the everyday banter that occurred among the various dorm rooms and their inhabitants. I no longer traveled with my closest friends to and from the Company area of operations for morning physical training, which meant that I did not eat breakfast with them after exercise. Over time, I found myself on the margins of the group. No one called to alert me to or invite me out for weekend excursions to restaurants, bars, and recreational outings, for instance.

When all that combined with the aspects of garrison life, I began to see in a more critical light. We low ranking privates were ordered to do ridiculous and pointless "dog and pony shows," like sweeping sand from the Company parking lot before high ranking officers who were chauffeured in multi-HUMVEE convoys, rolled into our presence. We were on the east coast of North Carolina, where sand is practically everywhere. Sweeping was a fruitless task, a way to "look busy" when there are no meaningful chores or training exercises happening. I began to see this aspect of military life as the flip side of the frontline soldier; the anti-hero who "bitches and moans" about picking up cigarette butts and about showing rigid obedience to people (some of whom I and my comrades jokingly called "dumbass" behind their backs) *only* because they "out rank" me. I was infuriated by my daily tasks, by the men that ordered me to carry them out, by the reasons given for the actions, and by my sense of anger about not being able to speak up.

On a personal level, I was exhausted. Dad remembers me starting to sleepwalk when I was seven years old, just after my mom died.[4] Initially it was bad. I was getting out of bed multiple times during the night. I would scream out, thrash around, sit up, stand up in bed, and, sometimes, leap from my bed in a full sprint and bash my legs into furniture. Especially as a younger kid, dad often made me sleep in his bed so that he could prevent me from hurting myself. Sleepwalking came and went in intensity throughout my youth and teenage years. It seemed the more I was stressed and physically worn, the more I was active in my sleep. This pattern re-emerged during Basic Training and at this later point in my military experience.

I don't recall my relations with my platoon members being adversely affected when they learned of my sleepwalking. I was surprised, however, when I found out that they were helping me at night when we were in the field. On one occasion, I sat up in my sleep and started screaming out for help during a large training exercise, when my squad was operating in an overwatch position. This could have been a lethal mistake in combat. No one said anything, but we all knew it. It was as if I believed that when I was deployed into the field my sleepwalking would cease. But I was wrong. I had fooled myself and was taken aback by the revelation. Sleepwalking, I realized then, was something that I could not simply turn off; it was a part of me, my history, beyond my control, beyond the control of the Army and my immediate superiors. It was a weakness associated with a wound, the death of my mom. I could not force from my memory seeing her body weaken and become frail and eventually succumbing to breast and (then) bone cancer and to the various chemotherapies and medications used in vain by the doctors. My sleepwalking continued to worsen.

In contrast to my youthful imaginings and popular TV commercials of what it meant to serve in the military, I increasingly began to see the repetition and confinement of garrison as a dead end. The life of a frontline soldier was not what I had expected. I got piss drunk every weekend with my friends and went to strip bars for entertainment. Then, Monday through Friday, I was compelled to train harder, to run further and faster, to carry more weight, to "drive on," to be "hard" and, perhaps most of all, to not be weak. "Pain," as was often said by my comrades and my superiors and just as often by myself, "is only weakness leaving your body." I started to realize, however, that there were some pains and weaknesses and frailties that could not be expelled; they were bound to you, part of your daily embodiment.

At some point, the training regime and way of living that I once organized my life around began to *suffocate* me. The meaning of the regime and the lifestyle didn't resonate anymore; it found no connection. The 37th's motto, which is displayed on every soldier's maroon beret and hangs above the entryway to most important offices around the battalion area, inscribes the social situation that I operated within and marks a good point of contrast: "Fortune and misfortune are all the same to the Man of Stout Heart." My heart, in some ways, had given out. I didn't care anymore. No longer did I strive to join the Green Berets. Even carrying the silver airborne wings seemed too great a burden.

The way I left Fort Bragg is indicative of the sense of disconnection that I felt and of the active rejection of the military that my actions embodied. One day during the late spring, after I had completed all of the exiting procedures required by the Army, I pulled my black Mazda pickup near the barracks on "smoke bomb hill," where I lived. My assigned room was on the third floor. I stuffed my clothes and unbreakables in large, 30 gallon black trash bags and dropped them three stories into the bed of the pickup, which I had backed directly below the stairwell balcony. I carried down my television, stereo and other valuable items and loaded them in the cab. Without saying goodbye, I drove away.

This takes me back to my dad's tears that summer day in 1996, when I slammed the car door shut and said goodbye to him. That moment of rejection was a long time coming; a fracture that started a few years earlier when, in the heat of an argument with dad over some issue that I no longer remember, I said: "I don't respect you. You didn't serve in the military and you didn't go to war like Grandpa Ed or Jack." We stood there, opposed to each other, with the living room between us. That is what I remember today; that image, those words and the tense feeling of anger, social distance, and physical proximity. I took a stand. It was a rejection of dad and an embrace of the heroic soldier figure. But the person that embodied those actions was no more. Or at least that self and the romantic notions of military service that were integral to its stability were comparatively insignificant given my concrete experiences and lived attitude. I left Fort Bragg and the military way of life and moved back home with dad. He was happy to have me back in the house and treated me differently, more like a "man" than a "boy." We took an extended car trip together that summer into the New England region of the US. I drove.

Yet, as life goes, my break with the military was more complicated than that. My social distance from the military and the identity and lifestyle that it entailed were not a function of my physical distance from the base. The autumn following my exit from the military, I started at a regional university near my dad's home. For years after I left the military, I continued to wake very early every morning, exercise daily, and draw from the discipline instilled by the training. I completed a BA in Political Science in three and a half years and decided to pursue a PhD because of that discipline which, as I alluded to earlier, was lacking in high school. I continue to borrow military metaphors and apply them to new settings: joking to friends who are worried about an upcoming exam that they just have to "drive on" through the concern; or jesting that the sweat and pain my wife's morning bicycle commute generates is only weakness leaving her body. Stories, experiences, and anecdotes about my time in the military serve me well in the classroom to illustrate points about various topics. And I've found that when people – ROTC students, athletes, veterans, anti-war activists, pacifists, and feminists – learn that I served in the Army, especially in a combat arms position, and then got out and repudiated that way of life, it positively connects me to them. The break, in other words, was never complete when I drove away in the Mazda. How could it be? The military is bound up with my body and memory and pedagogical style, my dad, the toys in his attic, the place that he lives, and the movies that we still sometimes watch together, Grandpa Ed, Uncle Jack, and his surviving friends whom I care for and see regularly.

There is no escaping my personal history, but "who I am" and how I make sense of the military has changed drastically over the past years. I went from offering up my mind and body as a sacrifice to the United States of America to a very different stance today: exuberant patriotism and nationalistic zeal sounds hollow and foolishly naïve, especially among those that have not fully committed their bodies and minds to the violent business of sovereignty and instead legitimate the state by paying taxes, by giving lip service to the virtues of the American nation-state, by voting in presidential elections, and by waving flags in support of this or that domestic or foreign policy issue. My experience before, during, and after the military and how I made sense of it has troubled my once unquestioned bond to the American nation and the foreign policy (Campbell 1998) efforts that constitute it. I have come to value and affirm my concrete connections to family and friends (who live around the US territory and the world) and to the place in the Appalachian Mountains that I call home.

Notes

1 In some instances, a corporal (E-4) can attend the Qualifying Course ("Q-Course") but most often soldiers holding the rank of sergeant (E-5) or higher are the recruits.
2 An Operational Detachment Alpha consists of 12 man teams with members trained as weapons sergeants, communications sergeants, engineering sergeants, and medical sergeants.
3 Basic Training is the common denominator among all Army soldiers regardless of their specific job. Advanced Individual Training (AIT) follows Basic Training; it

focuses on training soldiers in the basics of their individual jobs. AIT is where I began learning how to perform as a combat engineer.

4 Technically speaking, I have been diagnosed with "a classic case of parasomnia," to use the words of my doctor.

References

Blumer, Herbert (1986) *Symbolic Interactionism*, Berkeley, CA: University of California Press.

Campbell, David (1998) *Writing Security*, Minneapolis, MN: University of Minnesota Press.

Doty, Roxanne Lynn (1996) *Imperial Encounters*, Minneapolis, MN: University of Minnesota Press.

Gable, William B. and Edward H. Davis (1997) *An Oral History of Konnarock Virginia*, Charlottesville, VA: Virginia Foundation for the Humanities and Public Policy.

Goffman, Erving (1961) *Asylums*, New York: Aldine Transactions.

Goodman, Nelson (1978) *Ways of World Making*, Indianapolis, IN: Hackett.

Lofland, John and Lyn H. Lofland (1995) *Analyzing Social Settings*, 3rd edn, New York: Wadsworth.

McGuinn, Doug (2008) *Green Gold: The Story of the Hassinger Lumber Company of Konnarock, Virginia*, Boone, NC: Bamboo Books.

7 Waiting for the revolution
A foreigner's narrative

Alina Sajed

I grew up in communist Romania and I was 14 when the Berlin Wall collapsed and communism came to its end in Eastern Europe. Over the next decade of the 1990s, I learned to identify myself as a member of the "generation of transition," to grow accustomed to this strange label attached to young people of my generation, and to learn its treacherous nature. When 1989 came upon Eastern Europe and the communist regimes dismantled, I was finishing my eighth grade – the first crucial moment in the life of a Romanian student. I was supposed to be in the midst of grueling preparations for high school entrance exams, but I had no idea which high school might be suitable for me. Naturally, my parents had plenty of ideas … The December Revolution, as we call it, struck as lightning in my life: it was swift, dazzling, and life altering. For most Romanians, the collapse of a 45 years dictatorial regime was as unexpected an event as it was for the rest of the world. My family and I were visiting my grandparents in the countryside in the southern part of the country, and I remember my father's bewildered joy when he cried out to us: "Ceausescu fell!" He had tears in his eyes. I felt shocked, in utter disbelief, but also overwhelmed by a sense of hope that I had not experienced before. It felt as though two tectonic plates had clashed underneath my world and a volcano of possibilities was about to erupt.

However, as unexpected and sudden as it had all seemed, there had been rumors going on months before it happened. I remember kids in school speaking about the opening of borders of Czechoslovakia, Poland, and Hungary, and how their supermarkets were now stocked up to the brim with Western goodies! "Amazing," I thought to myself. "Imagine that!" Nevertheless, our chemistry teacher was quick to teach us that in spite of their abundant choices, they could not afford any of those goodies, because their prices were prohibitive. Not to mention that their youth were now rebellious and already addicted to drugs. "So," she said, "isn't it better in our country where prices are low, and everybody can afford to buy things? Why would we ever want to change this system?" "Buy what exactly," we asked astonished, "the empty shelves in our supermarkets?" We had heard from friends whose parents had gone on shopping trips in Poland and Hungary that things were changing there, that "there was more freedom" in those countries now, that they were Westernizing ... We listened to such stories in envy, imagining what it would be like if *we* ever set foot in a store stacked up "with everything"![1] But we never thought this would happen in Romania. It would have been impossible! Ceausescu had just been re-elected as the "beloved son of our country" for yet another term: it was a sunny cold day of November, and he had claimed that "even the sun is on our side!" My father had repeated this phrase bitterly when he came home from work; it was hopeless. We lived with the suffocating feeling that communism would last for eternity, that its immobility and fixity were so natural that *nothing* would dislodge it! Rumors and stories from elsewhere were all very good, but our everyday existence – in its repetitive monotony and predictability – was here to stay. A month later, Timisoara erupted, and within days riots spread like wildfire throughout the country, and people went out into the streets.

The wind of change was finally blowing through *this* country, which, for 45 years, seemed resigned to its fate. I remember walking around the streets of my grandparents' small town in December 1989, and imagining myself finally free ... I went into a small convenience store because I had heard that Belgian supplies had been brought in. I bought some jam and some shampoo, and I still recall the thrill of sophistication that I got from eating Belgian jam and washing my hair with Belgian shampoo! I thought to myself that now a whole world of possibilities had flung its gates wide open in front of me, all I had to do was step in. I was not the only one feeling that sense of euphoria.

On foreignness, strangeness, and other such creatures ...

> Some Balkan communities were only emerging from their forests at the moment when Lancashire workers were entering their factories.
>
> (Williams 1972: 22–23)

What was it like to live in communist Romania? many people ask me. Well, it was anything but boring. There were the constant and unexpected (sometimes prolonged) blackouts that were meant to "save the country's energy," which would leave us doing our homework in candlelight; the interminable and annoying queues for bread, meat, and Romanian Pepsi (!!!), during which you literally had to fight with other people to get to the front (no sense of the "civilized" and "polite" idea of personal space that I encountered in the West); the rations for milk, sugar, and oil; the constant disappointment at opening the fridge and finding it empty; the two hours a day of TV broadcasting most of which concerned itself with the visits that our "beloved father" paid to various factories and farms, and with the praise for his "wise" economic planning that made us "move forward on the path to communism" ... I will have to stop here because the list will be a very long one. These everyday experiences constituted my very first lessons in self-deprecation, which translated the lack of "everything" in our homes into a reflection of us as backward, uncivilized, and *outside* of Europe. This disease continues to plague Romanians' sense of self-esteem. Such daily disappointments were peppered by occasional encounters with Western magazines, smuggled by friends and family from Germany or France, which left us bitter and resentful about our own condition. I would spend hours mulling over the glossy pages of Western catalogs, admiring the clothing of women, and fantasizing for days about the gorgeous images of food, accompanied by recipes I did not understand, and whose flavors I could taste only in my imagination.

Ever since I can remember, I have always been fascinated by the notion of foreignness. In Romanian, the term for foreign, *străin*, also means strange, almost eerie. I have always had an ambivalent relationship with foreignness, simultaneously finding it alluring and irresistible, but also dangerous and unforgiving. So what did I perceive as foreign, as different? I grew up in Constanta, the second largest city in Romania after Bucharest, which lies on the Black Sea coast, in the Southeast of the country. This region enjoyed for hundreds of years (if not more) a sense of variety and diversity, as people from different ethnic and religious communities lived there together. The province had been part of the Ottoman Empire between the fifteenth and the nineteenth centuries. Therefore, there is a large Turkish community living there, and there are, or rather were at one time, also Arabs, Ukrainians, Greeks, Bulgarians, Albanians, Macedonians, Russians, Muslims, Catholics, Jews, and Orthodox Christians. Growing up, I had constantly been surrounded by difference, and I cannot say whether it is not this ethnic and religious diversity that left its most powerful impression on me. I was so shocked recently when I read an article on Constanta, which stated that in 1853, Romanians had constituted only 5.4 percent of the city's population, the majority being Tatar and Greek. How strange, as a Romanian, I was taught that this land had always been ours!

Thinking back, it always puzzled me how in that region the group that was conceived as most foreign and strange, that indeed triggered a "disconcerting strangeness" about itself, to use Julia Kristeva's expression, were the Macedonians. One would expect the Turks to be a target of "foreignness," as they had a completely different religion, with different holy days and customs, and a completely different language. Even physically, they could be distinguished easily from "Romanians" (especially since many of them are Tatars, a group coming from Central Asia). But oddly enough, it was not the Turks who were seen as the epitome of foreignness. It was the Macedonians, who share the same religion as the Romanians, whose language is similar *but not quite* the same as Romanian, and who were (and are still) identified as '*Aromâni*' (which could be translated as A-Romanians). I wonder what made the Macedonians the target of resentment and prejudice that came not only from Romanians, but from other communities as well?

In *Strangers to Ourselves*, Julia Kristeva talks about the "mechanisms" that elicit this sense of strangeness, of the uncanny. She suggests that the term *unheimlich* is not necessarily the opposition of the "familiar," that which is completely different from the "familiar," but rather the continuity into shadow of the sense of familiarity, which "should have remained a secret in the shadow, and it escaped to the surface" (2001: 270; my translation). It is thus this strange familiarity, the "immanence of strangeness within the familiar" that sets off the sense of discomfort and difference. It is the vague familiarity of Macedonians that triggered resentment within many Romanians, their similar *but not quite* the same religious and cultural traditions linked to Greek Orthodoxy; these traditions included differences that disrupted our claim to an "original" and "unspoiled" Romanian-ness. It is also the vague familiarity of their language, which was similar *but not quite* the same as Romanian, and which made me many times, as a child, think to myself: "I hate this language, it sounds like broken/spoilt Romanian." I remember vividly looking with a sort of resentment mixed with fear at old Macedonian women sitting on the ground outside talking in their "broken Romanian," dressed in black, with black scarves and the sign of the cross tattooed in dark blue ink between their eyebrows. I also remember looking at old Turkish women, dressed in vividly colored clothes, with scarves on their heads and their big semi-crescent shaped golden earrings and feeling a sort of curiosity and exoticism about them.

Another early encounter with "foreignness" happened when one of our Muslim friends got circumcised when he turned seven. It was quite odd that his family decided to perform the circumcision so late, but it became a reason for a party, as the whole neighborhood was invited to celebrate the "Muslim baptism," as everyone else called it. The children from the neighborhood had been his friends: we had been playing together for years and yes, we had always teased him by calling him "Ottoman." We never missed any opportunity of pointing out to him how heroically our Romanian people had fought and resisted the "Ottoman invasion" (the Romanians had also lost many battles against the Turks, but this was always conveniently left out of our conversations). Nonetheless, we were friends, and teasing each other was just part of friendship. But after the circumcision, especially since we knew what it involved, we treated him very differently. In our minds, his body now bore the mark of "difference." His mother had also made it clear to us that now he was a "true Muslim and a man." I guess we felt betrayed because we wanted to play with our Turkish friend whom we could always tease, not with a "true Muslim and a man."

Why was his becoming a "true Muslim" an impediment to our friendship? One explanation that comes to mind is that within our *imagi-nation*, Islam was the "other" par excellence. Although Romania as a "unitary state and homeland" was established in 1918, much of the history of the people of what was later to be known as Romania revolves around the centuries long struggles of resistance against the "Ottoman infidels." The fight against Islam and the heroism of Christians are very much part of the discourse that produces the idea of Romanian-ness. Even as children, history classes were extremely important in instilling in us this sense of national pride. It was not merely history but also literature classes that served to construct a discourse of a small but valiant nation, which attained greatness through its resistance to the Ottoman invasion. By his becoming a "true Muslim," our friend had suddenly distanced himself from us and unambiguously identified himself (or rather his mother identified him) as something we were taught to disdain and dismiss as "pagan," "unfaithful," "unfamiliar."

The West had always been present in the imagination of many Romanians as a mirage, as a promised land that cannot be attained (except by those fortunate enough), but also as *the* standard whereby we can measure our own worthiness. Communist Romania had a paradoxical relationship to Western culture: there was its capitalism, which, we were taught, represented a culture of excesses and depravity – the phrase "decaying capitalism" was constantly employed; but there was also its historical, literary, artistic, philosophical, and linguistic tradition that represented for us the Mecca of knowledge and civilization. This paradox meant that in school there was an in-depth indoctrination into all things Western: history, languages, and literatures, so that as students we had more knowledge of and interest in Western European history than we did in any other culture. The school curriculum was designed in such a way as to alternate, on a yearly basis, Romanian history and European or "world" history. Inadvertently perhaps, we always compared our own achievements with those of Western Europe, and naturally, we always found ourselves wanting. History teachers would remark bitterly that when Western Europe was undergoing the Renaissance, we were not "out of the woods" yet. My deep passion for French literature and civilization meant that I could recite the French royal dynasties by heart, that I had imbibed all of its classics. I was certainly more knowledgeable and more passionate about the plays of Pierre Corneille and Jean Racine, about the poetry of Paul Verlaine, and about the novels of Gustave Flaubert and Alexandre Dumas than I had ever been about Romanian literary works. And so I secretly fantasized that I was born in France. This type of francophilia was by no means extraordinary: as Romanians, we saw ourselves as the "Latin oasis in a sea of Slavic peoples," and regarded the French as our cousins. You see, the love affair with everything French had started in the nineteenth century, when many of the Romanian intelligentsia went to Paris for their studies. Lucian Boia, in a study on the link between history and myth in the Romanian imaginary, remarks that our affair with France started in the second half of the nineteenth century just as we embraced the discourse of modernization, which translated into an attempt to Westernize Romanian culture. This process of modernization also entailed a break away from our relation with the Slavic culture, of which Russia was the most important representative. We turned away from our frustrating relationship with Russia, and threw ourselves into the glamorous embrace of France, who was, after all, our Latin sibling in the West.[2]

I distinctly remember listening to my history teacher going on about the merits of Dimitrie Cantemir, an eighteenth century prince of Moldova, who is regarded as the Romanian answer to the Western European Enlightenment.

He was a prolific man of letters, whose work on the history of the Ottoman Empire had a considerable reputation in Europe. Upon being defeated by the Ottomans, he took refuge in Russia, placing Romania under Russian suzerainty. As I was listening to his lecture, my mind kept repeating a single thought: "I don't believe this! When Western Europe was in the full swing of Enlightenment, we had just produced our first history of Romania! How depressing ... instead of learning about Rousseau and Voltaire, we are learning about a guy who took refuge with the Russians!" I was in agony. "No wonder we are not part of Europe," I thought to myself. Teaching about the history of our relationship with the Russians at a time when Russia was what we perceived to be *the* cause of our misery was certainly an interesting endeavor. I looked at our interactions with the Russians throughout history through the lenses of a communist reality deprived of basic necessities and submerged in self-pity. And for that, I blamed the Russians. I *so* wished that my country did not share a border with the Soviet Union, and that we were located a bit more to the West. I was not alone in harboring such regrets. And the despair of our location in Europe remains an issue with which we have not yet come to grips. If someone were to ask me how I came to acquire a sense of what Romanian-ness is, of my identity as a Romanian, of my own (uneasy) location within the space of Romanian-ness, and of Romania's location within Europe, I would say that it must have been during my first 14 years of schooling.

On the paradoxes of acting ethically

I am reminded here of a quote from William Connolly, who states that "to act ethically is often to call some comforts of identity into question" (2002: xix). I found that indeed, throughout my life, my desire and/or impulse for ethical action has caused certain "comforts" of my identity to be called into question. The first time I had to call into question comforts of my identity was in 1992, three years after the "Revolution." While the idea of "acting ethically" may sound very pompous and self-righteous, especially when applied to a 16-year-old, perhaps a better way to word it would be that I questioned my own foundations in the spirit of a fairness that I then embraced. I was 16 when I chose a different religion for myself. It was not a conversion proper, since nobody tried to persuade me of a truth of which I had been unaware until then. Rather it was me who, having encountered the principles of the Baha'i Faith, felt that these suited me much better. It is not the choice I made that is particularly relevant here. While it was certainly a crucial transition in my life, I play down my choice here for several reasons: I am no longer a practicing Baha'i, and while I still acknowledge it as my religious belief, I suppose I went through a lot of soul searching during which I discovered "religiosity beyond religion."[3] However, the impact it had on my own sense of selfhood is significant. It was odd for me to see and feel how, because of my choice, my status changed almost instantaneously from that of an average Romanian teenager into that of a minority.

There are plenty of minorities in Romania: Hungarians, Turks, Catholics, Protestants, Jews, Germans, and so on. While their relation to the "Romanian nation and state" is not always a very positive one, no Romanian would actually blame them for who they are. Why? They were born in that particular tradition, they had inherited it from their parents and ancestors, as such, difference is/was *tolerated*, but not embraced. With me, my status as a minority was highly problematic and volatile: I was born an Orthodox Christian and I had "changed" my religion, betrayed my heritage. My status did not involve *being* but *becoming*. As such, I could easily be blamed for who I had become. At least this blame was constantly laid at my door, and every time it happened, I felt intensely angry. I could not stomach the hypocrisy that came along with it: to many Romanians, being Romanian meant, among other things, despising all those they deemed inferior, while protesting strongly whenever someone else (the West) made us feel inferior. I said to them: but being a Baha'i taught me to respect and revere all religions as sacred and unique, how is that wrong? And what would usually ensue was a long tirade on how one is *born* into a religion and therefore can never quit it, and on how Orthodoxy represents the true path to salvation for every Romanian. Well, if being a good Orthodox and a good Romanian means that I had to spend my life condoning the kind of intolerance and racism that comes with a particular (not uncommon) practice of Orthodoxy, then I was happy to quit!

My spiritual choice needs to be placed within the wider framework of Romanian-ness. This concept claims to enclose those features that supposedly define the "Romanian spirit" and the "Romanian uniqueness."[4] Orthodoxy is viewed, without exaggeration, as quintessential to the notion of "Romanian-ness." To be a "true" Romanian one *must* be an Orthodox Christian. Religion had been perceived as a refuge and resistance against the expansionary politics of the Ottoman Empire, of the Austro-Hungarian Empire, of the Polish, and of the Russians. During communism, it was one of the most important instruments of resistance against the regime. Therefore, the idea of "Romanian-ness" implies religious identity, linguistic identity, a common history of long struggles of resistance against "foreign oppressors," and the variety and beauty of the Romanian land.

Consequently, my becoming a Romanian with a different religion was viewed as a betrayal, an abandonment. Most people who found out I am not a Christian would be overwhelmed by a sense of incomprehension, and their first question would be: why have you abandoned your faith? All of a sudden, I had to constantly justify my choice and defend my newly discovered principles. As one of the principles I now embraced was respect and reverence for the sacred nature of *all* religions, I found myself defending Islam to many Romanians, although I was not a Muslim. This was an important change: I no longer viewed Islam as the ultimate "other" of Christianity, or of

Romanian-ness for that matter, but as a different spiritual path for which I had started to have immense respect. Instead of being happy to perceive other religions and cultures as mere caricatures, kept together by a sum of well circulated stereotypes, I discovered the beauty and complexity of Islam, Hinduism, Judaism, and ultimately, of Christianity itself as well. It was also the first time I inquired, in a more meaningful way, into non-European worlds. And so I had absolutely no patience with accusations that I had betrayed my heritage. I like to believe that since then I have changed my rash and impulsive ways, and developed a more nuanced view of their reaction ... I now find it amusing to remember the puzzled looks on people's faces when I said that I did not drink alcohol and why. They would reply: come on, *everyone* drinks, are you a Muslim or a born again? As much as I tried to explain I was not a Muslim, in their eyes it was all the same. There are many prejudices against Arabs in Romania, as many of them come there for business or studies. Interestingly enough, the same prejudices that I had seen aimed at others throughout my life, had been transferred on me as well, as my religion came from Iran, which in most Romanians' minds was equal to being an Arab and a Muslim.

A story from Urvashi Butalia's *The Other Side of Silence* (2000) comes to mind here. Butalia attempts to bring forward the voices of various people affected by the Partition. One of the stories is that of her uncle, Rana, who decided to stay in Lahore (which would soon become part of Pakistan), although the whole family had fled to India. In order to secure his possessions in Lahore and to escape harassment, he married a Muslim and converted to Islam. In an interview, he tells the author, his niece, that there had not been a day in 40 years in which he had not regretted his choice. He felt overwhelmed by a feeling of betrayal and he was never accepted by his family. This story somehow made me confront my own feelings of "betrayal" that had originated not from me but from people around me. It made me wonder: was this man feeling guilty for having abandoned his family in order to secure his possessions? Was he feeling a traitor for having converted to a different faith so that he would secure his material status? What had been the outer perceptions towards my "conversion"? What are the boundaries between free choice, constraint, and acceptance of one's "heritage"? Should there be such boundaries?

On entering Europe and rejoining the "civilized" fold

> It was us, the Eastern Europeans, who invented "Europe," constructed it, dreamed about it, called upon it. This Europe is a myth created by us, not only Bosnians, but other Eastern Europeans, too – unfortunate outsiders, poor relatives, the infantile nations of our continent. Europe was built by those of us living on the edges, because it is only from there that you would have the need to imagine something like "Europe" to save you from your complexes, insecurities and fears.
>
> (Drakulic 1999: 228)

After 1989, the deepest desire of most Romanians was "to enter Europe," to become European. My choice of pursuing a Masters in European Studies expressed this desire. To me, it was the ultimate opportunity to immerse myself in all things European, to become a member of the European nation, and proclaim to the world my Europhilia! The program was sponsored by the European Union, and its role was to train young people who would later become European experts once Romania joined the EU. After a year and a half of intense study about the diverse aspects of the EU, I had an epiphany. I had enrolled in a course on the history of Central and Eastern Europe. "This should be interesting ... " I told myself. I approached this course with the same attitude I had approached other classes on Romanian history, rolling my eyes and prepared to be bored to tears. However, I enrolled in the class because it was compulsory, part of a package on European history, culture, and civilization. But what happened was unexpected: I finally understood. I finally got it. For the first time in my life I felt proud to be from Eastern Europe; I understood its complexity and beauty. It did help that Professor Platon is a Romanian authority and a fantastic teacher. Nonetheless, I had never had any idea of the odd combination of historical accident, geopolitics, and even a sense of tragedy that played such an important role in constructing the idea of Central and Eastern Europe. I became aware, for the first time, of my own place within this region, of how my own bewilderment about the many identities I inhabited and tried to negotiate mirrored, to a certain extent, that of the region in which I was born and raised. I felt a pleasant sense of serenity and self-acceptance.

I learned that Eastern/Central Europe, more than simply indicating a geographical location, pointed towards *political* connotations heavy with the ambiguity that Eastern/Central Europe represents: according to Milan Kundera, this is a geopolitical space culturally Western and politically Eastern (Kundera 1984). But Kundera's statement still invokes a subtle lament for our cursed location and an implicit yearning for a closer link with the "West." I learned that "Western" and "Eastern" Europe are not two separate and discrete entities irrelevant to each other's destiny, but are bound together and constitute each other. There would have been no Western Europe as we know it without the Eastern one just as much as there would not have been an Eastern Europe without the West. And, most importantly, I learned that Eastern European societies are not failed attempts at being Western, they are *themselves*. But perhaps beyond these academic reflections, there was also a sense of my readiness to accept these ideas and a need to understand myself as part of a larger space and history.

In September 2002, I had the opportunity to travel to Coimbra (Portugal) to attend an intensive course in European integration, which gathered together students from various universities in Europe. Going through the passport check-up in Amsterdam's Schiphol Airport with a Romanian passport was one of the first lessons I received on European "integration." Needless to say, both my colleagues and I sported entire dossiers with the appropriate documentation and cash to prove that we were not "illegals," that we had no intention of remaining abroad, and that we would most certainly return to our countries. The passport officer made no efforts to hide his contempt for us, and shouted his questions at us, inquiring about the purpose of our visit, and about the seriousness of our intentions towards "Europe." We felt like criminals. We were not welcome.

In Coimbra, the European fold we imagined was ready to welcome us did not quite materialize. The students from Western Europe had very little interest in befriending those from the Eastern bloc, and we could not shake the feeling that we were the poor relatives, never welcome at the feast of Europe. We were joking among ourselves that no matter how hard we tried to join Europe "in style," we had to be content with joining the club through the "backdoor." One day, my Slovakian friend and I decided to brave unfriendliness and approached a group of students from France, Germany, and the Netherlands, who were basking in the sun and chatting away: "Can we join you?" They started laughing all at once, as if we had told the best joke. We looked puzzled and a bit confused. We then realized that what they heard was: "Can we join EU?" The irony was not lost on us.

Under the sign of Ovid

> We are all summoned to leave our homes, to heed the call of vastness, the call of depths, the voices of the stranger who inhabits us, the need to leave our homeland because too often she is not rich enough, loving enough, or generous enough to keep us close to her.
> (Tahar Ben Jelloun 2006: 266–67; my translation)

Leaving Romania and emigrating to Canada felt like going into a heart surgery without an anesthetic. It was in April 2003, and I was 27. When I handed in my passport for check-up at the Romanian border, the borderguard looked at the Canadian emigration visa and smiled at me: "Lucky you!" What I felt most vividly was that I was in the process of breaking ties, meanings, mind frames, and familiarities that I would never retrieve; that this was it, I would never return. I cannot justify this feeling except that I just knew it. This awareness had the materiality of an immense weight on my chest, and I could not breathe. On the flight to Toronto, tears were streaming down my face and I could not stop them, no matter how much I tried. I felt distraught not because I was leaving my "country," but because I was overwhelmed with the immense sense of loss I experienced at the moment. I had the feeling that I had lost my home, and as strange as it may sound I sensed I had lost myself. I was sure I would never adapt to this new way of life or accommodate to its requirements, in spite of the fact that I spoke English quite well. When I arrived here, everything around me told me: "this is not me; this is not where I am supposed to be." The first few months were the hardest. I could not hold back my tears every time I encountered something that reminded me of home: a song, news from Romania, anything. Every time I saw the trail of an airplane in the sky my eyes would fill up because I so wished I could be on that plane going back. I spent a lot of time searching for Romanian music, which until then I had despised and dismissed as "tacky." But most of all I was longing to speak Romanian to someone. The irony is that when I was living in Romania, there were times when I would tell myself: I cannot wait to leave this country! I am tired of all this corruption and intolerance! Not that I was looking forward to coming to Canada, that was not the case at all, but sometimes I found the "realities" of Romania overwhelming.

But why did I leave? The paradox is that I never wanted to leave Romania: while I admired certain parts of Western culture, I was not particularly fond of its current culture or lifestyle. From my own intuition, but also from stories told by friends and family who had lived abroad, I got a sense of a cold and impersonal society, in which I had no desire to live. I always told myself that I would love to travel and discover new places, but I would also like to have the option to come back "home." As I would find out soon enough, traveling and coming back "home" at one's will is not a universal luxury. How could I want to leave? All my cultural and emotional connections were "there." But there were more personal circumstances beyond my control, which I choose to leave unexplored. I remember praying fervently that my emigration papers would be stalled forever, or that the Canadian immigration services would find me unacceptable or that something would happen so that I would not leave. But it did not happen. And this is why leaving was extremely painful, because I *had to* leave.

Before I left Romania, I went one last time to my hometown, to Constanta, to visit my parents. My favorite place in Constanta is Ovid Square, which is named after the Roman poet, banished from Rome in the first century AD to the edges of the Empire, among the "barbarians" of Tomis (modern Constanta). It is not only Ovid's statue, dominating the square from its pensive heights, that has always inspired me. But the old quarter surrounding the square, the historical district, the old city, where various communities lived side by side, where you run into ancient Greek, Roman, and Thracian ruins next to an old mosque, which is near an Orthodox Cathedral, around the corner from a Roman Catholic church, not too far from an old and decaying synagogue. I grew up loving and despising Ovid at the same time: he was the great Roman poet of love, gracing our lands with his presence and his history. Yet, he had the annoying habit of constantly complaining in his verses about his exile among "barbarians" and "savages," far away from the splendors of Imperial Rome. "Hey, Ovid, get a grip! How bad could it have been?" I always felt offended by his whining, and thought he could have been more gracious. After all, we gave him a home in his exile! And yet, this time I harbored no ill feelings towards him, perhaps because I somehow knew that I was about to become a whining and ungracious migrant myself.

As an emigrant to Canada, I was plunged into my own foreignness in ways I had not expected. First, it was the matter of language: there was always (and still is) the accent that betrayed my "other-placeness." It seemed to me a constant struggle to put myself into another language. And interestingly enough, it was here that my own feelings of betrayal surfaced. It may sound odd, but I felt that I was not only forced to think, speak, and express myself in a different language, but also that I had to reinvent myself, to bring forward a sense of "who I am" that was quite foreign from the "who I had been" in Romania. One day I overheard a Turkish friend of mine speak in Turkish with someone. It struck me that her voice was different, it sounded as if a different person was speaking. She laughed and confirmed my feeling, she too felt different when she spoke English. I guess even my own perception of foreignness changed. It was not the immediacy of someone's looks or accent that evoked a sense of foreignness in me. Rather it was the way in which people related to each other "here" as opposed to how they related "where I came from." It was the mundane interactions and habits that struck me as strange: what people considered snacks, or the way they celebrated a birthday, or the way people said hello to each other, and many other things. My few encounters with Romanians "here" did not alleviate my sense of loss. Strangely enough, speaking the same language did not make me feel at home, nor did I feel that we were bonded by our experience of "foreignness." It was with people who came from completely different cultures and backgrounds that I felt most at ease, and with whom I could sincerely share my displacement. I felt I had so much more in common with them.

I have learned in the last couple of years that the feeling of "home" does not stem from speaking the same language or having the same holy days, but rather from a sense of shared experience and from a sense of human closeness that is almost inexplicable. What I share with my new friends in Canada are not only those similar responses that our being immigrant or foreign in Canada triggers in us, but also paradoxically those things we do not share, the various experiences from "back home." Although I cannot fully understand the backgrounds of my friends, I feel that it is precisely the presence of something that is inexplicable and yet that we all share which binds us together. But, above all, what connects us is a sense of loss, of something almost irretrievable. Nowadays, when I think of my home in Romania, I think of my mother's smile, my father smoking in silence, the many friends I left there, certain streets from certain cities that for some reason have remained imprinted in my memory, the cheap biscuits and sweets I used to eat as a child during communism and thought they were the best things ever, Ovid's whining and the haunting Black Sea, the feeling of overwhelming awe and joy that the sight of mountains unfailingly evoked in me every time I looked at them ...

"Mais où sont les neiges d'antan," said François Villon

> The fervor surrounding events can be deceptive: if that of the Eastern bloc countries is merely an ardent desire to be free of ideology, merely a fervent desire to imitate the free-market countries, where all liberty has already been

exchanged for technological ease of living, then we shall see once and for all what freedom is worth and know it cannot perhaps ever be regained.

(Baudrillard 1994: 29–30)

Last summer in 2008, I visited Romania again. I go back every other year to see my parents and my friends. My partner accompanied me, since I wanted to introduce him to my family. We visited some friends of mine, an old couple of teachers. Mariana Popescu had been my instructor and mentor throughout my elementary and secondary school years, when, like any self-respecting "diligent commie," I used to attend the literary circle associated with the Young Pioneers' Organization. Her husband is now a retired teacher. They invited us to their home, one beautiful July evening, and regaled us with Romanian-style barbeque and homemade red wine. We sat in the yard, under a grapevine trellis, and enjoyed the warm summer night, as Mr. Popescu recited to us a poem from Omar Khayyam. We asked them if they regretted the fall of communism. Mariana said both yes and no, her husband said yes. I asked them why. My former teacher explained that she did not regret it because living in a society without freedom was oppressive. Besides, going through the day knowing that your electricity and water might be cut off at any moment for an indefinite amount of time, and scrambling to feed your family on a daily basis, is not a good life. On the other hand, she regretted the loss of security of living, not having to worry about unemployment or about having a roof over one's head. However, what she regretted most was the education that we received, and the seriousness with which knowledge was seen. Her husband interjected that we might not have had much, but "we had books and we knew their value." He remarked that he definitely missed the "good old days." He had had the opportunity to travel to Russia, Mongolia, Czechoslovakia, and had enjoyed his career as a teacher. While he recognized that we were materially more prosperous today, he also felt we had lost ourselves, our sense of who we are.

I felt both touched and saddened by what they said. It reminded me of how I have felt ever since I have started living here "in the West." It is hard to put in words, but I feel that, in a way, I have lost a sense of freedom that I will never recover. I have come to appreciate the many opportunities I am offered here, which I would never be able to attain "back home." However, there is a price to pay for such luxuries, and I find myself wondering many a time whether it has been worth it. What I miss most is the freedom not to be assaulted at every moment by advertisements, publicity, consumerism, labels, information, pressure, deadlines, offers, sales, and so on. Such a sense of freedom is hard to explain or to describe. It is a peculiar peace of mind, a certain serenity to be-in-the-world without having to rush somewhere; it is a sense of lightness and even innocence. Do I miss communism? Like Mariana, I would have to say yes and no. I cannot regret the cold, the hunger, the threat of my parents being taken away if we criticize the regime in public, and the interminable queues for bread or meat. But I do miss not having much to watch on TV and being happy to read a book or play with my friends outdoors for hours. I do miss not having supermarkets and buying the freshest fruits and vegetables from peasants and not being bombarded by the labels of countless brands of shampoo or soap or clothing. I also miss the creativity and inventiveness with which we would make do with what we had. Above all, I miss the absolute sense of wonder and excitement that would overcome me every September, when my mother would buy me new notebooks and pencils before the beginning of another school year. How to make sense of the absurdity that in a repressive and impoverished society, there was a sense of freedom that simply no longer exists?

Watching *Good-Bye Lenin!* a couple of years ago felt like re-living my childhood during communism. There was a sense of nostalgia in the movie about a lost innocence that cannot be recaptured, which I found tragicomical. It is not a nostalgia for a better world that somehow disappeared, but for a different being-in-the-world that is now obsolete and irrelevant to our times. *Ostalgie* is not just a German phrase for missing life under socialism; it is a complicated feeling of simultaneous relief and anxiety, of confusion and bewilderment, of fragile hope and disappointment felt by many of my generation. No doubt a sophisticated theorist with postmodernist inclinations would read *ostalgie* as the commodification of history in late-capitalism, or as the domestication of dissent into marketable memorabilia. And no doubt it is that as well. But there is also a sense of yearning, which escapes such a reading, a yearning for a sense of lightness in a fast-paced world.

Every time I visit Romania, I am reminded that what I yearn for is lost. The life I left behind has transformed at an incredible rate in the last seven years. Walking through a park in Constanta in 2008 and watching teenagers on skateboards felt no different from doing the same in Canada. These young people had more in common with North American kids than they had with me. Listening to them speak to each other and watching them interact, I felt like a dying breed. I felt more at home watching Philip Kaufman's *The Unbearable Lightness of Being* or Donnersmarck's *The Lives of Others*, than I did in the summer of 2008 in Constanta. As a bewildered member of the "generation of transition," I entertained for a while fantasies of salvation from a regime in whose legitimacy we never believed. As a politically correct new subject of late capitalism, I am more bewildered than ever by the choices that lie ahead of me. A thought has been taking shape in my mind of late: that perhaps the "Revolution" never took place.

Notes

1 For the longest time, growing up in communist and post-communist Romania, this has been the expression that haunted the social horizon of every decision, desire, plan, or action of many of the people I have known. How many mothers in Romania told their children: don't you want to live somewhere where you have "everything"? "Everything" seemed to epitomize abundance, prosperity, the lack of lack, the end of misery.

2 I am obviously oversimplifying what is a very complicated reorientation in Romanian culture. It is noteworthy to emphasize that the "Romanian culture" to which I am referring now did not exist in the nineteenth century, since Romania as a "modern nation-state" was established in 1918 after World War I. What existed in the nineteenth century were a handful of Romanian principalities that had complex and sometimes puzzling relations. For a captivating analysis of the role of French culture in the Romanian imaginary, see Lucian Boia (2001).
3 I owe this expression to Naeem Inayatullah.
4 The concept of "Romanian-ness" found its most powerful expression in the philosophy developed in the inter-war period in the works of several Romanian philosophers, who had affiliations with the Romanian right, such as Constantin Noica, Nae Ionescu, Lucian Blaga.

References

Baudrillard, J. (1994) "The Thawing of the East," in *The Illusion of the End*, Cambridge: Polity Press.
Ben Jelloun, T. (2006) *Partir*, Paris: Gallimard.
Boia, L. (2001) *History and Myth in Romanian Consciousness*, Budapest: Central European University Press.
Butalia, U. (2000) *The Other Side of Silence: Voices from the Partition of India*, Durham, NC: Duke University Press.
Connolly, W. (2002) *Identity/Difference: Democratic Negotiations of Political Paradox*, Minneapolis: University of Minnesota Press.
Drakulic, S. (1999) "Bosnia, or What Europe Means to Us," in Agosín, M. (ed.), *A Map of Hope. Women's Writing on Human Rights. An International Literary Anthology*, Chapel Hill, NC: Rutgers University Press.
Kristeva, J. (2001) *Étrangers à nous-mêmes*, Paris: Gallimard.
Kundera, M. (1984) "The Tragedy of Central Europe," *New York Review of Books*, April 26: 33–8.
Williams, E.N. (1972) *The Ancien Régime in Europe: Government and Society in the Major States 1648–1789*, Singapore: Penguin Books.

8 Am I not that?

At the feet of elders

Sara-Maria Sorentino

> He knows in advance what he will find; the concrete experience is there to illustrate a truth already possessed.
> (Todorov speaking of Christopher Columbus, 1984: 17)

> Since we can never attain closure on the security we crave, never fill up our lack and make ourselves really real, we always need a devil to rationalize our failure and to fight against. As long as we do so, the chief cause of our problems will continue to be our attempted solutions.
> (Loy, 1996: 16)

> Something in the world forces us to think. This something is an object not of recognition but of a fundamental encounter.
> (Deleuze, 2004: 176)

While studying abroad in Ghana, I was told of a nearby rice-farming town named Dawhenya. After an early morning of false starts, wrong turns, and miscommunication, I found myself shuttling towards the unknown in a crowded tro-tro – dilapidated but magnificently intimate minibuses found, I later came to realize, in many parts of the so-called Third World. The unknown? Not entirely. I thought I knew the purpose of my journey.

I sought proximity with those about whom I had been reading. Not that I had a theoretically sophisticated understanding of a world system. I was slowly becoming familiar with the specialized language – SAPs, SOEs, IFIs, the IMF, privatization, deregulation, and liberalization. Account after account spoke of the devastation and havoc these institutions and their policies sowed around the world. I equated these failures with an absence of adequate knowledge, or a mystified false consciousness. It follows that I didn't want an undoing of my mystification. My formulation, reinforced by Chomsky-style fact presenting, was vague but ever present: learn more (raise my awareness), lessen the monetary greed (raise the bad guys' awareness), teach others (spread my enlightened awareness), and when difficulties of co-awareness are smoothed out we would all get along. I prepared by reading piles of books on Ghanaian political economy. Prior to departing, I had already written an introduction and conclusion to my Independent Study Paper, leaving gaps to be filled later. The thrill of a clear, efficient purpose served, I suspect, as an assurance of my mission and a guarantee that I wouldn't stray from my duty.

My time there was limited – Ghana for three and a half months and within that time frame, villages like Dawhenya for a day, maybe two if necessary. Even on this plane, however, holes in the narrative began to emerge: If all I desired were mostly predetermined inputs, then why was I traveling?

Dawhenya was the last stop on the route. Panic set in as the tro-tro approached its destination. I had trouble quelling doubts as to why I was there, what I would say, or what I was looking for. Anxiety of all sorts had been steadily surfacing and by this point in the trip I could no longer ignore the emerging crescendo. I wanted it to fade away. And if it were me, if I was it, I would have to fade away as well. Of course, I had forgotten that nobody in Ghana would allow a stranger's face to remain tense in isolation and confusion. Ghanaians have the extraordinary capacity to embrace strangers with more warmth than I have ever felt at home, while still holding tight to the necessary suspicion of my stated purpose. I may be misreading all these interactions. I have come to learn that my inherited tools of observation are trained to miss most of life's depth, and that this blindness, thankfully, is used by others to diffuse my more misguided attempts. But I'd still like to think that something in the smiles accompanying the greeting of *Akwaaba*, "welcome," to people who were aiming to destroy their cultures and communities wasn't mere irony. Their generosity continues to reverberate in my bones.

As we were alighting, the young man who sat next to me for the bulk of the ride inquired about my intentions in Dawhenya. I told him that I was a student learning about the Ghanaian economy and I had heard there were some rice farms in this village. He graciously offered to give me a bicycle tour of the area. We went to collect the bikes and Mark welcomed me into his home where I engaged in the usual round of greetings from his extended family. I had become skillful at anticipating and deflecting questions; a defense against being discovered as some sort of ghostly fraud and thereby of having a precious semblance of mutuality ripped away from me.

During the two mile trek into the heart of the fields, he told the story he's undoubtedly told so many times before while we surveyed the gravity of the destruction: a few green and lush fields and beyond that, a sprawling expanse of seeming nothingness. Dry, brittle, yellowish grass that spoke so much. Rusted trucks, overgrown irrigation systems, empty warehouses, and a presence that lurked all the more forcibly in its absence. He answered my clumsy questions with the care and patience of a son who stayed behind to tend the fields while the rest migrated elsewhere in search of work. In the rests between cycling, I hurriedly scribbled down the numbers: after the market was flooded by cheap rice dumped by the United States, the thriving community of over 3,000 farmers and their families had dwindled to 13.

Dwindled is not the right word, it is more like a forced expulsion. The transition from self-sufficiency to barren wasteland took a decade. The story was similar in the rest of the country and went hand in hand with the continual pressure to plant cocoa cash crops. Mark and I spent much of the ride in silence – both eerie and serene.

Back at his home, we talked for a while more. Although neither of us could fully account for what it was I was doing there, we could sit, riddled with all the contradictions, and share a coke and a few laughs together. This was perhaps the only day in the trip, and one of the few in my life, that I wasn't overcome by a desire to fill in a perceived nothing with something, anything. I have come to consider this stillness a rare and nourishing gift, the texture of which I've since attempted to cultivate. When it grew late, Mark hailed a passing car and I was ushered inside. I was dropped off at a tollbooth an hour and a half later and the newspaper boys assisted me in finding another ride that would take me the rest of the way. Moments later, a businessman in a white jeep offered me his passenger seat. I submitted to this flow with unaccustomed and appreciative ease.

That night at our flat, my friend Jenny and I didn't seclude our selves by playing Monopoly – a contraband purchase she and I attained at a nearby gas station. Nor did we perform our ritual excursion to the internet café or go to the Living Room, a place with separate movie rooms for rent, where we saw *Pretty Woman*, *Hotel Rwanda* and *Rat Race*.

I still can't shake something about the way Mark carried his sadness.

Dawhenya was the third and last farming location I visited during the independent study period. (Earlier in the trip, I wrote a mini-independent study on cocoa in the village, Morontuo, where we spent ten days.) I can't remember how exactly these and other interviews went. My sense of purpose steered the conversations. I suspect that those I was questioning humored my innocence and tolerated the arrogance of my privilege. I do remember one productively disastrous response to my arrogance. At a poultry co-operative, near the end of an interview with the manager, Nii, he looked at me steadily and leveled this indictment: "You will forget Africa. When you go home to America will you remember the people here? You have all of these ideals now but in time you will end up working for the IMF and World Bank." An inoculating dart finding its mark. The immediacy of my counter-protestations didn't miss a beat. I professed my commitment to the cause and my willingness to do anything to fight injustice. The forcefulness of my defenses, even now, serves as an indicator of the truth of the critique. Leaving that place, it began to sink in that the more I fought against his prediction the more it would come true. Could it be, I wondered, that my alignment with the World Bank and the IMF weren't some future calamity foretold, but a tragedy already present in my travels? That inside me was a struggle not only to forget but to make sure I did not remember? I remember inching toward and then shrinking from the sharp edge of these implications.

Two days later, I set out again to a village whose sustenance depended on pineapple exportation. A dedicated and obviously respected man had set up a small office in the center of town to chronicle the failed promises made to the farmers of this place. Many years ago, they were given farming inputs for a specific type of pineapple. But since then, a genetically modified hybrid variety with a longer shelf life and sweeter taste had become more fashionable in Europe. These new seedlings are outrageously expensive and the only farms that have access to them are pet projects of the World Bank. After a discussion in serious tones, this man, whose name unfortunately now eludes me, introduced me to several village elders seated together in the center of town. There were at least five men of sturdy stature, although my noted awe and admiration of this type of authority might be inflating my memories of a scene comprised of inordinately robust and towering presences. They seemed to be awaiting me, having heard, presumably, of my arrival.

Although unexpected, such visits, I learned, occurred with monotonous regularity. The tedium showed on their bodies: absent were the gorgeous Kente cloth robes I came to associate with initial ceremonial introductions, the men instead were clothed in modest T-shirts, trousers, and flip-flops. I read this less as a sign of surprise, and even less as a sign of disrespect but, rather, more as an indication of weariness. Too weary, even, to play the get-the-guilty-white-person-to-give-us-money game that has become a common recreational pastime in many parts of the country. I was told I was but one of many students from the universities that have come and gone, one of many bursting with hopeful enthusiasm and leaving the community empty handed. After protracted hesitation and negotiation, the advice they solemnly gave was that there was nothing I could do and that I needed to stop pretending.

This statement, of course, didn't emerge so succinctly all at once and it is probably beyond my capabilities to adequately gauge how, in a larger context, this fits with the rhythms of their frustrations. I do know something awfully powerful congealed and then struck hard in me, feeling both like a violation and an honest assessment of the encounter. I exploded into a fit of tears right there – the first on the trip, the first in a few years, and the first in a long, sustained series of similar outbursts.

I don't know if this was a ploy on my part for pity in another desperate attempt at avoidance or the beginning of a period of mourning over that thing I didn't know I had to lose. The poles of helper and helped passed into each other. The group of 80-year-old men, withered and proud, instantly gathered around to consol me. I often wonder if my outburst was bewildering to these men. Did they recognize something familiar in the suffering of my Western desire? Unsurprisingly, I have little memory of what happened next, but I do know I somehow made the four-hour journey back home to the little flat in East Legon, Accra.

I spent the rest of my official Independent Study Period in markets trying to track where the products being sold actually came from, staring blankly at a desk at an NGO, or trudging up and down stairs at the Ministry of Agriculture in search of someone, anyone, to interview.

Sixty-seven pages: the length of my Independent Study Project. I was proud of the number. And although I was beginning to feel intense bodily lurching, the power of this fantasy still shielded the written work from disruptions. It fit together nicely; just as I had imagined it. The redeemable characteristic of the document may be that tucked deep inside I included photos of Dawhenya, perhaps hoping to infuse some life into the sterility of my words and charts. Despite the clean, inviting binding, however, I haven't so much as opened the covers upon my return, not physically at least. In many ways I have turned the pages over and over, re-editing, re-inspecting, and repackaging the contents, contents that are stand-ins for my memories, memories that are manifestations of the most powerful forces I can conceive.

Some of the shattering was in the realization that the form, structure, and tone of my encounter served not only to obscure me from what it is I might be looking for but also to perpetuate the very problems for which I sought solutions. Needs and desires for travel went unquestioned and alternative possibilities for being and resisting unexplored.

I remember annoyance bordering on callousness at cultural differences, in spite, or maybe because of, the tolerance I prided myself in possessing. I remember passing notes and excessively yawning during a class on the aphorisms carved into the staffs of Ashanti chiefs, even as I professed a deep appreciation of culture. I sneered at a sewing lady in the market for continually getting my measurements wrong. I couldn't stand being stared at from the windows by children and adults of Morontuo for ten days straight. I said I would never come back to this god-forsaken place. I felt irritated by my body's incapacity to learn what seemed like relatively simple dance moves. I didn't even know I was doing it, but I divorced economics from life, from culture. I considered their music interesting but ultimately irrelevant in the fight for social justice. The music's cross-rhythms were drowned out by my ear's desire to create transparent harmonies of "social justice." To learn now in retrospect that even my ears have been trained not to hear ...

In one of the most disturbing interactions of the trip, I screamed at a man outside my tro-tro window peddling what amounted to a window shop of religious pamphlets and Christian memorabilia carefully balanced on his head that Christianity was an illusion. He walked away muttering angrily. I dismissed the entirety of the strong Ghanaian Christian faith as a disturbing remnant of the same package that arrived on the shores years ago. The passive recipients, I seemed to be saying, now needed to believe in something else. I made no attempt to accompany my Ghanaian families to church to explore how this Christianity might have taken different, creative forms.

Look at how I myself am now wedded to some variant of Christian confessionals. Am I hoping for forgiveness? I am working out how secularized faith in absolution might work to delay the endurance necessary for immersion into contradictory depths. This seems awfully important but theological studies are slow going, so I trust that the reader can patiently abide my muddled heresy.

I continue to wonder if there were any graceful moves to be made when ladies sharing taxi rides fawned over the shade of my skin or when men hounded me for marriage and for the promise of moving to America. I responded with symmetrical compliments, by insisting that I would be a lousy bride, and by exhibiting a despairing attitude towards costs of living in America. But this didn't seem enough. The wounds of history are impossibly deep on both sides.

More? I enjoyed being able to directly cross the highway that separated the university and the pizza shop. Students of Legon would walk down the road to the overhead walking bridge built presumably to facilitate passage across the busy road. But I soon learned that we white students didn't need to use the bridge: we could simply walk across the road and traffic would come to a halt. My path for easy access was already paved and I certainly didn't resist benefiting. I had experienced how my white skin literally induced tears in babies. In these moments I began to really feel the phenomenological sting of race. And now I learned I also had the power to stop cars. Along with my purportedly despised nationality, I had been granted the god like gift to jump across oceans.

I have trouble understanding why my legs made that leap. I wrote once that going to college in Ithaca felt like I was running from something but going to Ghana felt like I was running towards something. I do not understand what I was trying to say. Ithaca remained an empty screen in my imagination. As far as I recall, I projected very little on to the place, other than its distance from home. I didn't visit the school beforehand or investigate its credentials.

A few days before going to Ghana, doctors found that I had rather severe nasal polyps. Numerous diseases, apparently endemic to Africa, could induce an infection that would break through the potato-chip-thin bone between my nose and my brain, resulting in blindness or death. They urged me not to go. I laughed it off. Maybe physical death was nothing in comparison to the living death of suburban slumber...

One can, for the most part, make the claim that I never really traveled to Ghana – at least not while I was there and maybe not now. Perhaps the violence of it was the absence of a meaningful encounter. I experienced an encounter but only insofar as it didn't occur. On return, though, as I approached but never quite reached the land of supposed comfort and familiarity, I found myself re-traveling the paths to Ghana belatedly, inhabiting them differently upon reflection and reading, finding alternative parts of myself to draw from, discover, and create.

I still can barely speak to the intensity of the plane ride home. To do so would be to also explain, and perhaps dangerously explain away, the profound disturbances that continue to pry open the stability of what I consider my lived experience. I don't think any amount of time, distance, or counseling can dull the violence of those spasms. I tend to feel it as a profoundly intuitive glimpse into … well, into something with which all my habits and training can't quite catch up. The shattering of self, the crumbling of the ground and the sensation of being washed into and becoming this mess. Standing on a shore, looking at the patterning of waves, helpless at the awesome fury, and overcome with joy at their beauty. I had fancied myself to be taking something of a cool little dip – if I didn't wade too far in, I would be safe. But the undertow was deadly. Because of course, I was already drowning. That's not so hard to understand.

On the return flight, as my fellow students nostalgically anticipated their previous lives, it began to dawn on me that I didn't share their excitement. I was filled by dread. By the time we arrived in London, I was well beyond disconsolate. Through sobs, I kept saying that I wanted the plane to turn around. That's the only intelligible phrase I can recall uttering – that and nearly screaming at the cashier man in a leather shop, although I'm not sure why or what I was saying. In the NYC airport, as my friends left for their families or connecting flights, onlookers decried: "you can't leave her like that." But their planes were about to depart and so I was left to wander in a transit lounge for hours, waiting for my flight to Columbus. I bought a cheeseburger – something I had fantasized about during hot West African nights – but nausea overtook me. Lingering guilt about starving children compelled me to carry the Styrofoam box of leftovers on the plane, and it undoubtedly found its way to a fridge, where it was probably left, uneaten, for far too long.

The stillness in bodily responses to bumps in the night, the variations in the spaces over which my eyes linger – this is some of how I mark off the pre and post of the seismic rupture. A precocious eight-year-old friend was looking at some of my Ghana pictures and said: "that isn't you, you look happy!" Over the past break, I visited some of my closest friends from youth and they remarked upon the change. They never remember me crying; in fact they never remember our conversations even remotely approaching a level of seriousness. I use their interpretations of the narrative to try to respect the necessity of this pain.

The vulnerability of such moments is approached with jokes. It's both pathetic and understandable in a way. Forays into the terrifying abyss have been met by intense nightmares and hallucinations. The voices began as whispers – I don't know when they began to find audience in my ear. But the screams, oh, oh, those didn't take too long to come. I once read that the psychotic drowns in the same water that the mystic swims in with delight.

The language I've used to delay hasty interpretations after this breakdown goes something like this: "Look, something happened when I came back from Ghana and my entire universe felt like it fell apart." Trying to access this directly won't do the trick; I suspect it won't all suddenly make sense with the clumsy misappropriation of latent tools, especially given that how I've learned and lived and loved may be what induced this all in the first place. I've written along these lines in countless papers, emails, and journal entries to professors explaining why I can't quite focus on class material. It's a mark of their generosity that they gave me fairly good grades while I was doing minimal work on their course material.

Seismic catastrophe, maybe I'm exaggerating, it only took a year to smile again. But the facial stretching in the smiles feels different, more alive.

In a book I read, there was some imagery I liked. The author explains the self-enclosure of woman throughout time as different than the silencing associated with oppressed women by comparing the former to a larva:

> when the larva enters the pupa stage, it actually dissolves completely, turning into a kind of broth. While it is in its liquid state, the firm walls of the cocoon are vital to its survival. Over time, safely contained, it configures itself into a chrysalis, and at last it cannot be contained. The cocoon falls away, and the moth spreads its wings and flies.
>
> (Flinders 1998: 168)

She then speaks of cultures in which inward seeking and transformation is supported and guided by the framework of the community. Where stillness and non-action isn't seen as apathetic, docile, and cowardly.

I am not anticipating a glorious flight and revival after all this. I've been given the precious gift of reading and listening to powerful words and music, towards which my eyes, ears, and heart largely aren't attuned. The suspicion that I can't ever rightly translate this intractable gulf has turned into a massive conviction – almost everything I've read, the ethnographies of white western "privilege," seem to be saying that the most I can do is to nurture a receptive pupa-like place in me that can absorb anger and fear and love and emotions without immediately springing in search of causes. The strategy of reading has then become a preparation of what *not* to do; of starting to stop – if, given my legacy, this is even possible. The depths of colonization are almost awe-inspiring; the grip its most destructive elements have on me are so strong that I can barely see them. To believe otherwise would be to severely underestimate the intensity of my training, but it might also be to overvalue the perfection of the product and the smoothness of the operation.

I've made it a habit to attempt to compile a mental inventory of those things from which I shrink; these are things I cannot overcome by wishing them away. But the ways I attempt to address them speak to that which is unbridgeable. I begin to approach them and I feel the strain – my mind wanders, I joke, look away, throw up my hands, pose questions to deliberately distract, trail off with ums ... and give the appearance of being deep in thought when I'm really trying my hardest not to think. It's impossible. It feels impossible. Without these distractions my body descends into spasms. How to go on? When even the physicality of structures speaks of silences that ache with suffering? This is beyond heartbreaking. I don't know if I can say deep down I don't really care about the people I met in Ghana, as if the heartbreak is some kind of ruse. Because even deeper down, the impossibility of empathizing, that still feels like the real heartbreak.

Here's an element of my past, long forgotten, but resurfacing in ways. I was a little girl once. I read voraciously then. There were two libraries I would frequent – one next to our neighborhood park, which was within the distance of a bicycle ride, and the other just a short car ride away. A whole wall of that second library's structure was made of glass. In any case, the distance isn't so much at issue because after the taste of reading, I would have found a way to the library. The librarians knew me not only by name, but also by preference in books. It didn't take long before they were whisking me past the children's section and into the young adult shelves. And it didn't take long before I ate those up too. They took the liberty to reserve newly arrived novels they suspected would suit my fancy. I would emerge weekly, clutching plastic bags bulging under the weight of the books. I know my mother must have driven me to that half-glass library. But her presence there holds only faint traces in my memory. How did she feel about my habits? Did I have to beg her to take me? And why don't I remember this?

I read historical fiction almost exclusively. Slavery in the Americas and the holocaust of WWII were my so-called favorite time periods in the genre. I also built up quite the expertise in the flora and fauna of Madagascar from reading travel guides. What the hell was this little girl doing? What was I crying out for, what was I hiding from and what possible continuities was I intuiting?

I remember very vividly seeing ads of starving children and hotline numbers for abused children and thinking: *that's not me. I don't have it that bad. Suck it up. There is little I have to complain about.*

"I'm not that." The power of interpellation by negation at such a young age.

I was in fifth grade when the reading stopped. A sudden shift. My reading addiction was re-channeled into far less imaginative routes – primarily a nightly scheduled routine of sitcoms. That must have been soul crushing. I can still remember some of the time slots and their corresponding television shows: the Simpsons at 5:00 and 5:30. It is no surprise that a culture created on the basis of denial of genocide and systematized racism has carefully constructed structures that numb and ameliorate possible insights. Although these insights may only be based on the heuristic power of analogy, I'm somewhat convinced that analogies of victimization are more than mere devices, but instead are part of a historical dialectic, in which suffering there is intensified by ignored and repressed suffering here.

I have many questions. They swirl around. Many I have to bracket in order to speak at all. That thing, that thing that's speaking through me. I've written this all before. I know that. I'll need to write it again. I'm not sure why, or what this repetition means, if anything. There is something I am attached to – maybe it can be found in the times I cry quietly to myself that I am a good person.

I very much like this Rumi poem:

Search the Darkness

Sit with your friends; don't go back to sleep.
Don't sink like a fish to the bottom of the sea.
Surge like an ocean,
don't scatter yourself like a storm.
Life's waters flow from darkness.
Search the darkness, don't run from it.
Night travelers are full of light,
and you are too; don't leave this companionship.
Be a wakeful candle in a golden dish,
don't slip into the dirt like quicksilver.
The moon appears for night travelers,
be watchful when the moon is full.

(Rumi 1998: 47)

References

Deleuze, G. (2004) *Difference and Repetition*, 4th edn, translated by Paul Patton, London: Continuum.

Flinders, C. (1998) *At the Root of this Longing: Reconciling a Spiritual Hunger and a Feminist Thirst*, New York: Harper Collins.

Loy, D. (1996) *Lack and Transcendence: The Problem of Death and Life in Psychotherapy, Existentialism, and Buddhism*, Atlantic Highlands, NJ: Humanities Press.

Rumi, J. (1998) *The Rumi Collection*, translated by Kabir Helminski, Boston, MA: Shambahala.

Todorov, T. (1984) *The Conquest of America: The Question of the Other*, New York: Harper and Row.

9 Listening for the elsewhere and the not-yet

Academic labor as a matter of ethical witness

Lori Amy

My apartment in Tirane, Albania, is in "the block" – the area of the city occupied by the ruling members of the dictatorship that controlled Albania until 1991. This is now the most fashionable section of the City Center, just a few blocks from the offices of USAID, the United Nations Development Project, and the American Chamber of Commerce. In my little section of the city, I can rely on employees who speak English, the international language of development, to help me secure my Albanian cell phone, install a high-speed internet connection, and deliver pizza. Despite the fact that Albania is the poorest country in Europe, falling into what is often called the "second world," I can get almost anything I want in Tirane – designer clothes, electronics, cars, food, liquor, goods imported from all over Europe and America. These goods can all travel to Albania but Albanians cannot travel abroad. During the Hoxha regime, Albania was a closed society, isolated from the rest of the world. After the government collapsed, thousands of Albanians fled the country. Fearing an inundation of Albanian immigrants, the rest of the world enforced severe travel restrictions on Albanian citizens, making it extremely difficult even for business owners and leading intellectuals to travel for work or research. In the post-communist open-market era, foreign goods flow freely into the country, but the movement of Albanians is frozen.

I came to Albania through the complications of the cold war; a history into which I was born. I was born on an army base in Frankfurt, in the former West Germany, where my father was part of the military force dividing east from west, capitalist from communist. Before Germany, he served two tours of duty in Korea; after Germany, he went to Vietnam. I spent my childhood moving from base to base along the fences of the cold war. Much like the view from the balcony of my apartment in Tirane, my father embodied contradictions. At times he was violent, mean, angry, drunk, belligerent, a full spectrum of abuse. Other times he was charming, generous, funny, tender, his own version of loving. I was the youngest of the seven children that he helped to raise – three from my mother's first marriage, four that he and my mother had together. When I was 18, he disappeared. Less than ten years after retiring from the army he abandoned the civilian life to which he could never adjust and chased his dream of "living off of the land" – as he did in Korea and Vietnam.

To be in Tirane right now is, in many ways, to re-encounter Frank. There is an uncanny parallel between the tactics Enver Hoxha, Albania's last dictator, used to keep control of the country and the way Frank kept control of his family. Isolation, terror, surveillance. After Vietnam, Frank moved us – the four remaining children and my mother – to a remote army base in Alaska. Then, when he retired from the army he took a series of jobs in campgrounds up and down the Florida peninsula. I lived out my childhood on army bases, my adolescence in fishing-camps from the Florida Keys to the Everglades. When Frank left, our campground was six miles from our mailbox and the school bus stop. Living in fear of Frank's violence, grateful for moments of affection, moving constantly and so remaining isolated from people and things that could open up other ways of being – this history makes me feel that I share common ground with the Albanians who lived in isolation and fear under the Hoxha regime.

This ground-in-common is, of course, my projection. There is some distance between the academic job in the states that gives me the sabbatical time to do research in Albania and the international discrimination that makes Albanian intellectuals beg for one of the few scarce visas that will let them travel. And there is some distance between me and the Roma children I see sorting through trash in the dumpsters, looking for anything that might be of use – salvageable food or consumer goods. This movement between identification and critical distance frames the way I encounter Albania. It frames, for instance, the subject of my research: violence against women. Albania has become a source for the trafficking in women in the region (Tabaku and Stephens 2008). Ironically, the largely male forces deployed in the Balkans, from United Nations Peace Keepers through the many extensions of the interim governing structures, increase the demand for women trafficked into the sex industry. In an emerging market economy, women's bodies are commodities: cheap, in high demand, and disposable.

The violence I am researching tugs on many threads in my complicated tangle of history, emotion, projection, identification, and difference. There are parallels between the international forces in the Balkans and my father's military service in Germany, between the forms of violence my father directed against his family and the shape of violence against women in Albania. Even as I locate the ground I share "in-common" with the women whose lives I am studying, I walk uneasily because of my complicity with the forces of violence from which they suffer. Like this: after the collapse of the communist government, the economic and political ideologies driving my country hurt women and children. In the mania to make Albania a market economy, women lost jobs, social services were cut – including health care and education – and property formerly owned by the state was, by and large, redistributed to men. Gender stereotypes have gained new force, resulting in a 30% decline in women in government – there were more women involved in the political process in 1970 than there are today (IFAD 2009: online). Every woman, every child that I see on the streets, homeless, begging, reminds me of my complicity: American-style capitalism has both made America a rich country, from which I have benefited, and contributed to the poverty in many other parts of the world.

In this navigation of projection, identification, complicity, and critical distance, I try to distinguish the difference between the voices I carry in my head and the voices of the women to whom I listen. This is not easy – our internal voices can shout so loudly that they drown out the possibility of hearing. Much has been written about the importance of testimony in bearing witness to violence, to suffering, and to the traumas after which we must build anew a sense of self and world.[1] Working through such histories requires finding the language to represent our pain, crafting narratives that can make sense of what is otherwise incomprehensible and overwhelming. But testimony is only part of what is at stake in the process of bearing witness. We do not, in a vacuum, magically find words that can release the grip old wounds have on us. We find these words in relation: in relation to those that can listen both to the words we can so far speak and to the experience emerging through our exchange. Being present to the moments of rupture through which the unspeakable emerges is what Sarah Ahmed, in *Strange Encounters*, calls the condition of the possibility of hearing (2000: 157).

It is from this frame of the "condition of the possibility of hearing" that I want to discuss the place of the auto/biographical in academia – specifically, our relation to our subject matter. My opening vignette suggests some of the ways that auto/biography and our work converge: projection, identification, how the subjects we choose facilitate research, analysis, methods for gaining both a deeper understanding of, and a critical distance on, our troubled pasts. To follow Ahmed in her line of questioning, though, shifts the valence from the *individual* to the *relation*; when we ask what makes it possible to *hear* another's story, we are asking what are the terms of our speaking *and* hearing. We are asking about the relation between us. This shifts the meaning of "communication." The lecture, as the paradigmatic model of academic communication, stages communication as a one-way transmission of knowledge from teacher to student; "good" communication in this sense is understood as a speaker's skilled transmission of a message by virtue of which listeners receive the transmission and understand the message. On the other hand, communication, as a relation of testimony in which the dialogic scene bears witness to a past seeking its transformation, is quite the opposite. Communication as relation of speaking and hearing involves attending to "the other encounters, other speech acts, scars, and traumas, that remain unspoken, unvoiced, or not fully spoken or voiced" (Ahmed 2000: 156). "Communication" as a relation of witness, then, is precisely about opening a space for the presence of what is absent in our speech.

This is, I think, what Ahmed means when she says that "communication" is less a matter of the presence of the voice of the other than it is about opening "an unfinished, unheard history, which cannot be fully presented, even if it is not absent" (2000: 156). It is the presence of this unfinished, unheard history that I want to consider as I search for the place of the auto/biographical in my teaching, research, and writing. I would like to proceed by examining two inter-related threads: a classroom experience in the fall of 2008, teaching a freshman seminar on *Women and War*, and my recent arrival in Tirane, Albania.

***

Women and war

I agreed to teach a freshman seminar on *Women and War* in the fall of 2008 for two reasons. First, the university had just restructured the seminar to provide smaller class sizes and a greater emphasis on critical thinking and global citizenship. Second, I was preparing for a spring research trip to Albania, where I would be working on gender violence and globalization. The *Women and War* class provided an opportunity for me to bring some of my themes on Albania to freshmen. These issues – rape as a strategy of war, displacement and refugee populations, low-intensity conflicts and dirty war, torture, crimes against humanity, genocide – are difficult to discuss. I was acutely aware that 15 weeks of studying these things could throw some of my students into a state of crisis.[2] At the very least, I knew we would need strategies for dealing with the depression that is an inevitable consequence of sustaining a focus on violence. For some students, reading about the violence of war might bring up violence they had suffered in their personal lives. For these reasons, I believed that we needed to begin the semester by discussing the emotional consequences of spending so much time studying violence. Explicitly addressing our emotions in this way was fundamentally a relation of ethical witnessing – our conversation was not merely abstract: the work of looking closely at war in our world required us to encounter the emotional effects our looking involved.

My first step in this process of establishing relations of ethical witnessing was to ask students to write a short autobiographical introduction and post it to our online discussion board. What I asked was general: a few sentences about where they came from, why they came to Georgia Southern, and what they thought they would be doing in a course called *Women and War*. I also asked students to read what their classmates had posted. While they received credit for posting the introductions, I did not impose a grading criteria on the *reading* component; nevertheless, our course software showed that almost all of the students read at least half of the responses posted, many read all of the posts, and about one third responded to their classmates' writing. My own self-disclosure was equally important to this process. I believe that to encounter each other in an ethical relation of witnessing requires that we expose our own vulnerabilities by dropping the pretense of mastery. It also requires disclosing our stakes, our motives, and our desires. I told the students about my proposed research trip and about my hope of using our class experience to enter my work in Albania. And I shared my own history of violence in a childhood and adolescence with a father who suffered from the wounds of war in Korea and Vietnam.

These introductions helped me to think about how to present our topics and facilitate our communication. Most significantly, though, they helped me listen for those things that, though not articulated in the classroom, are nevertheless present. I discovered, for example, that one of my students was from South Africa. He described his father, who was in the Rhodesian special forces, as fighting against the "terrorists that now dictate Zimbabwe." His extended family is now dispersed in different countries. In this same class, an African-American woman described her fight with suicidal tendencies in the past and her ongoing struggle with racism directed against her. In between these two were a range of identities and histories; a number of white women from rural, religious, conservative families, a cosmopolitan woman from Haiti, a white woman whose mother fought for the passage of the Equal Rights Amendment, a white man who wanted to streak for peace. Knowing a bit about their backgrounds helped me to listen for what was not spoken – and maybe not speakable – in our classroom conversations.

Many in academia think such an approach is not "objective"; they fear and shun an open discussion of the violence that our scars bear. Those who do not want to, do not know how, or are afraid of such encounters, should listen to their body and decline to take up such methods. But those of us engaged in an ongoing struggle to understand and work through the violence of our lives and in this world have something to offer. Withholding this "gift" deprives all of us of an opportunity to encounter others and ourselves differently. When I say "gift," I do not mean that we are gifted, or that there is any special thing we bestow. I mean "gift" as a humble offering, from the heart of the struggle to co-create our humanity in the face of the very violence from which so many of us have suffered. And, in such encounters, our students have gifts to offer us.

My *Women and War* students made many offerings during the semester. One of them was their willingness to stretch towards this mode of bearing witness. Despite the initial confusion they were able to touch each other. They even found humor while discussing violence and suffering. Which is not to say that there were not tensions, resistance, angry moments, hurt feelings, and the need to navigate despair as we were encountering violence. All of this was present. But the structure of the class required us to come back together, week after week, and figure out what to do with these feelings. Much could have gone wrong in this project. We might have had an angry student who sabotaged the process. Students might have polarized against each other, remained stuck in the places they were hurt, angry, threatened. The fact that most of the students reached the end of the semester feeling like they had learned something valuable from the class and each other owes as much to the students in the class, the ways they brought heart and mind to our work together, as it does to anything I did. Their willingness and capacity to engage in this project of ethical witnessing is one of the most consummate gifts they offered, a gift for which I am profoundly grateful.

It was through the relation of ethical witnessing that we confronted the high tensions in the weeks after Barack Obama was elected President of the United States of America. I knew when I walked into the class the day after the election that, throughout the night, many of our students had been posting Facebook and MySpace warnings to friends to stay inside. They believed race riots would break out. To the best of my knowledge, there were no actual incidents of violence reported on campus, but students nevertheless feared *potential* violence. The election triggered powerful emotions within identity narratives connected to terms like "black," "white," "patriot," "terrorist," "Christian," "Muslim," "Arab," and "American." People fight and die from such emotions. These were also the kinds of narratives that we had been reading, writing, and thinking through for ten weeks. One of our jobs in *Women and War* was to think about how these narratives function as scripts for war and about how to re-write them. On November 5, election day, our discussion of how to re-write the cultural narratives involving violence became concretely grounded in our daily lives.

In the context of a course on *Women and War*, *knowing* that fears of race riots were running high among the students, we *had* to talk about this. The young woman from Atlanta, who had described having to fight daily against the despair she felt concerning the pervasive racism in the deep south, opened our discussion: "I almost didn't come to class today. I was afraid of being killed." She described the terror she felt while Obama gave his acceptance speech – she thought he might be shot, and that the general rage behind such an assassination attempt would be directed against her, a black surrogate. The young man from South Africa said he was afraid of America becoming another Zimbabwe. Other students were carrying the fears of their own family histories – white grandparents who had opposed integration and had used violence to prevent it, family stories about people being killed during the heyday of the civil rights movement.

The discussion was difficult to facilitate. It required the emotional labor necessary to *hearing* each other's emotions – a labor that entails maintaining a critical distance on our own emotional responses, looking for the histories behind others' responses, and seeking ways of understanding ourselves and each other through our encounter. Much of the time, the possibility of hearing is precluded because we are listening in too literal a way. We grab onto a word, a phrase, and pin it with a "meaning." We freeze it and miss its context, its nuance. Or we take a detail out of its element and appropriate it into our preexisting narratives. Hearing for witnessing calls for a different mode of encounter: it demands that we locate the scars we cannot see and linger in the emotional space out of which our words emerge; and it asks us to anticipate the future trajectory of our speaking and hearing relationship. Such critical and compassionate listening requires that we struggle with and through our own emotion. When fear is triggered and evokes a defensive anger, we are asked to step back from the emotion and ask: why am I feeling this? Why now? From where does my emotion emerge? Which ends does it move towards?

Hearing as a witness is to reach for a present consciousness in the moment of emotion that can trace its history and imagine its future. In this moment we listen to ourselves as well to others. My own rage against America's "war on terror," the way my heart breaks in the face of the racisms so prevalent in my culture – I had to listen to this as much as my students' responses. I found it hard work. It was the work of checking my own anger, my righteousness, of understanding these as defensive responses. I could not simply vent my rage when a white student said "now black people will feel like they can take revenge for slavery. White people are not safe." Instead, I had to ask: Why are some white people afraid of black violence? What histories are we carrying? And when the African-American students in class had to hear the fear and anger some of their white classmates were experiencing, when a young black woman said, out loud, "I was afraid to come to class today. I was afraid I would be killed" – I could not simply beg forgiveness from the students of color in class or magically produce the world without racism that I want for them, for all of us. Instead, I had to ask: How does a white student whose family fled Zimbabwe hear all this? What experiences of violence, of killing, has he lived with?

For each and every one of us, this conversation meant dredging up our histories of race-based fear – in rural South Georgia, where so much racist hatred lives and breathes and can still produce violence. It asked each of us to connect our emotional responses to our life experiences. And it asked us to understand the life experiences of others in the class, to imagine what emotion we would have, had we lived different lives. Most important, through this imagining we could ask: Is it possible for us, here and now, to find a way past our fear, our anger? Can we move through the force of an emotion that has the potential for violence? To an elsewhere not yet apparent to us?

Our conversation that day did not magically cure anything – not the war or racism or the histories of fear, rage, violence, and hate that trailed us into that classroom. But it did, I think, tap into what was felt but not seen between us. The stories we told placed fear (and the anger it suggests) into a context. Our anger, our aversion, our negative judgments ... if we do not look at these things, interrogate them, they can calcify and fossilize us into rigidity. To critically reflect on our own emotion, to encounter ourselves and each other with an eye to both the past and the future, can *move* us. Move us emotionally, in our empathetic responses to each other. And move us intellectually, in our expanded ways of seeing the world. As one student put it, encountering each other in this way:

> kind of brought out the best AND the worst in people, and I think it was very important to see both sides of the issues – the reason things are the

way they are ... I'm really glad that I learned in this class, and I feel like I've grown too and become more aware of what is going on in the world around me, and I really appreciate it.

Echoing this response, another student wrote:

this class has to make you think. For me, it made me want to be a better person. Not only for myself and the people that I love right now, but for my children's future, my grandchildren's future, for the world's future.[3]

A number of students expressed such sentiments. And the final evaluations for the class reveal that most students experienced our encounter – painful as it often was – as positive. Nevertheless, three students experienced our mode of encounter as negative. If we do not *want* to move, an encounter with forces trying to open us up and out is, at the very least, destabilizing, and, in the worst of cases, a perceived violence. Too often, when confronted with opposition, we feel the "other" to be an opponent – one to argue down, beat back. In extreme cases, we can feel the threatening other to be morally "bad" – not just on the "wrong" side of an argument. To have open disagreement in class required confronting our tendency towards such emotional responses. It required this of me, too. I do not want to have to admit to myself that I can move from disagreement to dislike, can respond defensively to being called into question. I want to think of myself as above this. But I am not above it; I have not transcended the ego-bound messiness of my own contradictions. In the classroom, my students force me to practice what I preach: they force me to look at my own emotional responses, to examine the assumptions, prejudices, ideologies shaping them. They demand that I move past my knee-jerk reaction to reject and dislike the students whose ideologies, beliefs, and ways of being oppose mine.

When we can encounter each other as ethical witnesses, we may – if we are lucky, if the conditions are right – inhabit the classroom as a relation of becoming. As a site bringing us back together, week after week throughout a semester, the classroom constitutes neither a beginning nor an end. Rather, it is a movement from the now to the not-yet. The classroom as a site of becoming is only possible, however, when we are willing both to risk speaking and assume the responsibility of hearing – hearing not simply what is said at the moment, but, rather, listening for both the histories and the futures that might be emerging through our articulations. This kind of listening is, I think, indicated in the response of a young woman who, though uncomfortable in the post-election discussion, nevertheless stood in a relation of ethical witness to a classmate from a very different political position. She says, in the beginning of her response:

The discussion we had in class today was in a way biased and uncomfortable in my opinion. I felt that those of us that were unhappy with the election had no say in the discussion. I know we had the opportunity to talk when we wanted, but I felt like no matter what we would never be right.

She closes her response with a comment on the African-American woman who spoke of her fear of being killed by white people angry with the election of a black man as President of the United States of America: "[She] is a great speaker and she has a way of getting her opinion across so powerfully. She is very understanding of others and open to all views."

This student's honest grappling with her own emotion is a gift that forces me to similarly grapple with mine, to move beyond my own initial reaction and find the common ground between us. This reaching out to touch and opening ourselves to be touched is what Butler (1997) calls the linguistic and social occasion for the transformation of self and other. Part of what is at stake in our speaking and listening is the possibility of hearing *ourselves* differently. We can encounter our own contradictions and find language to speak about what we did not realize was in us. We can tell a story that we've told a hundred times before, but, when this story is told in a different context, to a different audience, with a different response, it can take on new meaning. In the *Women and War* class, the students who were devastated by Barack Obama's election forced me to call into question my own elation – an elation that was as staked in fantasy and projection as was the mourning the McCain supporters were experiencing. Obama cannot magically fulfill my fantasy of an end to poverty, war, racism, anymore than McCain can fulfill people's desires for security and protection. One of the most important gifts students brought to our class, then, was the willingness to voice criticism, to articulate opposition. They forced me re-see my own fantasies and projections.

***

Tirane, Albania: spring 2009

This necessary work of seeing and hearing, of being in relation *through* difference, is what I think of as the work of love. This is work I find easy to take up from my newly established location in Tirane, where I have come to study gender violence in what is euphemistically called a "transitional" society.

I fell in love the day I landed. Jet-lagged and disoriented, I was stopped in my tracks by this scene: on one side of me, a construction graveyard, on the other, a ministry building. Directly across from the uniformed guards patrolling the building were haphazard deposits of amputated concrete, barrels, derelict construction equipment. In the midst of the rubble, poorly marked and easy to miss, a twelfth century Ottoman wall is partially excavated. It was discovered when a twenty-first century construction project unearthed one of the thousands of such archeological treasures to be found in virtually every city in Albania. Framing this scene were half-constructed buildings; some new construction that had come to a halt, others the falling-down buildings of the old communist regime. In this free-fall through the chinks time makes in the architectural accretion of centuries, I fell in love with everything that spoke to me through these fissures.

One of the things speaking through the stone traces of three centuries is the force of love through which our lives endure. The concrete detritus – in the graveyard next to the ministry building, from the crumbling communist buildings with their trademark ugly and bad construction – speak the transience of our individual lives, the cycles through which what we build up will come down. They tell the story of entropy, decay, the destruction our wars make. But they also tell the story of Eros: the force up, the life drive that rebuilds, grows, perseveres. As with, for example, a phenomenon common in Albania: a large number of unfinished but nevertheless lived-in buildings.[4] These structures have first and second floors that are completed and inhabitable, but the top floors are skeletons, frames waiting to grow. The reasons behind this phenomenon speak to the collision of capitalism and communism. In a country that went overnight from the virtual abolition of private property to a cut-throat capitalism in which pyramid schemes collapsed the economy, these houses tell the story of people scrambling to make homes when property rights are in dispute, without banking and credit and government protection, piece-meal, with the money sent home by relatives working abroad. If a family can secure – occasionally by law, but just as often by sheer force of will, sometimes violence – a piece of land, they build as much as they have money for at any given moment. These buildings speak simultaneously of poverty, civil war, the scars of communism and capitalism gone haywire, and of perseverance, love, hope, and the steady work of building a future. Those unfinished floors can expand to take in married children, newborn babies, and extended family.

I immediately reverberated to this place, to the ways in which it opens up to "other speech acts, scars, and traumas" (Ahmed 2000: 156). It would be easy to say that I fell in love with the pride, suffering, pain, endurance, spirit, desire, dignity, and heart of the people and this place. While that would not be un-true, it is equally true that I have projected onto what I see a quality of feeling from a childhood still present in me, an attachment formed too early to be conscious of how it moves me. How much of the beauty I can see through the concrete detritus around me echoes the still-rebuilding West Germany into which I was born, the rubble from the earthquake that crumbled Valdez, Alaska, in 1964 – a rubble in which, as a child, I played. It is important to remember this, to listen in myself for all of the ways that I am bringing the unarticulated traumas of my father's cold war to my experience of Albania. To attend to the histories we carry with us, to look for the projections that shape our responses, is to take up the work of love. It is to seek in the other, not an image of ourselves that we want returned to us, but an opening of our vision that allows for a re-seeing; to see ourselves differently.

To take up, here, the work of love as a matter of ethical witness means sitting with the scars and the traumas palpably present in every person, every street, every building – in, quite literally, *everything* that I touch. I knew, before I came here, the facts and figures of "development": 50% of the economy "grey" or "black" market, the government heavily "corrupt," basic infrastructures still lacking – electricity, water, roads, hospitals a hodgepodge of first and third worlds. But I did not know that Albanians are still living in the prison of their borders. Everywhere I turn, another person – a doctor at a health conference I attended, the chef at my favorite restaurant, my next-door neighbor's brother, the cleaning lady's son – has had to go illegally to another country for education. It seems a small thing to ask: give me a visa, please, so that I can learn how to perform surgery, cook, program computers, or run a business. To obtain a visa, applicants have to provide official letters of invitation – almost impossible to attain given how little contact Albanians have with the outside world. If they are lucky enough to find an outside contact and obtain the precious documents they need – the letter that invites them to come to x or y or z country to attend a semester of school, a training program, a conference – they still need to prove that they have the money in advance to support themselves for the full duration of their stay. As an American traveling to Albania for research, I needed nothing but my passport. I got my ticket three weeks in advance and my visa at the airport in Tirane. Because of the accident of my birth and my American passport, I enjoy the unearned privilege of unrestricted travel while my Albanian friends endure the degradation and humiliation of being held captive by borders we have invented.

I love walking the streets of Tirane. I love this city's complexity, its contradictions. This "love" is, I know, partly the projection of the cold-war Germany into which I was born, split down the middle, its architecture still bearing the scars of the second world war, of the modernization it was undergoing. It is partly that, in the sorrow this city reveals, I touch old sorrows of my own – the violence my father brought home, the shame that marked me, a child of poverty and violence. But, beyond all of these projections, there is something in Tirane I am trying to hear – the possibility of a story that might emerge through the ruin of the capitalist and communist worlds colliding. One register of this ruin: 30% unemployment, rapid mass migration to Albania's few urban centers that leaves villages abandoned, raw sewage spilling into city streets, non-existent public services, millions of people disenfranchised. On the opposite end of this spectrum, the spring 2009 exhibit on communist oppression in the National Museum.

Walking into the exhibit, the first thing you see is a barbed wire installation running almost the whole length of the exhibit room. Behind the barbed wire is a continuously running film. The exhibit proceeds via a circumnavigation of the room, requiring the visitor to pass behind the barbed wire and enter the world of the victim. On the walls are mounted images from the communist period: trial scenes, buildings in ruins, the rooms where the tortures were performed, pictures of victims who were imprisoned, tortured, executed, killed in uprisings. Taking up an entire wall of the exhibit is an installation with the names of victims – a roll call of the dead. As an attempt to articulate the scars and traumas of the pasts trailing us, this exhibit asks us to listen for the before and after of these images. A before: many of the photographs are mug shots that were kept in each prisoner's file. In the corners, you can see an elliptical discoloration, the outline of the paperclip that fastened image to documents. Rust, maybe? Or blood?

The reddish-black trace left by the paperclip speaks other stories. A human being, behind a desk, file folders, documents of accusation, arrest, notes from an interrogation, the details of imprisonment. The means of death. My imagination runs to clichés: an ashtray overflowing with butts, the dregs of coffee gone cold, an ugly metal desk. There is an afterwards in this trace, too. The family beside me searching for the names of loved ones who were killed. The disillusion in the streets, where so many of the city's poorest people come to the despairing conclusion that things were better under communism. In the trace of this paperclip, I hear the raw pain of enduring traumas, both "communist" and "capitalist." This exhibit exists not only as a testament to a past of suffering, violence, isolation, terror – it exists also in dialogic relation to the push for free markets, for development, in the midst of a city strewn with household garbage. Leaving this exhibit and walking the streets of this city that I have already grown to love, I am moved to ask: *what is it to which this moment bears witness?* If we put the exhibit on victims of communism in direct communication with the ravages of capitalism, is it possible to forge a relation of speaking and hearing, an ethical relation of witness that enables our movement from the now to the not-yet?

Here is a concrete example of what I mean: the Albanian Students Abroad Network organized their second annual conference, Bridging Perspectives for a Shared Future, in Durres, Albania the last week of April 2009. Students from all over the Balkans – Kosova, Macedonia, Greece, Bulgaria, Albania, Croatia, Serbia – attended the conference, which was designed both to build relationships among identity groups navigating histories of opposition and to develop intellectual capacity in the region. At dinner the second night of the conference Evetar, a young man from Kosova told me:

> I was ten years old when the war came. The things that happened in the war, I did not do them. They are not my fault. That Serb over there, he was ten years old, too. He is not responsible, either. We can't keep hating each other for the things that happened when we were ten years old. We have to learn how to live together now.

Working towards both brain-gain and peace-building, these students were engaged in what Tzvetan Todorov calls the practice of exemplary memory. Exemplary memory connects us to the suffering of others and to the world around us. Whereas remembering in a literal way rehearses, over and over, the wrongs we have suffered and so feeds hatred and rage, exemplary memory brings the past into the present in order to affirm life over death, love over hate, hope over despair, and compassion over violence (see Todorov 1996).

To remember in this way is to re-member for the futures we have to make. Remembering for a future is a creative act. It is a way of re-mapping shattered psyches, fractured bodies. Young people born into the Balkan wars, carrying the legacy of the capitalist–communist divide, organized themselves around the need to imagine a future of peace and stability. And they conscientiously, conscientiously, organized themselves as a site of becoming; the conference intended to build relationships, networks, concrete actions for the futures they imagine. Less than a month after this conference, I received a text message from a young journalist who had attended. He wanted to organize an international conference that would bring together students, leaders in government and business, and the media to address the important issues facing the Balkans in the process of integrating into the European Union – would I help? A week later, I met him in Tirane, where we stayed up all night working on the proposal for a conference that thinks both in terms of concrete action-steps today and generational change in the years to come. Including issues such as the role of the media, minority rights, physical/psychological borders, higher education, and motivating and mobilizing youth, this conference calls the traumas of the past into dialogue with experiences in the present as part of a process of imagining a future.

These students are doing exactly what Ahmed calls for when she reminds us that we have to ask not only "how did we arrive here, at this particular place?", but also how does the "*here-ness* of this encounter ... affect *where we might yet be going?*" These students, navigating the carnage of the capitalist–communist collision, have the job of remembering as a birthing, a labor that generates and transforms the social world (Jelin 2003: 5). Such a birthing requires relations of ethical witnessing, a way through the calcified detritus of our hard-line ideologies and a path into the compassionate address of the flesh and blood body.

***

Here and there

When I started teaching at the University of Tirane, I didn't know what to expect of my students. Would they be different than my students in the states? Would I have to change my teaching methods? Across language and cultural barriers, how would we communicate? Within the first half hour of class, these students showed me the silliness of my worries. The range of their responses – wit, humor, earnestness, intelligence, play, compassion, sorrow, pride, a desire to learn and grow, boredom, fear, curiosity, confusion, amusement – were similar to my students in the US, similar to mine. In the messy work of navigating our old wounds and desires for a future, my students, both "here" and "there," sustain my hope, show me, day after day, the possibilities for the futures we have to make. Through my students, I find, over and over again, that we *can be open* to relations of ethical witness if these relations are opened to us.

This essay, for example, is a product of ethical witness. After reading my first draft, the editors sent back this critique: would it be possible for me to "let go of the explicit, political, polemical, pedagogical" voice masking the range of messy emotions that accompany teaching as a mode of encounter? Would it be possible for me to be more honest about the fears, confusions, the oh-my-God-what-am-I-doing feelings that come with every class in which a student is angry, hurt, exposed, vulnerable – in which *I* find myself angry, hurt, exposed, vulnerable? I took this critique as a call to witness the ways in which I use theory, research, the authority of the citation, as armor shielding me from my own doubts, fears, confusions. In as much as my ego will let me, I have tried to respond to this call. It is a partial response, I know. But I believe that it is precisely through the ways that we find to drop our defenses, to expose ourselves to an/other, that we might re-compose ourselves and our world.

We do not yet know the location, the composition, of a world beyond our violence. It has not yet arrived, or we have not arrived to it. My driving question, for my life and in my work, is: How do we keep in progress the temporal movement from this now of our violence to the not-yet of its re-composition? Is it possible, through our encounters, to open up to the elsewhere and the not-yet?

Notes

1 See especially Felman and Laub 1992; LaCapra 1998; Das 2007; and Miller and Tougaw 2002.
2 See especially Felman 1992.
3 After the difficult discussion about the election, I asked students to write about what they heard, felt, to reflect on what they experienced as happening in that conversation. And, at the end of the semester, I asked them to critically reflect on their experience of the class. In these reflections, as well as in the course evaluations, students' responses overwhelmingly affirmed the value to them of engaging in this project of ethical witness.
4 For a more complete discussion of this phenomenon in the Balkans, the Middle East, and North Africa, see the excellent exchange on the blog Aqoul (2005). Factors impacting such building practices include rapid population growth, poor regulation, lack of mortgage financing, disputed property rights, and the workings of the informal economy.

References

Ahmed, S. (2000) *Strange encounters: Embodied others in post-coloniality*, New York: Routledge.

Aqoul (July 3, 2005) "Cairo's collapsing buildings," available at: www.aqoul.com/archives/2005/07/cairos_collapsi.php (accessed July 1, 2010).

Butler, Judith (1997) *Excitable Speech: A Politics of the Performative*, New York: Routledge.

Das, Veena (2007) *Life and words: Violence and the descent into the ordinary*, Berkeley: University of California Press.

Felman, Shoshana (1992) "Education and crisis, or the vicissitudes of teaching," in *Testimony: Crises of Witnessing in Literature, Psychoanalysis, and History*, New York: Routledge.

Felman, Shoshana and Dori Laub (1992) *Testimony: Crises of witnessing in literature, psychoanalysis, and history*, New York: Routledge.

IFAD (International Fund for Agricultural Development) (2009) "Albanian Gender Profile," available at: www.ifad.org/english/gender/cen/profiles/alb.htm (accessed June 28, 2009).

Jelin, Elizabeth (2003) *State Repression and the Labors of Memory*, translated by J. Rein and M. Godoy-Anativia, Minneapolis: University of Minnesota Press.

LaCapra, Dominick (1998) *History and memory after Auschwitz*, Ithaca, NY: Cornell University Press.

Miller, Nancy K. and Jason Tougaw (eds.) (2002) *Extremities: Trauma, testimony, and Community*, Urbana: University of Illinois Press.

Tabaku, Arben and Sarah Stephens (October 2008) "The Albanian Initiative: Co-ordinated Action Against Human Trafficking," *The State of Efforts in Albania to Combat Trafficking of Persons, 2007–2008*, United States Agency for International Development, available at: www.caaht.com/Drafts/SAT%202007_08%20Rpt_CAAHT_Eng.pdf (accessed July 1, 2010).

Todorov, Tzvetan (1996) *Facing the Extreme: Moral Life in the Concentration Camps*, New York: Henry Holt.

10 To realize you're creolized
White flight, black culture, hybridity

Joel Dinerstein

My first official interview for a tenure-track job was for an African-American literature position at The Citadel, the military college in South Carolina. I was 41, it was my first year on the academic job market, and I considered it a courtesy shot: my dissertation advisor was a friend of the chair of the English Department. I knew The Citadel would prefer to hire an African-American to a Jewish-American so I considered the interview a practice run with little at stake.

It was 8:30 am, and I was the first job applicant to walk into the hotel room. The early hour had its advantages: I got a peek into the backstaging of search committee dynamics, a small plum for the still-aspiring novelist living inside me. The chair was a genial, charming professional in his early 50s, who welcomed me warmly. He was flanked on one side by a nervous junior faculty member just out of the shower, a thin young woman (one of the department's first, I'd heard) swathed in a gray power suit. On the other side sat a dissolute white Southerner of about 55, slightly balding and with a pockmarked face; he ignored me to attend to his hangover. Sitting sprawled on the couch, braced up by one arm, he took occasional peeks at my application letter and refilled his coffee mug every eight minutes or so.

The chair took the first round and tossed two lobs: (1) "How would you teach an African-American survey course?"; (2) "How do you help students understand the relationship of African-American literature and canonical Euro-American literature?" Then he threw a curveball: "What if we asked you to cover another period in an emergency, say the British Literature survey or eighteenth-century literature?"

"I'd love to," I lied without missing a beat. "To teach Swift, Defoe, and *Joseph Andrews*? That would be lark for a semester – I'd frame it around satire and the picaresque as the subtext for the Age of Exploration. Since it's not my expertise, I could have fun with it ... well, at least, after catching up on the scholarship." That satisfied him, and I was thankful for my undergraduate English BA: extrapolating from my American Studies PhD would have been, shall we say, a *drag*.

The chair ceded the floor to his junior colleague. I don't remember the first question, only her second: "What drew you to African-American literature?"

"Well, I was born and raised in Brooklyn, New York, in the midst of white flight." I caught her eye to see if the term was familiar; it isn't always anymore, and wasn't. I explained: "I loved growing up in Brooklyn" – I retain a writer's relationship to it as the space of home – "and in the five years of my early adolescence, my neighborhood changed from white to black. In 1969, my high school, Erasmus Hall – the oldest public high school in the nation – was 70 percent white, and one of the best in New York. By 1974, when I was a junior, it was 80 percent African-American and Afro-Caribbean (Haitians and Trinidadians, in particular). In five years, there was a complete turnaround in the neighborhood's population. My family was one of the last to leave – among my white friends – since my parents waited for me to graduate.

"At the time I wondered why everyone was moving. I knew of the race riots there before my arrival, but, to me, the neighborhood didn't feel any different. In my *junior* high school, there was a great deal of racial tension; by high school, it had evaporated. I worked at a candy store every night from 5–10 pm and did not feel unsafe on the streets. I didn't understand what was happening; what was more important, I consciously wondered why no one talked about it." That much I said to The Citadel's search committee; I kept the after-image to myself. Turning the corner from Ocean Avenue onto Church Avenue for the last time as a resident, on the way to the subway station, catching the June sun full in my face and thinking, "What happened here? And why didn't anyone discuss it?" I walked to the D-train station and headed to Forest Hills, Queens, a neighborhood I refused to bond with in the summers between college years. When I entered SUNY Buffalo that September as a 16-year-old freshman, I was already nostalgic for my Brooklyn childhood.

"In my early 20s, I was an aspiring novelist and my subject was white flight," I locked eyes with my interlocutor, who was probably ten years my junior. My unpublished first novel ran to a thousand pages, and I started the research by reading African-American novels about urban life. I wondered: What did blacks think of other groups moving out because they moved in? There wasn't much directly on the subject – oddly I thought then, but I understood later. I read a bunch of James Baldwin and Amiri Baraka, Paule Marshall's *Brown Girl, Brownstones* and David Bradley's *South Street*, *The Autobiography of Malcolm X*, essay collections by Julius Lester and June Jordan. Those works led me to memoirs of civil rights leaders ... John Lewis and James Forman, I remember, and many others. And when I say 'I understood later,' I mean that only in graduate school did I realize African-American novelists were busy reinscribing black experience into all of American history."[1]

I paused and took a drink of water. No one said anything. I filled the space with repercussions.

"Anyway, I was also a free-lance rock critic in this period and was constantly reading books on blues and jazz, as well as musicians' autobiographies. I don't want to digress too far, but suffice it to say, I'd become something of an autodidact on race relations. Or maybe an amateur American Studies scholar or ethnomusicologist.

"I moved back to Brooklyn a few years after college in the mid-1980s to teach at an inner city junior high. While writing the novel, I lived about three-quarters of a mile from the corner where I grew up, and often walked around the old neighborhood for inspiration, eating Jamaican beef patties and coco bread. Almost everyone assumed I was a cop – I could see the fear, and it was certainly unwarranted physically; I realized it wasn't common for a white guy my age to walk around the neighborhood confidently, as if it was his own turf.

"While writing the novel, I read African-American novels hot off the presses: Toni Morrison, Alice Walker, John Edgar Wideman. I consider Ralph Ellison and Albert Murray artistic and intellectual mentors. For my dissertation on the relationship of jazz and industrialization, I interviewed Murray in his Harlem apartment one afternoon for four hours. It was, for me, the archetypal master/apprentice experience, and one of the high points of my life." I stopped to remember.

My response lasted about four minutes. The pause when I finished lingered for at least 20 seconds. In a thin, strained voice, the woman said, "That's ... just ... not the answer I was expecting."

Ever the eager job applicant, I replied simply, "What were you expecting?"

She rearranged herself into a more formal sitting posture. "I thought you'd say something like ... there was a seminar paper you were working on and you realized there was a useful angle to explore it in an African-American text. In the process of your *research*, you found it a rich vein for exploring American culture ... and that's how it became one of your areas of study."

You gotta be kidding me, said my internal Brooklyn street-kid voice.

"Well ... that's not what happened," I said, dropping my eyes.

I realized right then that *was* probably a common way for a Euro-American scholar to come to African-American literature. *That's the lamest thing I've ever heard*, the Brooklyn street-kid voice was riled. The Kid has good instincts and can leap micro to macro in a single bound. He quickly, internally, turned on my scholar-self: *Is she saying that's a common way for scholars to find their fields of inquiry and expertise?* Yes, I believe she is, I&I thought. *Well*, the Kid yukked, *at least that explains all the mediocre scholarship.* To my scholar-self, it also explained the wry look I'd often seen on the faces of senior scholars when I launched into an extended exquisition on my work. It wasn't the ideas but the passion that worried them: it meant I'd lost "objectivity"; it meant, *I&I guessed*, there might be something emotional lurking beneath the "pure" intellectual inquiry. *Yeah, right.* It meant a white guy who wanted a career should not do black studies.

Well, jesus-H, of course, The Kid jumped back in. But this is what drives me – intellectually, kinesthetically, spiritually, philosophically. In some way or other, I have always studied race and ethnicity, African-American music and culture, American identity and the African diaspora: these arts, tensions, and conflicts are at the core of my chorography. I self-identify *co-equally* – culturally speaking – as Jewish, Italian, and African-American *straight outta Brooklyn*, from foodways to streetways (urban cool pose) to my ways *wit' woids* (Brooklyn accent, Jewish cadences, Italianate dialect profanity, the African-American vernacular). In my jelly-roll soul the embodied philosophies of African-American music and dance – from swing to Coltrane, from the lindy to Monk to the mashed potato – have been the artistic forms that most illuminated my mind, body, and soul. The attraction was originally cultural and organic rather than sociological and political, and it was never rebellion for its own sake: meaning, I wasn't originally driven to ideas of social justice because "slavery is the original sin of America" (as Senator Bill Bradley first declared in 1992),[2] although if some kind of reparations – whether economic, redemptive, or psychological – are not forthcoming, the nation is doomed. Rather, this was all knotted together in the emotional tangles of my childhood, as amplified through literature, history, music, sociology, psychology, philosophy, and anthropology. And it all ran and rumbled in my veins like the city's subway system, slowing down long after rush hour to just *two trains running*, as the old Muddy Waters song went, "one run at midnight/and the other one runnin'/just before day" (Waters 2006).

It's our only path to inner peace, The Kid moaned. I *had* to grapple with race issues the way every true writer or scholar *has* to write. I *had* to get to the root causes, and if not actually conceive of solutions (at least intellectual or artistic ones), lose the thread of fate I&I'd spun my life on.

I spent the 1980s researching the novel on white flight. I read everything from J. Anthony Lukas's *Common Ground* to Joel Kovel's *White Racism* to Ralph Ellison's *Shadow and Act* to Nat Hentoff's jazz criticism. I read any novel or memoir that grappled with race relations, from John Lewis's *The Making of Black Revolutionaries* to Alice Walker's *Meridian* to Saul Bellow's *Henderson, The Rain King*, before stumbling on what was, for me, the masterkey: Thomas Pynchon's unwieldy epic masterwork, *Gravity's Rainbow*. I read it six times in the 1980s. Pynchon figured a group of South African Hereros as the return of the repressed – as revolutionary guerrilas who survived the massacres of German colonialists in South-West Africa to haunt the Fatherland in 1944 – piecing together a V-2 rocket through sabotage and the black market (nice pun, that). It is beyond the scope of this essay to explain the novel or its influence upon my considerations of race. Suffice it to say that, for my purposes, Pynchon had asked nearly every crucial question about race within a global context. He didn't answer them, but charting Pynchon's map catapulted me into the next stage of my own intellectual atmosphere like a booster rocket. From there, I could only fall to earth on my own intellectual fuel, buoyant (if lucky) or self-destructing (if not).

And she was expecting some cocktail-party esoterica I once extrapolated from a couple of fraught African-American texts? So wondered The Kid on the verge of becoming credentialed. I was at that moment 41 years old and had not spent my 30s as an impoverished graduate student hoping to stumble on some interesting intellectual nugget I could refine into a career.

As I tell any graduate student who asks the right question: "If you're passionate about your research, at some point you'll recognize that it's meaningful on a personal level because you're researching yourself. Only you've externalized the questions."

Which brings us back to me.

Interlude: an embodied headnote

Mike Pearson uses the term "chorography" to refer to the intertwined scholarly and personal excavation of one's intellectual work, a narrative summoning that creates a texture of connotation and denotation, a poetics of existence (Pearson and Shanks 2001: 64). A second invented term, "mystery," represents (and puns upon) the tripartite discourse necessary for such self-excavation: the experiential, the cultural, and the academic. That's the scholarly side. Blues musicians in the early twentieth century used the term "mixtery" to imply that any mystery requires a mixture of narrative and philosophical perspectives (Edwards 1998: 597). That's the vernacular side. Here I remix Francisco Varela's concept of the embodied mind – within the human organism – such that it functions as an autopoietic system (i.e., holistic, interactive, improvisatory, responsive to the world) into an idea of cognition as embodied grooves. In other words, the habits we inhabit (in the Humian sense) become rote musical grooves propelling each of us through the daily dance – call it a cognitive soundtrack – until a given experience or set of data requires a new response. When new data, or a new experience, disrupts the groove, a new one must be found. The process of creating a new embodied groove slowly emerges through experimentation or critical engagement; ignoring the message of the new experience, stimulus, or database is what we call denial. That's the cognitive side.

The mixtery of mystery is an attempt to narrate the shifting embodied grooves by which I have moved (personally and intellectually) through the alleyways of race relations and American culture. It is a network of thought – of call and response – that occupies more musical space (and more grooves) in my autopoietic system than any experiential core besides my family. And finally, to square the circle, "chorographer" bleeds easily into choreographer. *As a scholar of African-American music, dance, and culture, and as an American Studies theorist attendant to what Ralph Ellison once called the "complex fate" of American identity (Ellison 1995: 189), I humbly submit this essay as a narrative of the intellectual dance of my life.*

And now, Mr. Narrator, back to an old embodied groove.

Blues was from somewhere

In one of my attempts to become intellectually literate outside of academia, during my early 20s I read a spate of intellectual comic book guides, _ *For Beginners* (e.g. *Nicaragua for Beginners, DNA for Beginners, Einstein for Beginners*). Apparently at the age of 16, Einstein asked himself, "What would the world look like if you were riding on a ray of light?" (Schwartz 1979: 8). The writer suggested that Einstein spent his whole life answering that one question. With apologies to Einstein, my intellectual life is analogous. For my entire life, I have been pursuing answers to two intertwined questions I asked the day I left the old neighborhood: "What happened here? And why doesn't anyone discuss it?" Both were codes for several underlying questions about the core *dis*-ease in American society: (1) "What's race got to do, *got to do* with it?"; and (2) Stuart Hall's question, "What is this 'black' in black culture?" (Hall 1993).

I began with music, or rather, *it* – the music – began with me. I spent most Friday afternoons buying used records at Titus-Oaks Record Store next to my high school in a search for lyrical poetry, mood-elevation, illumination, communion, and my own voice. I was a rock&roller, but as the Muddy Waters song goes, "The Blues Had a Baby, And They Named It Rock and Roll," so I also immersed myself in the blues. I often wondered about the musicians who created it. A few years later, I read Amiri Baraka's *Blues People* and in the preface, he declares: "blues [was] one beginning of American Negroes" since it represented the first "relation of the Negro's experience in this country in *his* English." For Baraka, blues language and its form – first-person subjective, rhythmic meditations – established the first poetics of African-American existence in English, and marked "the Negro's conscious appearance on the American scene." At the time, I knew nothing of the musical precedent of the spirituals and wondered instead: from what cultural storehouses did blues musicians draw? (Baraka 1963: xii).

In high school, I picked up much of what I knew from the liner notes of recordings by the likes of Skip James, Muddy Waters, John Lee Hooker, and Bukka White. Apparently, all these musicians came from the same 90-square-mile area of the Mississippi Delta. How could that be? How was it possible that one of the most impoverished, oppressed, uneducated pockets of American society produced a musical genre that changed the world's music and dynamited its dancefloors? As a musico-cultural fact on the ground, blues upends the center-periphery model of artistic influence and the base-superstructure economic model of cultural knowledge. I came up with my first amateur theory midway through college. I wondered: If I was a genius born into an African-American family in the Delta, what would I become? If I was a gifted and talented kid, what would this community support? Music, preaching, teaching ... *maybe* writing. Maybe a student might break free of the sharecropping and domestic work, encouraged by teachers or guided by sheer will to find scholarships to law school or medical schools via historically black colleges. But what if your calling found artistic resonance – not to mention ethnic affirmation – in the music of your own community? To use the African-American vernacular, what if you were a "bad man" (like Robert Johnson), or a "race man" or "race woman" (like Muddy Waters or Memphis Minnie), or even a modernist artist on your own terms (like Skip James or Howlin' Wolf)?

You might be a blues singer or musician: the internal dissident, the outlaw insider, the liminal wandering anti-hero of southern African-American culture. Let the preachers claim in their envious exhortations that blues was "the devil's music"; you'd call yourself "the devil's son-in-law," as Peetie Wheatstraw did. You'd be valued within the community for your mobility, freedom, and sexual adventuring – like Luzana Cholly, the hoboing blues guitarist idol of the young Alabama boys in Albert Murray's *Train-Whistle Guitar*, or like Shug Avery, the cosmopolitan lesbian blues singer of Alice Walker's *The Color Purple*. You'd be the secular conduit for wisdom and good times, for dance and critical engagement, for public meditation and private exorcism. The blues musician's resistance to social definition – by both the dominant society and the ethnic group – was embodied in individual style, artistic tensions, and African-American modern poses of public blackness (e.g., pimp, diva, hustler, dandy). With the important exception of post-1945 jazz, African-American musical genres have often functioned as a social medium for its community. As Chuck D said about early hiphop: "Rap music is the Black CNN." As an artistic antecedent of hiphop, blues instructed, entertained, and rejuvenated black audiences; bluesmen and blueswomen created a temporary community in live performance analogous to the call and response of preacher and congregation.

To accomplish these objectives it had to be dance music, something I only realized after musical pilgrimages to The Checkerboard Lounge on Chicago's South Side in 1986 and to Mississippi Delta jook joints in 1991. As Zora Neale Hurston's Janie reflects at the end of *Their Eyes Were Watching God*: "you got tuh *go* there tuh *know* there" (Hurston 1998: 192). At the Checkerboard, a few middle-aged couples casually got up to dance a slow, relaxed boogie to piercing, electrifying Chicago blues that seemed to sear my skin. In Delta jook joints, people danced with serious facial expressions, signature moves, and inter-generational partners (75-year-old women with 30-year-old men, and vice versa). Instead of registering the guitarist's high-end wailing in their facial expressions (or, say in air guitar), the dancers held to the rhythm underneath. It was all in the spirit of deep play, a polyvalent community ritual of self- and collective expression: the live music had a depth and texture that rooted you to the ground and demanded a physical response. As Ralph Ellison summed up this vernacular philosophy in *Juneteenth*, "keep to the rhythms and you'll keep to life" (2000: 131).

In the bathroom of the Blue Diamond Lounge in Clarksdale, Mississippi, a working man standing next to me in his early 40s – blue overalls, trucker's cap, a short salt& pepper afro – asked curtly, "Are you having a good time?" I answered: "Yeah, yeah, I'm having a *great* time. "Well," he said quietly and with a hint of a threat, "don't have too good a time." His meaning was clear – or seemed to be – and changed the tenor of the evening. First, I think he meant this isn't *fun* for the people who live here: it's critical engagement of their lives as predicated in music and dance, a combination of emotional release, aesthetic communion, and spiritual rejuvenation. Second, don't come down here for your "bit of the Other" (as Stuart Hall renders it) without understanding that we tolerate your presence and might change our minds at any moment. The dancing, the music, and the communality of critical engagement in these jook joints struck me as every bit as serious as anything I'd ever read through the lens of ethnomusicology.

Concerning blues, I began with this question: how could a primarily agrarian culture produce artistic forms, language, music, and styles that an urban, industrial society, supposedly more evolved and advanced, would want to appropriate? Academically speaking, a scholar could write this paradox off as an internal critique of modernity through primitivism (i.e., as nostalgia for community), or as an example of popular music as narcotic pablum (Adorno 2002: 450), or as a form of cultural slumming. Yet if one theorizes that consumers enjoy appropriating black music, kinesthetics, and style as cultural production that primes the pump of a self-reflexive superior racial identity, what explains the global power and influence of African-American music and dance? By definition, such universal acts of embodiment cannot constitute passive, distanced racial desire if the dominant social group "eat[s] the Other" (hooks 1992: 41), or further, if the colonized ethnic group has successfully created a counterculture of modernity (Gilroy 1993: 1) over the course of a century. What if we instead take seriously the claim that there was (is?) a fundamental "need [or lack] in white culture" for self- and cultural expression (Smalls 1998: 137) such that African-Americans "create the move and grooves of every generation" for a dysfunctional dominant society (Keil and Feld 1994: 99)? Don't we need better theories than "love and theft" by whites (Lott 1995) to account for an artistic model of creation and economic distribution that makes global youth want to fight for their right to party and protest, and in the process, embody African-American musical and dance practices? Certainly we need better theories of art and aesthetics to explain, to take just one example, James Weldon Johnson's observation in his 1934 autobiography that "the Negro drags his captors captive" in music and dance. After watching whites come to Harlem for a decade, Johnson reflected: "On occasions, I have been amazed and amused watching white people dancing to a Negro band in a Harlem cabaret ... in a word, doing their best to pass for colored" (Johnson 1934: 328).

Every time I'd read such quotes in graduate school, The Kid would crack wise to the apprentice scholar: *So where are the scholars creating a vocabulary for the "love" half of "love and theft"?* And the apprentice American Studies music scholar wondered back at him: So why *have* Afrodiasporic music, dance, physical gesture, and slang become the global lingua franca of modernity? *They don't even* ask *that question*, The Kid rolls his eyes. Too invested in their own political identity, maybe, I suggest. *Ya think?* And the scholar rolls his eyes too, and I&I laugh and try to have some perspective.

But I'm getting ahead of mystory. Because before reading any of the theories I just riffed in shorthand, I taught middle school in the Fort Greene section of Brooklyn, and realized I knew nothing about *race* at all. So I wrote a novel about it.

Exodus

I never had the faith in myself as a writer to simply work a shit job and pursue my authorial vision. Instead, after college, I earned a teaching certificate and took a job at JHS 265 in the Fort Greene section of Brooklyn. I lasted six months in a school where 11 (11!) first-year teachers quit in the first month. The failures of inner-city schools were no longer news and I had nothing to add to the work of Jonathan Kozol and others except my Emperor's-New-Clothes testimony. Through an exchange with Nat Hentoff, my experience became a cover story in the *Village Voice* (Dinerstein 1985), complete with a photo of yours truly on the cover, looking slightly crazed. Four months later, I was a guest on *Donahue* for an episode about the failures of public education. I played the role of white-guy-in-the-ghetto, even if the nation was past caring about that narrative. The best part of my 15 minutes of fame was that it kept my parents off my back for a few years. At 27, I was going nowhere – a bum, a loser, a derelict – but maybe I was the kind of bum who writes a best-seller or something. Seven years later, I entered graduate school after gigs as a rock critic, public relations writer, and word processor operator, all of which were in support of my fiction habit.

Just after *Donahue* I began writing my first novel and, over the next five years, I produced an unwieldy thousand-page manuscript. As a work of fiction, it was, at best, a glorious mess. I made a typical mistake of the first novelist and tried to do too much: interweaving white flight and my Jewish family, the twilight of urban neighborhood life and the economics of urban poverty, the history of blues and a white kid's apprenticeship through rock'n'roll. The climax contained an amazingly naïve solution for the nation's race problems: African-American inner-city secession as self-governed entities. In my (partial) defense, such ideas were in the air: in Boston, the Roxbury secession initiative *was* put to a vote in 1990. In the novel, the idea of *secession* was meant to be not only an irony of US history but a synthesis of Malcolm X's urge to self-governance, Fanon's theories of psychological oppression, and the model of extant self-contained communities such as the Amish and the Hasidic Jews. I finished the novel in 1990, and set its final act in Crown Heights, Brooklyn, the neighborhood where I was born. In an odd historical irony, the Crown Heights riots occurred the following year.

Near the end of my novel, there is a re-imagining of the Exodus story. At the age of 70, the retired obstetrician Doc Beyer has left his wife and comfortable Florida retirement to return to Crown Heights, the home of his old practice, where he becomes an orthodox Hasidic Jew. Doc Beyer takes in the novel's protagonist, the 25-year-old singer/songwriter and junior high school teacher, Andy Lerner. (Yes, that's *learner* – the pun of a heavy-handed apprentice writer.) Their relationship stemmed from a coincidental meeting years earlier when they both realized Dr. Beyer delivered Andy to Mrs. Dorothy Lerner in 1959. Then one night, during one of their frequent fights about music – swing vs. rock'n'roll – Doc Beyer drinks too much schnapps and narrates his dream of black empowerment.

African-Americans from Brooklyn purchase two huge, contiguous parcels of land in Northern Georgia – "parcels the size of counties, you understand, Andy" – and in large numbers, they walk away from the inner cities. Along the old Post Road (Route 1) and frontage roads, along interstates and across bridges, thousands of African-Americans marched, their numbers swelling every day with walk-ons from New Jersey, Delaware, Virginia, Tennessee. As an indictment of the treatment of African-Americans in the US, this *self-chosen* people marked the territory with their dissatisfaction. For comic relief, I had various recording engineers embedded in the ranks doing field recordings of music, either spontaneously sung on the march (blues, spirituals, Motown, hiphop) or in the huge encampments at night, often at local airstrips. In the novel, Doc Beyer believes the only way for African-Americans to gain the true respect of all whites was first through separation, then through historical understanding and ethnic/religious training comparable to Hebrew School, and most of all, through ownership of one's own cultural production. As narrated, the goal of secession was to set up a sovereign state, a nation within a nation, and incorporate; in other words, Doc Beyer's vision was based on the model of Israel crossed with Jewish-American experience. After narrating the million strong black exodus to Canaan, Georgia, Doc Beyer falls asleep; Andy covers him with a blanket, thinking, not without sympathy for the old man, "Just another version of sending blacks back to Africa."

Then he takes out his guitar and improvises an ironic one-off blues for that evening:

> Ain't never been hungry, baby,
>   and I never been cold –
> No I can't say I ever been all that hungry –
> ... and I ... ain't never been ... real cold –
> Yeah, I got them middle-class white-boy blues –
> ——hmmm, and it's the dullest story ever told.
> Yes, the dullest story ever told.

The title of my novel was *child of rock'n'roll*. Each layer of puns in the title was intentional, up to and including that "rock and roll" was originally an African-American vernacular term for sexual relations. (As in the Chuck Berry line, "we were ... reeling, rocking and rolling until the break of dawn.") I thought of the narrative voice as "participant-observer first person": in each chapter, the 25-year-old reflecting narrator remembers a certain interesting day and jumps into it, narrating in present tense an approximation of his 17-year-old (then 19- and 21-year-old) consciousness. I wanted to preserve the voice and *mentalité* of being 17 in the 1970s while writing between the ages of 27 and 32. At the time, it occurred to me that this might be an interesting conceptual slant on how reggae musicians refer to the first-person narrating subject as "I&I," even if Jamaicans mean the communion of one's self and the deity Rastafar-I. For my purposes, "I&I" declares a social subject through a paired personal pronoun; as such, it could serve as a concise, emblematic critique of Western individualism. Certainly I was more interested in the layers of self than any declaration of social or religious communion or community, but I was aware of the implication and wanted such connotations in the mix.

In effect, contemplating "I&I" was an early run at my long-term current scholarly project: how to theorize a creolized *American* self-concept. In other words, under what conditions might all Americans affirm or aspire to a creolized social identity built on the assumption that to understand the process of being an American, one must claim a historical and social mixture of cultures that is as much Native American, African-American, Irish-American, Mexican-American, or Jewish-American, as whatever one's actual ethnic descent might be. As a repudiation of all essentialisms, it reflects an oft-quoted statement by African-American playwright and director George C. Wolfe: "We're all mutts." There are obvious criticisms to make of any attempt on my part to theorize a creolized identity: that it's just another white male attempt to universalize the self; that it is a fuzzy multicultural construct of individualism created to evade the atrocities of colonialism and modernity; that it encroaches upon the historical victims of white racial oppression and steals their souls for rejuvenation. As any cursory reading of my work would reveal, my objective is exactly the reverse. I take as a starting point that "whiteness" is a constructed racial formation built on four pillars: colonialism, capitalism, Christianity, and technology (Dyer 1997: 16–18; Dinerstein 2006). My intention is instead to provide a theoretical framework to take a first step towards discrediting the Eurocentric myths of superiority and progress, of rational intelligence and the color-coding of human development. My objective is to *re*-cognize and deconstruct the West's identity politics since the Renaissance.

Only in retrospect have I realized this idea of the creolized self was implicit in *child of rock'n'roll*. Andy Lerner is a child of American popular culture, the polyglot nature of which is not only disproportionately African-American – like the term and music "rock and roll" – but improvisatory, adaptative, integrative, "jazz-shaped," as Ellison once called it (Ellison 1995: 586). Late in the novel, Andy relates Doc Beyer's exodus fantasy of African-American empowerment to an older black activist character named Robinson; he seeks approval and cross-racial solidarity against Doc's regressive escapism. "His idea's not crazy," I have Robinson respond, "or at least not completely crazy. In an all-black state, kids could learn the history, philosophy, and arts *from the dark side*," Robinson gives a fiendish laugh. "To gain an appreciation of a culture of survival – same as Jewish kids in Hebrew school, like the Doc said. Same as the Passover Seder ritual. And that would have to be taught by black teachers to black students. That we may have to secede to succeed at this transmission? Sad, but not totally crazy."

Robinson's statements reflect my admiration for the philosophical hybridity of African-American authors raised in all-black towns, Ellison and Zora Neale Hurston in particular. Along with Langston Hughes and Albert Murray, Ellison and Hurston affirmed equally Southern black vernacular and American democratic philosophies. Through their writing on music in particular – Ellison on big bands, Hughes on the blues, Hurston on spirituals – I understood how Duke Ellington's orchestra was, quite simply, the public display of democracy: first, it provided aesthetic exemplars for negotiating the relationship of the individual to the community; second, it was a public display of citizenship, with its opportunity for self-expression (the solo) within one's responsibilities both to one's section and the collective groove. In 1957, Ellington wrote a short essay about how big bands exemplified the necessary harmony of unique individuals that made for a successful democracy, a social reality then unavailable due to entrenched racism. "Bands are made up of all kinds of personalities," Ellington wrote, and each band's distinctive sound can be comprised of "a polyglot of racial elements that includes Indians, Germans, Jews, Negroes, Swedes, Frenchmen, Belgians and southern whites" (Ellington 1993: 296).

Reading Ellison, Hurston, Murray, and Hughes also sent me back me to Emerson's call for an experiential imperative. I'd always found this best stated in Walt Whitman's poem, "A Child Goes Forth":

> There was a child went forth every day;
> And the first object he look'd upon, that object he became;
> And that object became part of him for the day,
> or a certain part of the day,
> or for many years, or stretching cycles of years.

To re-*cognize* a new existential perspective – that of any object, any person, any Other to Self – ideally, one might be*come* it, learning to flow to a new groove. *Ideally*, I mean; it's rarely attainable. Yet and still, once processed through empathy, this new groove becomes part of the self, and can permanently impact how one sees, hears, and feels events and encounters, increasing one's intersubjectivity. Such a child might understand himself or herself within a framework of organic hybridity. As Albert Murray declared in *The Omni-Americans*, the United States is "an incontestably mulatto culture" (Murray 1971: 22). Logically then, any child raised within its normative conventions becomes socialized as such. If any American child absorbing popular culture absorbs not only African-American culture, but many other ethnic cultures, he or she is no longer white (not culturally speaking, anyway).

I was such a child. So is any child of rock and roll. *Or* funk. *Or* hiphop. Or (going back) ... of the swing era. Or of the jazz age.

As for my novel, that first half-blind groping after these ideas ... well, when I sent it to agents, a few were kind about my vibrant writing style, but there were no takers. You can imagine the wild success of a thousand-page novel chock full of such meditations on race, culture, and identity, all built around a thin plot.

I had the first of several early midlife crises.

I was 32 and needed a sphere of work. I boiled down the possibilities to journalism and a doctorate in American Studies – a field suited to my inquiry, I knew, from scanning the orals list of a friend in SUNY Buffalo's program. I was also encouraged by a friend with a tenure-track job at NYU, who suggested that one goes to graduate school to learn how to "say the sayable": to learn methods and theories within a community of scholars in which I might frame contributions to the intertwined fields of race relations, American music, and African-American culture.

Not for nothing had I named my protagonist Andy *Lerner*. He wasn't me, but rather, a narrative agent – a learning vehicle – upon whom I spent five years riding into the far academic turn of the mixtery.

So what: swinging into the future

I'll begin the end of mystory with a quick sketch of the book that came out of my dissertation, since it satisfied the first phase of the inquiry I'd begun at 16. In *Swinging the Machine: Modernity, Technology, and African-American Culture Between the World Wars* (2003), I theorized a dialogic relationship between African-American music and technological society. Jazz musicians had stylized train rhythms and sounds into a sonic grammar that Albert Murray once called "locomotive onomatopoeia." Through the iconic musical figure of the train – as in swing-era classics like "Take the A Train," "Chattanooga Choo-Choo," and "Tuxedo Junction" – jazz became a global popular music due to its transmutation of the capitalist engine of industrialization into deep play for dancers around the world. By integrating train rhythms and factory rhythms, and by stylizing the machine aesthetics of mass production – repetition, flow, power, and propulsion – into popular music, jazz musicians created a dance-centered modernist music that helped neutralize oppressive technological systems.

This act of artistically *swinging our machines* represents an overlooked heroic act of popular modernism. It is my theory of what Samuel Floyd calls "the power of black music": African-American musicians integrated machine aesthetics into popular music. The creation of a "techno-dialogic" of jazz and industrialization was then (and remains) a global artistic contribution that cannot be overestimated. Moreover, the stylization of aural soundscapes into new rhythmic idioms has become an ongoing artistic triumph – that is, an act of socialization every youth generation repeats (e.g., in hiphop, techno, and electronica currently). The successive aesthetic influence of African-American music remains an artistically self-aware cultural adaptation both resistant and assimilative, and defies nearly all artistic paradigms. In most cases, African-American music has worked its way not from the center to the periphery, but from the ghetto to global capitals. Moreover, the music has been produced by an ethnic group with low prestige within the dominant society and yet its expressive culture has colonized the bodies of ruling classes all over the world. To take just one example, the very notion of free-style individual dancing in modernity derives from African dance, not the couples-centered paradigm of European culture, whether courtly or folk.

One might still call this primitivism. That remains the conclusion of many scholars I respect, but I find this analysis historically unsatisfying. The agrarian landscape and its pastoral ideals no longer compelled industrial workers. The proletariat (and everyone else, too) needed their bodies and minds retooled and recalibrated for a technological society. African-American music traveled globally to bring the news of John Henry: rev up your bodies or become physically and spiritually exhausted as attendants of the world's machines. Within a restrictive space of social protest, African-American expressive culture urged all comers to find rejuvenation in music, dance, kinesthetic flow, and the tactile pleasures of the human body – all of which sounds good to me. The move from agrarian to industrial society demanded cultural forms of adaptation; Western culture had deluded itself by over-valuing rational thought. Beholden to Christian dualisms of flesh/spirit and body/mind, European artists could not (and did not) provide forms for the liberation of repressed minds, bodies, and souls. Yet as many scholars of music and dance of the 1960s pointed out, for this rich cultural legacy, no equal gift has been returned to African-Americans from American society (Keil 1966; Stearns and Stearns 1994).

Certainly I had made a self-destructive career choice, only it was never a choice. Not for nothing is scholarship a *calling*, that secularized sonic metaphor for a transcendent cosmic vibration that knows your name. Yet I was indeed triply challenged on the job market: I had a PhD in American Studies, which English departments often believe (wrongly) lacks literary rigor; my dissertation had more to do with the cultural study of African-American expressive culture (and music) than with modernist literature, per se; I was perceived as a white scholar doing work in African-American Studies, with all the marketplace liabilities of such a narrative. Since mystory ends well (for now), let's say the ends have justified the journey, and leave it at that. Actually, no, let me instead pay my respects to my colleagues at Tulane, who assessed my work as valid right from the initial interview at MLA. Yet so battered was I by the job market's ego-crushing fractals I barely realized I'd landed the perfect job for a jazz scholar until a month after the move to New Orleans, when I found myself dancing next to the tubas on my first second-line parade.

Nearly every Sunday from Labor Day through the end of June, a second-line parade takes to the streets of New Orleans, as organized and sponsored by a Social Aid and Pleasure Club (a fraternal society), free and open to all.

Over the course of four hours, a second-line parade carnivalizes and colonizes public space: they are little cultural miracles of democratic resistance. In second-line parades – rolling block-parties, really – if you're walking near the brass band, you need to dance or walk in time; it's uncool to simply stroll along like a spectator near the band. The musicians depend upon the energy of the second-liners (the dancers) to form a physiological call-and-response analogous to the musical one. In terms of cultural practice, African-American music is *participatory*; spectators need to *roll wid it*, or get the hell out of the way. This advice has been shared with me more than once, sometimes gently and sometimes with hostility. On one parade three years back, there were so many Euro-Americans clogging up the roiling forward movement that several older African-American men turned a veiled threat into a chant fitted to the brass band's propulsive marching beat: "If you ain't gonna roll/if you ain't gonna roll/get the *fuck* on … out of the way."

I'd landed on the streets of one of the last living local African-American musico-cultural traditions. Moreover, I am able to participate, observe, and support the local knowledge of its embodied philosophies, ones that have – in national contexts, in every generation – colonized Euro-American and global bodies, voices, language, style, humor, and kinesthetics. In its community-building and emotional release, the second-line parade inverts the 1970s advice of George Clinton and Funkadelic, "*Free Your Mind … And Your Ass Will Follow.*" In surrendering self to the flow of the street, one might say the implicit directive is to *free your* ass … *and your* mind *will follow.*

My right to the dancing of this attitude has been validated and affirmed in about the same measure as it has been questioned and resented. Once a toothless, older African-American woman in a long, sleeveless one-piece white gauze shirt – half-hospital gown and half Yoruba ceremonial dress – tapped me on the shoulder from behind. "Go 'head," the 70-year-old woman nodded towards my midsection. I knew she meant that I should dance for her. I danced a bit and she shook her head slowly, then more emphatically and demanding, disapproving. Thirty seconds later she shouted her frustration: "*Show me what you* got!" And so I did, sinking low into one of my signature moves, a low-center-of-gravity squat where I shift my hips and roll ball-to-toe. For two minutes, she watched me with a level gaze as she danced lightly, a bit of a flamingo thing, kicking high from one step to the other. Then she nodded: she was satisfied I had submitted to the music and turned away.

The Kid grumbles at my complacency. *Maybe you're a careerist after all.* Say what? I bristle. *So you wrote a book, so now you have an intellectual cohort. So what? How does this create any active social change, how does it do anything except support your intellectual habit?* It was important to get a job I loved, I shot back, to live somewhere I felt I belonged. *And now what?* And now what … what? I throw down with The Kid. *Maybe it's all still acting-out from our Brooklyn upbringing; maybe you always just wanted to be down with the Brothers.* Oh, come on. *And all you've done is some intellectual version of that.* Well, then I've failed, haven't I? I mean I participate, but other than a few colleagues, it's not like I'm part of any social or political activism here; I am not, in any sense, down with the Brothers. *That's what I'm saying,* The Kid cuts me, *that's what I'm saying.* He takes a breath. *So the fuck what?*

The Kid hits me with the core question of my field: the *so what* question. It is no doubt the toughest question of all once you've finished an article, a book, or a project. "*So what do we* know *now that we know* this?" What does it help us understand? How does it lead to new frameworks or actions?

I wished The Kid dead at that moment. But I can't afford the emotional costs. I&I are the child that went forth. So I answer him in a scholarly fashion:

Afrodiasporic musics represent the first intimations of a global culture that remains unrecognized as such as yet. Often in tandem with Latin musics, Afrodiasporic musics and grooves have colonized the world's dancefloors for more than a century: working backwards from hiphop, reggae, and Afropop to funk, souk, disco, and mbaqanga, from soul and rock& roll and calypso to samba, tango, and swing. Why? What does it mean? *So what?* The Kid presses me. So: In the opening pages of his classic theoretical text of African-American music, *Stomping the Blues*, Albert Murray appropriated Kenneth Burke's aphorism about literature for African-American music: it is "equipment for living" (Burke 1938; Murray 1976: 16). How does it prepare us and for what? In *Black Talk*, American Studies scholar and jazz musician Ben Sidran's study of the role of orality in African-American music, he offered his readers a revolutionary subtitle: *How Black Music Transformed Western Literary Values* (Sidran 1981: xii). The omnipresence of music at every level represents a complex movement away from language, literary narrative, reading, and highbrow culture – the artistic servants of Western hyper-rationalism – to orality, aurality, and dance, to the sonic resonances of the ear and the body germane to all local cultures. What does this transformation portend? Such a crossing from literature to music in the twentieth century represents a major categorical shift in global aesthetics, epistemologies, and expressive individualisms.

So ... what does it mean? I don't know, I concede to The Kid, I'm *thinking* about it; I'm *feeling* my way hopefully towards some useful framework. I want to help scholars ask better questions. That's all I&I can do for now.

My inquiry these 30-plus years has led me to believe that this creolized self is emergent – the *panhuman*, as I tentatively call it (Dinerstein 2006: 591) – and it is already *culturally* present in global music and dance. When I was commanded, "Show me what you got!," I understood this directive to mean the following: African-American music and dance provides cultural practices for individuality that must be uniquely self-expressive and yet surrender to the rhythmic flow. To have *processed* and internalized this struggle suggests a willingness to work for social change. Such willingness can be read on the body and in the grain of the voice (I believe), and in Afrodiasporic societies, often enough, each and every member of a community considers him- or herself a self-empowered aesthetic judge of cultural expression. In other words, imitation of perceived African-American moves is for wannabes, poseurs, and wiggers.

To understand the embodied philosophy of African-American music, one might start by taking seriously James Brown's command "to get down with your *bad* self." And then to *realize* ... that self is *creolized.* Call the *pan-human* simply "the dancing of a [new] attitude," to invoke Burke again (Burke 1973: 9), by which we may yet all swing into the future together. If the minds, bodies, and embodied grooves of industrialized nations have been colonized by such cultural forms, the creolized self needs to be theorized, criticized, and negotiated.

So you think that's it? That now you're fighting the good fight? The Kid mocks my self-congratulatory rhetoric.

My scholar-self surrenders to The Kid: my work is a lifelong inquiry; my objective is to create new frameworks for considering self and society, rights and responsibilities, I&I. *Yeah, right. You're a utopian dreamer. Always have been.* The Kid is impatient; always has been. The Kid is neither becalmed by stability or accomplishment, nor by place, home, tenure, or turn of phrase. The Kid still wants the good society through full recognition of others (and Others). But I&I have always agreed on our definition of freedom: the belief that every other person is as good and equally important as you are – existentially speaking, that is, without regard to race or class or income level, gender or religion or nationality, history or mystery. With liberty. And justice. For all.

Yeah, right, The Kid says, and throws on Bob Marley's "Redemption Song," the version by Johnny Cash and Joe Strummer, and I&I, well, we turn it *way ... up ... loud.*

Notes

1 I understood later through two works: (1) Carlo Rotella's *October Cities* (1998), a study of postwar urban literature that juxtaposes the postwar novels of white ethnics with those of non-white ethnics to reveal the economic issues of this displacement; (2) Keith Byerman's *Remembering the Past in Contemporary African American Fiction* (2005), a work which traces out the concerns of contemporary African-American authors.
2 Senator Bill Bradley on the US Senate floor, March 26, 1992. It can be accessed at his website, www.billbradley.com.

References

Adorno, T.W. (2002) *Essays on Music,* Berkeley: University of California Press.
Baraka, A. (1963) *Blues People,* New York: Morrow Quill.
Burke, K. (1938) "Literature as Equipment for Living," *Direction* 1: 10–13.
——(1973 [1941]) *The Philosophy of Literary Form,* Berkeley: University of California Press.
Dinerstein, J. (1985) "Diary of a Mad Teacher," *The Village Voice* 30: 18, 21, 23.

——(2003) *Swinging the Machine: Modernity, Technology, and African-American Culture Between the World Wars*, Amherst: University of Massachusetts Press.
——(2006) "Technology and its Discontents on the Verge of the Posthuman," *American Quarterly* 58, 3: 569–95.
Dyer, R. (1997) *White: Essays on Race and Culture*, New York: Routledge.
Edwards, B.H. (1998) "The Seemingly Eclipsed Window of Form: James Weldon Johnson's Prefaces," in O'Meally, R.G. (ed.), *The Jazz Cadence of American Culture*, New York: Columbia University Press.
Ellington, D. (1993) "The Race for Space," in Tucker, M. (ed.), *The Duke Ellington Reader*, New York: Oxford University Press.
Ellison, R. (1995) *The Collected Essays of Ralph Ellison*, New York: Modern Library.
——(2000) *Juneteenth*, New York: Vintage.
Gilroy, P. (1993) *The Black Atlantic: Modernity and Double Consciousness*, Cambridge MA: Harvard University Press.
Hall, S. (1993) "What is this 'Black' in Black Popular Culture?" *Social Justice* 20, 1–2: 101–14.
hooks, b. (1992) *Black Looks: Race and Representation*, Boston, MA: South End Press.
Hurston, Z.N. (1998 [1935]) *Their Eyes Were Watching God*, New York: Harper/Perennial.
Johnson, J.W. (1934) *Along the Way*, New York: Viking.
Keil, C. (1966) *Urban Blues*, Chicago: University of Chicago Press.
Keil, C. and S. Feld (1994) *Music Grooves: Essays and Dialogues*, Chicago: University of Chicago Press.
Lott, E. (1995) *Love and Theft: Blackface Minstrelsy and the American Working Class*, New York: Oxford University Press.
Murray, A. (1971) *The Omni-Americans: New Perspectives on Black Experience and American Culture*, New York: Avon.
——(1974) *Train-Whistle Guitar*, New York: McGraw-Hill.
——(1976) *Stomping the Blues*, Cambridge, MA: Da Capo Press.
Pearson, M. and M. Shanks (2001) *Theatre/Archaeology*, New York: Routledge.
Pynchon, T. (1973) *Gravity's Rainbow*, New York: Viking.
Rotella, C. (1998) *October Cities*, Berkeley: University of California Press.
Schwartz, J. (1979) *Einstein for Beginners*, New York: Pantheon.
Sidran, Ben (1981 [1971]) *Black Talk*, New York: Da Capo Press.
Smalls, C. (1998 [1987]) *Music of the Common Tongue*, Middletown, CT: Wesleyan University Press.
Stearns, M. and J. Stearns (1994 [1968]) *Jazz Dance: The Story of American Vernacular Dance*, New York: Da Capo Press.
Varela, F.J., E. Thompson, and E. Rosch (1993) *The Embodied Mind*, Cambridge, MA: MIT Press.
Walker, A. (1982) *The Color Purple*, New York: Harcourt Brace Jovanovich.
Waters, M. (2006) "Still A Fool," [song] *The Definitive Collection*, Geffen/Chess (record label).
Whitman, W. (1960 [1855]) "A Child Goes Forth," in *Leaves of Grass*, New York: Penguin.

11 Goodbye nostalgia!
In memory of a country that never existed as such[1]

Wanda Vrasti

Rigoberta Menchú was a liar, an inventor, and a manipulator. I, Wanda Vrasti am none of the above. I am a scientist, an academic, an expert, and a professional. I am trustworthy and exact. I am a bearer of degrees, I carry business cards, I bring evidence when I write, and I make sense when I speak. Naturally then, neither do I write well, nor do I have any captivating stories to tell.

Goodbye nostalgia!

Communism is like 9/11. Everyone has a story of where they were and what they were doing at the time. And everyone, when prompted either on a long flight or in a volume like this, will want to share it. Looking at the steadily growing shelves of memoirs on communism, there are roughly three types of stories: those written by former "enemies of the state," detailing the horrid experiences of forced incarceration in prisons, work camps, and mental institutions; memoirs written by political dissidents, disturbing yet tolerated elements who managed to stay out of prison, read foreign books, publish here and there, and even retain a marginal political voice; and, finally, stories written by "average" people, people who are neither dead nor in exile, people without historical scars or elected offices, whose stories revolve around their everyday lives "in"/"under" communism. If earlier texts were written either by people who died (usually in prisons), ran away, or were granted the heroic title of "survivors of communism," the more recent raconteurs witnessed the Revolution in their adolescence. The generational shift comes with a transition from writing history to producing memory: instead of the heroic sagas of exceptional historic figures we now hear the mundane experiences of commoners, instead of describing the atrocities of authoritarianism, recent communist memories focus on the seemingly trivial effects of living with cultural censorship, and economic lack. Their anecdotal, and mostly humoristic, evidence comes from the school years spent under the vigilant eyes of autocratic teachers or holidays spent on the grandparents' farm in the countryside. They speak of first loves and first break-ups. They provide endless lists of missing consumer products, and detailed descriptions of the ingenious improvisations meant to replace them. The single most poignant feature of these accounts, however, is the deep melancholy caused by the total eradication of a world of meaning, regardless of how cruel, senseless or absurd this world might have been. This melancholy is anathema to the generations before us.

The German film *Goodbye Lenin!* (2003), where a son has to replicate the manipulative tools of the communist regime to prevent his mother, who has just recovered from a coma, from finding out that the regime has collapsed, could easily belong to this final category of melancholic memoirs. In drawing in equal measure upon historic resentment and nostalgic aesthetics, the film manages to strike a significant blow against communism while portraying the past in endearing colors.

Shortly after the film was released, the *New York Times* featured an article about the warm and fuzzy feeling of "Ostalgie" (a mélange of nostalgia and the German word for east) that began to take hold of both East and West Germany, albeit in different ways, during the 1990s (Bernstein 2004). The article was centered around the "Documentation Center on Everyday Life," a museum located in the German provincial town of Eisenhüttenstadt on the border with Poland, which experienced a surge in visiting numbers thanks to the success of *Goodbye Lenin!* "About 10,000 a year come to look at transistor radios, jars of Bulgarian plums, schoolbooks, plastic water glasses that never seemed to come in the right colors" (ibid.). Although on the surface, Ostalgie seems to be a return to the good ol' ways, it works in rather unexpected ways: "*Ostalgie* is not what it seems to be – it is a symptom less of East German nostalgia than of West German utopia" (Boyer 2006: 363, original emphasis). This because it reduces the "cultural heritage" of East Germany's authoritarian past to a bundle of consumer goods that can be easily divorced from their political economic context and subsumed to the vacuous aesthetics of commodity fetishism.

Goodbye Lenin! – perhaps not surprisingly because, after all, it was produced by a team of West Germans – works according to the same logic as the Eisenhüttenstadt museum, turning communist memory into memorabilia. History is reduced to a plethora of artifacts to be admired in museums, photographed during city tours, purchased in souvenir shops, collected, and resold at exorbitant prices. The moral of the story is that East Germans, although perhaps critical of the side effects of reunification effects (including higher medical expenses, unsubsidized living costs, industrial restructuring plans, rising unemployment, and growing crime rates) are consumer subjects too. In *Goodbye Lenin!* Alex is consumed by his inability to obtain the right brands, his sister is obsessed with replacing socialist goods with their flashier Western equivalents, and their mother is overjoyed at finally obtaining the Trabant[2] for which they had been waiting for years (Boyer 2006: 376). Despite historical differences, consumption is the common humanity that brings together all post-89 Berliners – a perverse twist on Chancellor Willy Brand's epochal slogan "*Jetzt kommt zusammen was zusammen gehört*" ("Now comes together what belongs together"). Communism might have pampered its subjects with greater subsidies, greater job security, more reliable social services, and a generally slower pace of life – hence the ostalgist mood – but it is equally vulnerable to the fantasies of capital. No matter how quirky and comforting the socialist landscape may have been, Alex and his family cannot reach political maturity unless they fully subscribe to Western models of conduct, consumption, and citizenship.

Ostalgie functions as a Western utopia because it refuses to take seriously the political ambitions, programs of government, or historical force of communism. Void of any political content, of anything that might render it controversial or dangerous, communism becomes the domain of the derisory and the ridiculous. When the Iron Curtain was finally lifted, what we saw were not grandiose acts of resistance or the frightening remains of a complex mode of social organization, but malfunctioning transistor radios, schoolbooks painted in the colors of social realism, and rows upon rows of canned food, as if millions of people had been duped into trusting and fearing a political regime that had nothing to rely on but empty slogans and budget deficits. Just like the native tribe that was once condemned for its cannibalistic inclinations, but whose almost-extinct cultural and gastronomic uniqueness were nonetheless stored in the "consultable record" of humanity (Geertz 1973: 30), the history of communism was stripped off of its once fearsome connotations and handed over to museum curators and marketing specialists. In their hands, communism became a sum of absurdly humoristic elements, a heritage site preserved and presented for the eyes of tourists, anthropologists, and collectors. This is multiculturalism at its best!

Goodbye Lenin! also says something about the larger narrative and aesthetic conventions communist memoirs must respect to be deemed authentic and persuasive. It sets the disciplinary margins of a genre that has become a hit with art-house film buffs, comparative literature students, architects, museum curators, and travel agents. The rules are as follows:

1. To use communism as the backdrop or subject of an auto-ethnographic piece, communism must be stripped of its affective and aesthetic value. Greyish colors and sordid life stories are encouraged.
2. The memoir must acknowledge that, just like the Roman or the Aztec Empire, communism is a bygone civilization that, albeit historically fascinating, borders on the tragic and the absurd.
3. While communist memoirs may deal with such universal human experiences as love, friendship, or joy, they must never forget to point out how unmistakably sad and miserable life under communism really was and, in doing so, formulate some sort of a normative desire for progress. Anything else would be inaccurate and nostalgic.

Post-communist beginnings

My own story of communism is relatively short because I was only a child when it came to an end. With the exception of a brief three-months period in first grade when I was elected (sic) president of my class and became a "hawk of the homeland," as patriotic elements between the ages of 7 and 14 were called, I don't recall any personal encounters with authoritarianism. I never had any confrontations with officials, I never stayed in line for precious food rations, and I was never forced to participate in parades or youth volunteering programs. Not even my parents have spectacular stories to tell. They were neither party members nor political dissidents; they had neither fled into exile nor participated in the Timişoaran Revolution.[3] But unlike my parents, I don't even *remember* what it was like to live in communism. The little I know is a purely bookish experience drawn from the memories of others.

My parents and friends tell me I have nothing to say about communism. Not having experienced it first-hand is like being a second-rate member of the historical community, blessed but silent. It was not until I left my post-communist landscape that I realized there was something I wanted to say. But how can I convey how fortunate, even grateful, I consider myself for having grown up in a place that lived on both sides of the 1989 turn, without glorifying something I am expected to denounce? How do I explain that I think (the legacy of) communism has taught me things that you cannot be schooled in, while knowing that I am writing in memory of a past that has never existed as such?

Just before Christmas my parents sent me off to a nearby village. This was not the place where my grandparents lived – the place I assume most overprotective parents sent their children during the Christmas holiday of 1989. Still, in the winter of '89 my parents *had* to send me off to Jebel, a village just outside my hometown. In those days, my father worked as a medical doctor at the psychiatric hospital just outside the village. As any doctor, he was a figure of authority useful both to the state and the villagers, but infinitely more precious to the latter. He was the person to go to when you needed medical attention, *any* type of medical attention, from cough medicine to emergency surgical interventions. He was also someone who could clean the streets of the village drunks, the criminally insane, and abusive husbands, all of whom preferred to stay in a mental institution than serve a sentence in an overcrowded prison. Also, elderly individuals who were no longer welcomed at home, homeless people banned from the public eye, and disturbing social elements of all kinds found their way to this institution, which was more a mixture of reformatory, elderly home, and half-way house than a conventional psychiatric hospital. More importantly, my father was helpful when ever someone needed a note to avoid military service, trial, and even imprisonment. For services and favors rendered, people would (re)pay him in German chocolate, American cigarettes, and coffee of a variety of origins, not to mention hoards of live or less alive stock, smoked ham, cheese, fruit, eggs, home-made moonshine, preserves, and canned goods of all sorts. These arrived most abundantly during Christmas but also in steady rations throughout the year. The meat went into the freezer which was twice the size of our fridge. The cigarettes along with most of the coffee and the moonshine were stored in a special cupboard in the living room to be "recycled," that is, exchanged against valuable services other "acquaintances" could provide – tickets for spa retreats, subsidized holiday packages, access to foreign-language kindergarten and schools, and passports.

That winter I stayed for almost a month in Jebel at the house of a hospital employee. Christmas had come and passed, then New Year's. When the beginning of the second school term was postponed, I realized that this was not a regular vacation, but an exile. I was in hiding. But life in Jebel was hard to argue with. The family I was entrusted to indulged me on every occasion. Even in the village, wherever I went, there were desserts, snacks, fruits, and smiles welcoming me. People knew I was "Dr. Vrasti's daughter." These flummeries would never have happened in my home town. My mother would have undoubtedly discouraged them. But, aided by the flurry of events happening back in Timişoara, I went on to enjoy the longest ever winter holiday.

When I was eventually allowed to return home, my parents and I had lunch in the living room like we always did on weekends. The table was set in the kitchen and then arduously transported amidst clinkering cutlery and spilling sauces to the living room where my mother tried to make up for the lack of a proper dining room. Everything seemed normal, as if nothing had happened or changed in my absence, as if I had just gone to the countryside on a school vacation, when we all knew that, in reality, I had no grandparents to visit in the countryside, the second school term had been endlessly postponed, and there had obviously been some political turmoil going on. Eventually, my parents filled in the blanks. Apparently, in my absence they had taken a few walks downtown to watch the protests but then quickly returned the moment they saw tanks and heard bullets. One night, in our neighborhood, they saw a man being shot in a confrontation with the military. (Years later the public would still demand to know who shot at civilians after the fateful night of December 22nd: "*cine-a tras in noi, dupa decembrie douzeci si doi?*"). A few days later, friends of theirs, who played in a band, sought refuge in our apartment after making an appearance in the opera balcony. Together, they watched most of the Revolution on TV, like everyone else. The events unrolled with a fury and speed no one could keep track of. In no more than six days the regime fell apart like a badly staged puppet show. When things regained their mundane normalcy, my father was nominated director of the psychiatric hospital in Jebel and my mother was offered the leading position at the cooperative she was working for because most of the other employees turned out to be party members and traitors. In a few years time the cooperative would go bankrupt. By then my mother would be re-certified as a public notary, profiting from Romania's real estate boom, while my father toured the world doing research for the WHO. Ten years later the three of us would emigrate to Canada.

I am a member of the *post*-communist generation. I spent my adolescent years in "a period of transition" which unfolded against the backdrop of earlier times. Communism was constantly invoked and referenced in history classes, during dinner conversations, in the newspapers my parents (and later I) read, and in the yearly televised anniversary of the Revolution. But it was always done as a warning sign or an impetus for change. Let us give up on our socialist atavisms and make a radical turn to the West. The most fortunate of embraced Western models through the "visa lottery," meaning they were successful in the US immigration program. Others opted for the Canadian or Australian point-based immigration system. Yet others had to settle for seasonal low-skilled work in Spain, Italy, Greece, Ireland, Israel, Austria, and Germany. Those who stayed also had to emulate the West, which would be described in the media by the political and intellectual elite or by those "gone outside" (*plecati afara*). Often, we would receive guidance from our diasporic co-nationals in the form of books and newspaper articles that did not shy away from adopting an explicitly didactic tone. They contained advice and examples for how we were to conduct ourselves following occidental models of government, civic attitudes, and lifestyles. I too participated in this grand endeavor by detecting and discarding anything that remotely resembled or reminded me of communism: from historical materialism to impulses of solidarity, from community activism to acts of vigilantism, from organized self-realization programs to cosmopolitan normative ambitions. Little did we know that many of the principles and values we were trying to rid ourselves of were considered desirable attitudes and sensibilities in the West. Particularly confusing was the overlap between the liberal democratic requirement for social capital and civic virtue, stressed by Western political thinkers from Tocqueville (1835 [1961]) to Robert Putnam (2000), and the Marxist-Leninist penchant for government through communities, voluntary work, and associational life.

In 2007 the Romanian weekly *Dilema Veche* dedicated an entire issue to the question of volunteering. It concluded that decades of forced "patriotic labor," followed by the socio-economic brutalities of structural adjustment plans and rapidly changing lifestyles, made Romanians unable to fulfill the demands of a vibrant civil society. Add to this the fact that the national "mentality" is proverbially suspicious of next of kin and government, and the verdict is clear: post-socialist Romanians were uninterested in performing the good works of altruism despite the obvious secondary benefits they entail, including trust-based social networks, psychological satisfaction and recognition, and symbolic capital (Voicu 2007). It seemed that modern Romanian subjects were only passively and reluctantly performing their citizenship, which, the newspaper declared, was a major hurdle for a country whose single most ardent wish was to leave its marginal role in Europe and join the "civilized world."

Who's afraid of communist youth?

Romania, the summer of 1953: Sweat and enthusiasm are running high for the preparation of the Bucharest International Youth Festival to be held in August of that year. One of the main goals of this year's festival is to abolish the parasitic attitude, identified by the teen magazine *Scânteia tineretului* as one of the greatest perils threatening communist ideals (Ilieş 2004). Even if, at times, the social parasite turns out to be an honest individual, she is still dangerous in resisting the socialist work discipline and in refusing to work towards the realization of new norms of production. So, after a prolonged slumber, the country's youth, together with its brothers and sisters visiting from capitalist countries, embark on a mission of homeland beautification. Amidst songs of joy and good spirit, boys and girls flex their muscles on shovels to transform a garbage infested ravine into a splendid park. In Mamaia, volunteers are planting trees along the sea shore. In Iaşi, it is reported that 70 students have planted 12,000 trees in two hours. This amounts to 85 trees per student per hour, that is, more than one tree per minute. These achievements have a contagious effect upon the country's factory workers, who are also eager to fulfill and surpass their production norms, as well as upon the inhabitants of Bucharest who, overjoyed, propose to join in Sunday voluntary labor (Ilieş 2004).

Communist ideology rested on the assumption that human nature was fundamentally malleable and receptive to the transformative and progressive qualities of organizational life. Consequently, it was obsessed with planning, optimizing, and monitoring the future of the socialist community. Immediately after the Bolshevik Revolution, Lenin opposed the "leftist fraction" of the Communist Party and their plan to dismantle all workers' unions and other professional organizations. Contra Trotsky, Lenin argued that, within the new historical context, these organizations were far from being redundant and they would function en masse as "conveyor belts" for the realization of the communist vision. Stalin would take over this ambition and increase the number of arm's length organizations to include unions, cooperatives, factory organisms, women's groups, press groups, cultural-educational organizations, and youth organisms. The purpose of these vanguard organizations was to recruit and train the new socio-political elite to engineer a progressive political subject (Tismăneanu 2006: 138).

One problem remained, however. Despite its fascination with neatly regimented mass conduct, Marxism-Leninism expressed an inherent skepticism towards large groups of people. Youth groups, in particular, demonstrate this ambivalence. On the one hand, thanks to their relative flexibility and receptivity, it was thought that the communist youth would spearhead the transformation of the entire body politic. On the other hand, however, the vices threatening the moral fiber of this demographic, that is, laziness, apathy, and cosmopolitan inclinations, instilled constant fear and mistrust in those orchestrating these changes. The solution to this conundrum was to increase and tighten the organizational ropes that would shape the "new man" from an early age onwards (Tismăneanu 2006: 139). Teens and young adults were going to be monitored and regulated more closely than any other demographic group with the help of youth groups, student bodies, extra-curricular programs, and cultural initiatives.

One of the most urgent areas of reform concerned young people's attitude to work. Unlike the "antiquated man," that is, the bourgeois subject, for whom work was merely an instrumental activity meant to ensure his livelihood while augmenting the wealth of others, the "new man" would be a worker par excellence. He would perceive work as a moral necessity; work would be his second nature, his *raison d'étre*. As opposed to the laborer who perceives works as tedious, alienated drudgery but submits to it to sustain himself and his family, the worker gains personal meaning and a larger sense of purpose through his professional activity. Work, in Marxist-Leninist ideology, is the medium through which political events, national celebrations, communitarian ideals, and personal skills and talents are expressed. "Work is the most convincing form of expression of human solidarity and the joy of life" (Boia 2005: 137). Teens and young adults must submit to this work ethos from an early age onwards lest they become "*cosmopoliți*," meaning, individuals corrupted by occidental tastes and hedonistic vices, including denim wear, long hair, rock and folk music, idling and loitering.

By the end of the Cold War, the Russian *Komsomol* (*Kommunisticeski Soiuz Molodioji* – Communist Youth Union) was counting 15 million members – most of whom were the children of laborers and farmers. *Komsomol* also acted as an umbrella organization for the Pioneer Organization, which included middle school students ages nine to 14, and the Octombrist Organization, targeting pre-school children up to the age of eight (Tismăneanu 2006: 140). In Romania, *Uniunea Tineretului Comunist* (Union of Communist Youth) numbered one million members by the end of the 1980s. In 1983, 90% of ninth-graders belonged to the UTC and in 1988 the number rose to a staggering 98%. From the tenth grade membership in UTC became mostly automatic and compulsory. Those who did not belong, did not refuse participation, but were most likely expelled or excluded based on meritocratic and political criteria (Cioflanca 2006). All of these organizations had as their primary goal the formation of a "new man" through associational networks, voluntary work, and patriotic sentiments.

The collective memory from these times is divided. Some city folks remember the so-called voluntary work days, field excursions, expeditions, and festivities as days of love and idyll in the country side, and a welcome break from the sordid routine of school discipline and ideological education. Others are bitter in their recollection, denying that there was ever a moment of bliss among the staged glory of communist youth. Nonetheless, both sides agree that no one from the youngest pioneer to the university student, from class leader to commanding instructor, from parents to teachers took these voluntary work responsibilities seriously. Endless successions of reports, journals, instruction, recitals, oaths, more reports, parades, and salutes were nothing more than generations of youngsters "pretending that we care so they leave us alone" (Bot 2008).

The politics of idleness

At age 17, a year before I graduated from high school, my mother somehow managed to obtain two Canadian visitor visas and promptly booked us on a tour of the universities of Southern Ontario. The European employment market was overcrowded and insecure, she claimed. North America, of which Canada proved the more accessible and affordable part, provided an alternative model of human organization, work ethics, and civic spirit. Her determination could not be argued with. It was not because the quality of the Canadian post-secondary education system left no doubt in her. Rather, her ambition that I study and, eventually, settle down abroad was personal and political in a way you could not disagree with without automatically vexing her entire worldview. Her hopes for me were in fact the ambitions she herself would have liked to pursue. Or so I felt.

My coming of age was somewhat belated. Like most other Romanian teenagers, I had not worked a single day in my life. It was expected that I would get good grades, go to university someday, and move out on my own when I got married, but beyond that I had no responsibilities to attend to. Everything from school sandwiches to vacation money was provided by my parents. So when my parents gave me three choices – attend law school in Romania and take over my mother's six-figure earning practice; pursue a "solid" social sciences degree in Canada, for example, political science was "solid," anthropology was not; or do whatever I wanted at my own expense, which basically boiled down to going to film school – I knew, in reality, I only had one option. The third option was impractical and implied a fairly ridiculous post-pubescent running-away-from-home type of scenario. The first option was not truly an option. Not emigrating was something my parents would have had even greater difficulty accepting than not following their professional advice. It had been their most ardent wish to emigrate and that wish only escalated in the years following the Revolution, when their disillusion with the indigenous political class and national culture reached new heights. To them, and to my mother in particular, not emigrating meant letting another generation go to waste in a country for which they had nothing but resentment. They had never dared to swim across the Danube or claim refugee status pre-1980. A mix of quotidian responsibilities and vague hope for a more "civilized" Romania had kept them from emigrating even after the wall came down. But now that I was about to attend university abroad, they would finally have an excuse to follow. And so, there was only one option.

After two weeks of comparing tuition prices, campus sizes, facilities, and geographic distances, after two weeks of interviews and appointments with guidance counselors, ombudsmen, and international student liaisons, applications were collected and final decisions made. Back home, my teacher asked me to prepare a presentation on "lessons learnt" in Canada, a country which for citizens of the post-communist bloc is still untouchable beyond costly application procedures and one-way plane tickets. I said: "There people care, they don't just pretend. Volunteering is essential to ensuring admission to more competitive study programs, better-paid jobs, and more reputable career paths. But, even beyond that, people just seem to genuinely care." Like a tourist, I had scouted the Ontarian valuescape by conversing with diasporic family members and university admission officers or glancing at campus bulletin boards, recreational centers, and newspaper ads. Although my notes were highly impressionistic, this was the one fact that had made the strongest impression upon me.

Having grown up with cautionary tales of youth organizations and patriotic work programs, my post-socialist generation imagined "the West" as the complete antithesis of everything we were taught to detest. In my high school years I venerated a long list of American dropouts, bums, social menaces, and morally maladapted characters. The rosy smell of nostalgia still envelops these times of difficult-to-obtain Henry Miller and William Borroughs novels, Tarantino and David Lynch films, or the records of Leonard Cohen, Nick Cave, and Tom Waits. Together with my parents' generation who, although significantly more prudish and conservative, had a soft spot for turn of the century French *ennui* and Jerome K. Jerome's *flâneurs*, we envisioned America as a vast geography of rebellion and enjoyment. Watching them, we cultivated a kind of idleness that was more of a political statement than a pseudo-Eastern state of contemplation (or complacency). Our idleness was nothing but noise and fury, uncompromising values, lifestyles rough at the edges, dreams of conquest, sharp tongues, and short attention spans. It was not idleness of the uncompetitive non-materialistic kind that one usually finds in hippies or of the righteous kind one sees in radical ecologists and vegans. Our idleness was bad for you. It was the idleness of refusal like in Melville's *Bartleby*, the bohemian idleness of Absinthe-soaked Paris, and the wasteful idleness of the Beat generation. It wasn't that we aspired to laziness, but we did not want to participate in the sentimental education on care and compassion endorsed, in late liberalism, by espresso-sipping artists as well as cappuccino-gulping businessmen (Brooks 2000: 10). Doing nothing and, implicitly, not caring about anyone "was much more than a lack of activity. [It] offered itself as a deep basis for identity" (Lutz 2006: 276). In "a culture obsessed with purpose, pragmatism, and productivity" or, in our case, patriotism, parades, and pioneers, doing nothing – whether in bodily or affective terms – was not a neutral act. It is what we now, in retrospect, like to call resistance, but which we then had no language or patience to theorize.

It was not until I left Romania that I realized how romantic these Western fantasies were: not only were my Canadian colleagues and neighbors willing to produce, participate, and parade with a zeal and enthusiasm I had never before encountered, but they were also prepared to commit their bodies, time, and labor power for free. I arrived in my post-industrial, advanced democratic, and Western-based adoptive country only weeks after graduating from high school. My first encounter with North American campus life was far from the Timothy Leary type of imaginary I had secretly fantasized about.

Frosh Week, with its color organized teams of screaming (post-)pubescent youth, proved a more fruitful recruiting ground for the great American Boy/Girl Scout Association than for an anti-nuclear protest. Though, I have to admit, I would have had little interest in either group chemical experiments or anti-chemical protests. Not recognizing these signs of apathy, one day, an over-eager employee of the international student office at my university recruited me for a volunteer job. I was to set up a booth in the campus concourse on those specified days when all clubs, charities, and associations, along with a few select businesses, get together to vie for the extra-curricular time of students. Our idea was to match domestic and international students for them to exchange language skills. Had it not been for the poor enrolment rate, lack of foreign language speakers, and an imminent university staff strike, maybe the idea would have worked and cohorts of bi- and multilingual students would have patrolled our campus. What good came out of this initiative were a few boosted-up résumés, mine included, which featured a boisterous self-description as the founder and organizer of *Talk Swap*.

Over a century ago Tocqueville argued that what distinguishes democracy from despotism is the presence of a vigorous associational life to cement a free, stable, and participatory society (Cruikshank 1996: 244). Strangely enough, associational networks never lacked in the Eastern bloc. On the contrary, they flourished to an extent and at a speed rate Robert Putnam could only dream about. It is not the absence of civic institutions or their failure to promote trust, cooperation, and freedom that separate liberalism from communism. Communism is not the despotic opposite of democracy, as the liberal argument goes. It embodies only a more rudimentary conception of the rationale and operation of government. Communist rule subjected its citizens to repressive, unappealing, and often drab programs of government that encouraged citizens to cheat, poke fun at, and desert from its tutelage. Liberal democracy, on the other hand, is based on a more gentle, participatory, and seductive types of authority that claim allegiance through a combination of self-rule and quasi-voluntary acts without, however, working towards the emancipation of political subjects (Cruikshank 1996: 245–46).

While communist regimes tried to abolish the parasite by disciplining the body politic and appealing to dogmatic patriotism, post-industrial democracies adopted a more refined strategy to promote a vigorous work ethic, one that was in line with democracy's preference for consent over coercion. Management theorists were among the first to realize that conferring on workers a sense of achievement, personal meaning, and a possibility for growth was a more effective strategy for improving productivity and curbing absenteeism than trying to inculcate a conformist type of worker morale (Boltanski and Chiapello 2005). If workers were given greater autonomy over their time and greater input in their work, their productivity, commitment, and satisfaction would increase to a level where the whole doctrine of work ethic would become redundant (Lutz 2006: 271). Where labor tapped into workers' passions and potentials, where the employment sites reproduced the atmosphere of domestic and recreational space, where rewards appealed to workers' deepest desire for self-expression and-realization, the age-old distinction between work time and free time collapsed (Hymnowitz 2001) to make room for the "pleasures in work" formula – an ironic play on the infamous "joy *through* work" slogan (Donzelot 1991: 251, original emphasis). The revolutionary insight of management studies was that meaningful and rewarding employment can create the fantasy of quasi-voluntary work. Work that smells like force, exploitation, and boredom quickly becomes vulnerable to (collective) resistance, as the "revolt against work" movement of the 1970s demonstrated (Ross 2008). However, when work fosters self-esteem, empowerment, and personal growth, workers participate with a zeal and dedication that no amount of material insecurity and exploitation can compromise.

In the transition from industrial proletariat to post-industrial "souletariat," or to put it in Foucaultian terms, from the government of the self to self-government, management studies killed the slacker once and for all in a more efficient and definitive way than communist rule ever could. The rise of creative, affective, and autonomous work brought on the demise of anti-establishment figures that used uselessness and wastefulness as their strategy of political revolt. The slacker's moment of glory in popular culture became history (Lutz 2006: 289). Inactivity became unbearable unless it was used either to recharge one's batteries for more work or to advance one's extra-curricular range of interests and skills. Doing nothing became "the most difficult thing in the world," "the most difficult and the most intellectual," as Oscar Wilde put it, both because of the social stigma of "laziness" and the unbearable semiotic emptiness of inactivity (Lutz 2006: 55). Doing nothing is not about having nothing to do, as in the case of unemployment, old age, disability, or clinical depression. Doing nothing happens in spite of existing alternatives. The difference between the two is that having nothing to do, that is, living off welfare, is a tolerated albeit despised social position, whereas choosing to do nothing is a blatant defiance of the value system that binds together workers, employers, and even the unemployed. The latter is a much more difficult stance because the biggest threat to the idler is not social stigma, but the inwardly turned aggression of guilt and shame. For the idler to endure the latter, the choice of doing nothing must be a political one.

Thinkers from Socrates to Nietzsche and Foucault have elaborated on the ethical work involved in making the self into a work of art. The self, they argued, could be molded through ascetic and rigorous activities to help it achieve ethical virtues and aesthetic perfection. Although they did not provide a list of what those activities might be, only a monstrous imagination could have predicted that in the post-industrial age the standard of reference for such self-work would be the résumé template, the self-help bookshelf, or the human resources guideline. I never volunteered again. And, more than that, I made sure to choose a profession where I am rarely evaluated on my leadership skills, problem-solving aptitudes, and extra-curricular activities, most of which I am still unsure as to what they mean.

Communism was a "simpler" time

In a deceivingly awkward-looking interview given by Slavoj Žižek on the Bostonian television show NiteBeat (but which in my opinion proves his utterly brilliant and charismatic character), and later featured in the autobiographic film *Žižek!* (2005), the Slovenian rock star philosopher explains that, when faced with the obligation to visit grandmother on a weekend, a child is faced with two possibilities. If he happens to have an authoritarian father, who regardless of the wishes of the child, will demand that the visit takes place, the latter has no option but fulfill his father's injunction and pretend to enjoy it. If, however, the child is fortunate enough to have a tolerant father who has been diligently schooled in the art of so-called "postmodern" parenting, he will be given a choice. The child is free to decide whether he is going to visit grandmother against his wishes or neglect his familial obligation. The second father, Žižek argues, is more perverse and, in fact, more restrictive than the first. Whereas the former maintains an "honest" separation between what is really desired and what is pretended to be desired, the latter erases this distinction, calling for a perfect congruence of the two. In the second scenario the child must visit his grandmother *and* like it. A similar parallel could be drawn between the communist memory of my youth and the liberal democratic present I am now a part of.

It seems to me that, even at the risk of committing a sacrilege against all those who ever lived under communism, the subjects of authoritarianism had it easier. It seems ridiculous to argue such a thing in the face of the monumental records of imprisonment, torture, and the violation of universal human rights that went on in the Eastern bloc. Of course, the liberal critique stands. But the claim I want to make here refers to a different, more mundane and partly less sensational side of life under communism. It refers to the millions of people for whom authoritarianism became a more or less mundane occurrence, which colored their textbooks, sense of fashion, musical and literary tastes, living arrangements, professional choices, holiday destinations, and fantasies of a "better world," but which only rarely interrupted it. In spite of how "insensitive" this argument may sound, there is a distinction to be made between, on the one hand, Communism (with capital C), which was responsible for the most exceptional aspects of the regime and was prominently featured in Western media, and, on the other hand, communism (with small c). The latter was a mode of social organization that structured rather than disrupted everyday life. Writ small, communism, I argue, was a "simpler" time in the sense that there still existed a firm and unambiguous ethicopolitical separation between compliance and rebellion, acquiescence and irony, discipline and enjoyment, productivity and uselessness, enthusiasm and apathy. If nothing else, communism presented its subjects with a landscape of clear ethico-political points of reference. In its perverse usage of megalomaniac five-year plans, kitschy aesthetic, and doctrinarian language, communism created a massive rift between public dogmatic injunctions and private acts of defiance, between the ambitions of professional, administrative, and political authorities and the ideals, language, and performances of its subjects, between subjection and subjectivity (Yurchack 1997). Instead of creating an overlap between pleasure and productivity as flexible capitalism does, or between political subjects' sense of self and their acts of citizenship as liberal democracies do, communist rule offered a plethora of liberating outlets for apathy and slacking, playing and cheating. It is through indifference, rather than through active resistance, that communism was eroded over the years (Cruikshank 1996: 242; Yurchack 1997: 186).

To say that communism was a "simpler" time is not to romanticize what has passed, but to seize upon its immense humoristic and transgressive potential. That potential is carried on even in the memory of communism. There is not a single communist memoir, at least from the contemporary generation, that does not border on tragicomedy. I always have to laugh out loud when I read about the ingenious strategies people had for holding down a full-time job without doing any real work or about the elaborate strategies they had for obtaining a Western cultural product or owning a Western consumer good. Similarly, there is not a single communist memoir that fails to point out the subversive potential of public displays of boredom, slacking, and double-speak. These texts are equally useful in challenging liberal appeals to voluntary work, able bodies, and enthusiastic minds. The fact that self-rule is increasingly moving into the direction of the therapeutic proves that technologies of government are becoming increasingly savvy and sensitive (Rose 1990). Especially now that affect, altruism, and autonomy are being used as liberal-capitalist outlets of individuation, we must remember the value of resisting and refusing power through joking, yawning, or idling.

Postscript

As I write these pages on the smallest laptop ever invented, I hear the heavy tropical raindrops hitting the tin roof above my head. Because of the rain I can miss work today and write instead. My work these days consists of clearing out weed gardens, planting trees, building pathways, making compost, and whatever else is needed in Nueva Juventud Park in the Peten district of northern Guatemala, where I work five days a week. Technically, I am a volunteer although I pay to work here and my funding sources pay me to do research on the subject of volunteer tourism.

Over six years have passed since my last volunteering experience, but the phenomenon has not ceased to puzzle me. What has always fascinated me about volunteering is not what I could get out of it, in terms of social networks, psychological rewards, or normative citizenship, but the fact that I had no use for these rewards. I neither craved nor appreciated them. I eventually started wondering whether there was something wrong with me: Did I suffer from a post-communist allergy to collective identities and programs? Did I inherit my co-nationals' proverbial apathy to their next of kin? Could I blame this on some deep-buried atavisms from my past or was my aversion to volunteering somehow politically justifiable? When these questions failed to leave me alone, I decided to make them into research questions. Volunteering landed on the chopping table of my dissertation work.

Notes

1 *Goodbye Lenin!* (2003).
2 Type of automobile produced in East Germany before 1990 and a hit throughout the eastern block. Despite its flaws, the Trabant was considered to be of superior quality to the Romanian Dacia, the Czech Lada, or the Soviet Volga.
3 Timișoara has an iconic place in the Romanian landscape. This is the city where the revolution began. It is also my home town.

References

Bernstein, R. (2004) Eisenhüttenstadt journal, "Warm, fuzzy feelings for East Germany's gray old days," *The New York Times*, January 13, available at: www.nytimes.com/2004/01/13/international/europe/13GERM.html?scp=1& sq = Warm, fuzzy feelings for East Germany's gray old days& st = cse (accessed July 1, 2010).
Boia, L. (2005) *Mitologia științifica a comunismului*, Bucharest: Humanitas.
Boltanski, L. and E. Chiapello (2005) *The New Spirit of Capitalism*, New York: Verso.
Bot, I. (2008) "Corp de pioneer," *Dilema Veche* 5(216), April 6, available at: www.dilemaveche.ro/sectiune/tema-saptamanii/articol/corp-de-pionier (accessed July 21, 2010).
Boyer, D. (2006) "*Ostalgie* and the politics of the future in Eastern Germany," *Public Culture* 18, 2: 361–81.
Brooks, D. (2000) *Bobos in paradise: The new upper class and how they got there*, New York: Simon & Schuster.
Cioflanca, A. (2006) "Rolul UTC in angrenajul totalitar," *Revista 22* 16, 876, December 22, available at: www.revista22.ro/rolul-utc-in-angrenajul-totalitar-3329.html (accessed June 24, 2009).
Cruikshank, B. (1996) "Revolutions within: self-government and self-esteem," in Barry, A., Osborne, T., and Rose, N. (eds.), *Foucault and political reason: Liberalism, neo-liberalism and rationalities of government*, Chicago: University of Chicago Press.
Donzelot, J. (1991) "Pleasures in work," in Burchell, G., Gordon, C., and Miller, P. (eds.), *The Foucault effect: Studies in governmentality*, Chicago: University of Chicago Press.
Geertz, C. (1973) *The Interpretation of Cultures*, New York: Basic Books.
Goodbye Lenin! (2003) [film] directed by Wolfgang Becker, Germany: X-Filme Creative Pool.
Hymnowitz, K. (2001) "Ecstatic capitalism's brave new work ethic," *City Journal*, available at: www.city-journal.org/html/11_1_ecstatic_capitalisms.html (accessed September 25, 2009).

Ilieș, C. (2004) "Sa starpim atitudinea de gura-casca," *Cahiers de l'echinox: Litterature et totalitarisme* 7: 199–292.

Lutz, T. (2006) *Doing nothing: A history of loafers, loungers, slackers, and bums in America*, New York: Farrar, Straus and Giroux.

Putnam, R. (2000) *Bowling alone: The collapse and revival of American community*, New York: Simon & Schuster.

Rose, N. (1990) *Governing the soul: The shaping of the private self*, London: Routledge.

Ross, A. (2008) "The new geography of work: Power to the precarious?" *Theory, Culture & Society* 25, 7–8: 31–49.

Tismăneanu, V. (2006) *Comisia prezidențiala pentru analiza dictaturii comuniste din România: Raport final*, available at: www.presidency.ro/static/ordine/ RAPORT_FINAL_CPADCR.pdf (accessed July 26, 2008).

Tocqueville, A. de (1835 [1961]) *Democracy in America*, New York: Schocken Books.

Voicu, B. (2007) "Între realitate și speranța," *Dilema Veche* 4, 169, May 7, available at: www.dilemaveche.ro/sectiune/tema-saptamanii/articol/intre-realitate-si-sperante (accessed July 21, 2010).

Yurchack, A. (1997) "The cynical reason of late socialism: Power, pretense and the Anekdote," *Public Culture* 9: 161–88.

Žižek! (2005) [film] directed by Taylor Astra, USA: Hidden Driver Productions.

12 Shaping walls
Moving through Lanka's forts

Nethra Samarawickrema

In the winter of 2006, when I returned home for Christmas break, I spent my first week in Galle, a port-city on the south coast of Sri Lanka. It had been a year and a half since I last came home, a year and a half in which I began to sense, with urgency, that something had gone terribly wrong with the way I had run away to America. Professors, books, and friends brought me face-to-face with the fact that it was more than just the liberal arts education that drew me to the US. I was beginning to realize my move was inextricably connected to global currents of power and colonialism. So, during my 2006 winter break, I returned to the country I thought had little to offer me (save perhaps its curries – my tongue stubbornly retained the relationship the rest of my body and mind tried to break), aching to see what I had blinded myself to while my eyes turned westwards.

It was fitting then, that in my first week home, I found myself in Galle. Colonialism was woven thickly into the history of Galle. It was Galle that the first Portuguese ship washed into in 1505 beginning the first wave of colonization. It was also in Galle that the Dutch built their sprawling fortress during the second wave of colonization. Colonialism, which seemed a distant phenomenon when I studied it in school, now felt intensely close. Traveling to Galle I wondered how I would react to its presence in the old buildings of the city. I would soon see that it was a place of many revisits and reconfigurations. But before I venture into my time there let me first describe my own return home.

***

At first it was the visceral thrill of being in Sri Lanka, the usual high of an international student returning home. I woke up at four in the morning and ate my second dinner, delighted that my mother had made all my favorite curries. I spent my first evening by the sea and gulped in long breaths of ocean smell. I sweated while walking outside. Properly sweated. I settled into my routine of morning walks with my father. At night, I curled up with my mother.

But the predictability ended there. "Sri Lanka looks different to me," I wrote to my friend Jason who was spending the break in Pennsylvania. I felt surprised, unsettled. Sri Lanka looked different, not only because it was speedily becoming westernized, not only because the army barracks that had disappeared in the few years of "ceasefire" had multiplied tenfold and now appeared on almost every street corner in Colombo, but also because I was perceiving my surroundings in a different way. Something within me had begun to shift over the past three years and these shifts were showing me things I hadn't seen before.

It was within the confines of my home that I felt this change most intensely, especially when I spent time with Missiya, Sushila, and Lionel who did the cooking and cleaning in our house. I still can't recover from an incident that took place a few days after I arrived. I was chatting to Sushila by the stove as she added spices to a curry, speaking to her not because I wanted her to do something for me, not because I was saying hello while hurrying out of the kitchen with a cup of tea, but because, for the first time, I wanted to chat with her. We were laughing at something when I suddenly noticed Sushila's face, the fullness of her cheeks, the darkness of her skin, the wisps of gray in her hair, her wide smile. The thought crossed my mind, "Oh, she's a person!" As we laughed, I felt momentary surprise at this recognition that I was talking to another human being. It was as if I had seen her through an unfocused lens all this time – a lens that made me perceive her solely by the role she played in our house. Now, writing about it, reliving it, what I feel most is shame.

In the next few days, slowly, with a sickening feeling, I started feeling the presence of people I hadn't paid attention to. Each time we drove down the roads, waves of panic hit me as I noticed the people walking in the streets, rushing into overcrowded buses. Over and over again my eyes adjusted to what I was seeing as my mind reassessed the values that had made them invisible to me. It felt strange to realize that people could disappear from my vision because of their constant visibility. And yet, in the past, they hadn't completely disappeared. I had been conscious of class differences when I lived in Sri Lanka, but mainly as a marker that separated the educated, "well-to-do" us from the "not-so-well-off" them. I had accepted the disparities in wealth as normal and natural simply because it was what I had always known. I used to think that the only thing to do was to help, in any way we could, "those" who weren't as lucky as we were. It never occurred to me that there was something amiss with the economic structures we were all a part of. Now, suddenly, the boundaries of "us" and "them" were loosening; I was noticing a likeness that made the inequalities jarring and difficult to bear. In the class Understanding Capitalism, I had encountered the disturbing term "Necroeconomics," the economics of death. Its definition encapsulated the concept that the creation of wealth required the simultaneous creation of poverty. This term rang in my ears as I tried to grapple with the shifting light through which I was beginning to see the people and places around me.

And now, there was another word that refused to leave me. *Unfair*. The word rolled around in my mind with increasing intensity. *Unfair*. An English word. One English word among the many English thoughts in my head.

It was a word that began to eat into me, sucking my breath like a mango seed when people at roadside stores, in three-wheeled taxis, in my father's construction sites called me "madam" and acted deferentially in my presence. *Unfair.* The word made me do things I hadn't done before. It made me desperate to interact with people to bridge these gaps. I felt edgy and restless whenever I spent a length of time inside my house. I avoided using English and urgently spoke in Sinhala to everyone I met – people driving taxis, people working in shops, people selling vegetables. I talked to them as if I could claim allegiance with the lower classes in my country as easily as I had previously rejected them. Each day I ploughed through the conversations, despite all the times I cringed when people teased me about my anglicized Sinhala and despite all the times they inquired about which country I had grown up in. Like them, I too wondered, "which country had I grown up in?"

Still, alongside the disquiet, the guilt, the hurry to get to know the "real Sri Lanka," something else was unfolding. My body was breathing as though it hadn't breathed in a year and a half. I drank in the movement in the streets, the madness of the traffic, the changing tones of the sea, and the sound of my friends teasing each other in "Singlish," the hybrid of Sinhala and English. And as I padded about my house, barefoot, and absorbed its open spaces, its colors and textures, a sense of stillness, connectedness, and rest washed over me. I felt as though something within me that had been numb, like my fingers in the winter chill, was slowly tingling back to life. In this first week, I swung like a pendulum between waves of panic and waves of relief. And I carried my aches – my longing for Sri Lanka and my pain at who I was in Sri Lanka – with me to Galle.

***

My previous trip to Galle was sudden, unexpected, and brief. It took place two years before this visit, in the Christmas of 2004. Our car joined the long line of vehicles streaming southwards, carrying bottles of mineral water, clothes, rations, and whatever we thought would be useful for those who lost their homes in the Tsunami. As we drove to Galle, I felt startled by my inability to recognize or pick out the familiar sites that marked the drive I knew and loved as a child. Instead, I beheld strange displacements: huge fishing boats jutting out of houses, toilet seats sitting on rooftops, and a deathly silence in the streets, much like the ghost towns I had seen in the villages bordering the war zones of the north of the island. And now, driving along the coast two years later, I marveled that Galle had regained its life and rhythms. How it had reconstituted itself, I would only later see. For the moment, I felt a rising anticipation upon approaching this resilient city.

***

I soon found myself in the Dutch Fort of Galle. Initially built to a small scale by the Portuguese, the Fort was later expanded and strengthened by the Dutch when they took over the port-city and its natural harbor.

Shaping walls 155

As I mentioned before, while growing up in Sri Lanka, I had considered colonialism to be distant and bygone. But the classes I took in Ithaca – Global Fury, International Conflict, and Understanding Capitalism – brought it closer, alerting me that the distance I experienced from colonial history was connected to my inability to see and perhaps bear its proximity. So that day, as I walked towards the Dutch Fort, I expected to feel intense anger upon standing in front of it.

But I was surprised at my response. I could still sense an imposing power emanating from the Fort's walls and feel the might of the thick granite ramparts that encased what would have been a sprawling city in the eighteenth century. It was impossible not to perceive the authority and force in the Fort's structure, even though parts of it were fading and crumbling. But what struck me most was the way this magnificent beast had slowly been changed, slowly been reclaimed, by the culture it once held in a colonial bind.

Then I remembered why I used to get excited about visiting the Fort as a child, why I had considered it very much a part of my country. Within the Fort's imperial walls, a small city thrived. In those childhood visits, I would excitedly run down its narrow streets and pathways looking for little shops where people were making and selling crafts. The Fort was home to many local communities who had lived there for generations, who had honed and passed down specialized skills in lace making and jewelry and gemstone carving. Now, returning to the Fort, I spent several afternoons walking alone through the tiny roads, going in and out of shops, talking to people selling things, asking them about the place, slowly absorbing what I was seeing and hearing.

I met Fatima, a lady who owned a jewelry store. She told me that her family had been living in the Fort for six generations, producing and selling jewelry, a trade the Moor community she belonged to specialized in. During the conversation that went on for two hours, she told me about her neighborhood and showed me different houses, counting the number of generations each family had lived there, highlighting the kinds of trade or craft-making they engaged in. I found to my surprise that within the Fort's walls, Sinhalese, Tamils, and Muslims lived in the same neighborhoods and even spoke each other's languages. As I walked around, I could see what Fatima meant. I passed the old Dutch Reformed church built in 1754 and smiled as I found, not too far from it, a temple and a mosque. The missionaries wouldn't have been too happy about that, I laughed. Life had gently crept back through the Fort's granite walls, and inside it, I could sense the pulse of the small city.

I left the tightly knit streets and made my way towards the ramparts that overlooked the sea. As I walked, I glimpsed a scene that captivated me. In the Fort's sea-facing wall, within the rectangular openings from which cannon once fired, a particular kind of life was thriving. In each embrasure punctuating the vast granite facade, protected from society's view, young couples huddled together capturing a few moments of privacy. Needless to say, public display of romance is risky business. As I ran my eyes along the length of the rampart I digested the fact that these couples had sought refuge in the walls that once housed the death cannons of the Dutch. They had gravitated to the Fort and claimed it as the space to hold their trysts. I walked past them, giggling at the irony. These shifts in meaning struck me as surreal and almost poetic; I hadn't anticipated such evocative encounters in a place that embodied colonialism and control. Each reconfigured space I stumbled upon gave me a renewed sense of vitality.

There were other shifts though, that took me aback, that dulled the spirit of agency I sensed in the city. In the following days I learned about the recent ripples of change unsettling the Fort's communities. One woman pointed to a new cafe and told me that a few years ago, it had been the ancestral home of a local family. But they had sold their house to a foreign investor and left the community, as many other residents had. Later I would learn that the government was encouraging foreign and local investors to buy property in the Fort, renovate the buildings, and open up businesses that would draw tourists to the site.

As I walked down Church Street, the main thoroughfare of the walled-city, I began to realize with a sinking feeling that the Fort was on its way to acquiring a new, stylish, sexy face. Many of the old buildings had been renovated and inside them, boutique hotels, high-end stores, and cafes had opened up. And these exclusive, expensive textile, clothing, and craft stores were fast replacing the small, family owned jewelry and craft shops that had thrived for generations. Many of the families that had made a living by selling their crafts to the local and foreign tourists found their livelihoods threatened with the arrival of the boutique hotels that drew tourists who gravitated towards the more expensive stores. I was told that one by one, many families had accepted the large sums of dollars offered by foreign and local investors and left their ancestral homes in the Fort.

My father and I spoke about these changes one evening as we walked around the Fort. Usually, I feel closest to my father when I walk with him. His architect's eye is able to perceive shapes, space, and light in a way that is beyond my grasp. Walking beside him, I often feel the buildings and streets come alive. But that evening was different. He was incensed. "This place is falling into shambles," he said, angrily pointing out several crumbling colonial houses along a narrow by lane. He was appalled that the historic site was not being well maintained. It was only when we found our way back to Church Street and came upon the sight of the hotels and cafes that my father's spirits picked up. The architect in him delighted in the fact that the old buildings had been restored, preserving the exterior facades of the colonial architecture and, at the same time, blending the colors and textures of Sri Lankan art into the interiors. He carefully examined the buildings to see their fusion of eastern and western, traditional and modern aesthetics.

Throughout the walk, my father spoke. "The Fort must be renovated and restored. These old buildings are crumbling and the residents have no sensitivity to maintain them," he said. "I'm glad that foreigners are buying up the old houses. They're preserving them in a way that our people can't be bothered to," he said. And then, seeing my frustrated look, he responded, "There's nothing wrong with expatriates giving a new look to the Fort. The people who live here can take the money and find other places to live." "The important thing is that this site, its art and culture are preserved," he said. As he looked around the Fort, he told me what he envisioned for it – that it would become a place full of restaurants, cafes, and galleries where local and foreign artists could exhibit, listen to music, and host cultural events. "You have to think of the bigger picture," he said. "Rebuilding the Fort is important, not just because it is a historic site, but because it'll help tourism to thrive. Unless tourism picks up, our economy is doomed," he said.

"The Fort needs to be restored," I agreed. "We need to find ways of sustaining ourselves in this crumbling economy," I agreed. "The old houses are beautiful and need to be preserved," I agreed. "But, beauty at the cost of what?" I argued. "What's the point of restoring the Fort without sustaining the life within it?" My father picked up his pace. "There's community here, there's vibrancy," I persisted. "The people I spoke to have been living here for generations. They complained that the place feels different, that their neighborhoods are changing, that they can't compete with the expensive stores." I walked faster to catch up. "As for the restaurants and cafes in which 'culture thrives,' can't you see that the character of the Fort is not there, but in the neighborhoods, in the family owned shops?" My frustration grew as we walked on, looking around at the hotels, "Who can afford to stay in these places? Doesn't it bother you that this Fort, this hallmark of colonialism, is now being repopulated by yet another wave of expatriates and tourists?" My father shrugged me off.

The next morning, while mulling over our conversation, I made my way up the slope of Church Street and came to the old mansion at its far end. The Fort was full of old buildings belonging to the different colonial eras and one could easily pick them out by their distinctive architecture: by the verandas lined with pillars rising up to meet the slanting roofs; by the arched openings of the building facades revealing the porches they enclosed; by the insignia that peeked beneath the layers of dust and grime that had coated the walls over the years. The old buildings rose above the small shops and houses that crowded the streets, but as they faded and crumbled their beauty and power had muted with age. The mansion on top of Church Street however, looked different. Unlike the other dust-darkened old buildings on that street, this one had been renovated, preserving the old architecture. It was now the Amangalle Hotel, which charged up to $400 a night. The paint was fresh. The mansion looked very much alive.

I felt unnerved, walking past the Amangalle. The building itself was striking but it was the sight unfolding through its columns that caught my attention. As I passed by the open porch I could see, seated around the low wooden tables, clusters of well dressed foreign tourists sipping tea in the veranda, being served by barefoot, sarong-clad waiters, mostly young men.

In many ways this image is a familiar sight in Sri Lanka. But, in this renovated colonial mansion, this hotel that was accessible only to the wealthiest tourists, it was a sight that jarred me enough to pause. I was reminded of the distance I had felt from colonialism as I grew up, even in places like the Fort. The scene in front of me now brought alive the past and gave it a sudden, startling proximity.

That evening, I returned to the hotel where we were staying, disheartened and sickened by the gentrification in the Fort. I was tired of arguing with my father and frustrated, as I wanted to feel close to him. Well aware that the Lighthouse was one of the most expensive hotels in Galle, I walked towards its terrace feeling torn. I was incensed at what I had seen that day, at the echoes of colonialism speaking through the hotels of the Fort. At the same time, I was in pain and badly wanted contact with beauty. I looked around the Lighthouse and slowly found myself drawn to its architecture, despite my anger. Its open spaces and the colors reminded me more of a temple than a hotel and there was something about it that spoke to my yearning for home.

Perhaps it was the intensity of this need and the difficulty of sitting with the angst and finding a different kind of beauty that one of my aches shoved the other down and I hungrily took in the space with its long, dark walkways lit by clay lamps, its mural paintings on the walls, the colors and textures I had missed for so long. I curled up on a chair and sat watching the waves hurl themselves against the rocks below, drinking in the stillness that came in the arrangement of space with its temple-like architecture. Regardless of the voice telling me that this was a temple we were paying 14,000 rupees to spend a night in, regardless of the voice telling me that the Lighthouse, although outside the Fort, was a part of the structure of tourism that had a deeply destructive impact on the Fort's community, I couldn't stop myself from soaking in the beauty.

Before long, the anger I had directed outside, turned inside. I had become attracted to the very hotels I was incensed about. The discussions in my classrooms in college came back, about how the desire for the exotic other was as much a part of colonialism as the efforts to control and exploit. All around me were elements of Sri Lankan culture, taken out of context and thrown together to give the tourists a generic exotic "native experience." I was offended by this selling of culture, and yet here I was, in my yearning for home, drawn to the architecture of these hotels.

But as I began paying attention to this hunger, although my frustration and anger remained, my thoughts shifted somewhat. Perhaps there was more to these places than an attempt to give tourists a cheap rendezvous with the exotic. I realized, suddenly, that perhaps my yearning felt so soothed by these hotels because it was akin to the very yearning that created them. In the sixties, a little over a decade after independence, many local artists and architects renewed their interest in traditional crafts and vernacular architecture. Until then, it was the British, Dutch, or Portuguese colonial architecture that fashioned most urban houses and government buildings. My father's generation of architects and artists brought back vernacular forms and designed buildings that spatially, structurally, and colorfully embodied old Buddhist and Hindu temples. I'm guessing that the movement to create public spaces that evoked the folk and pre-colonial forms came from a desire to reconfigure meanings and to recognize beauty in the traditional art and architecture that had been changed, undervalued, and cast aside by colonial forces.

I left the Lighthouse and returned to the Fort before heading back to Colombo. As I walked around looking at the Fort, I thought about its gentrification and painfully sensed that what was looking back at me was a beautiful shell emptying of its life and its spirit. I thought about how wealthy Sri Lankan investors and foreign hotel companies were swooping down on the Fort with the power of their dollars, using its setting to recreate a colonial experience, this time through tourism. As I passed the boutique hotels in the renovated colonial buildings, I recalled how their interiors contained forms of vernacular art, with their uniqueness blurred from being thrown together with a mish-mash of artifacts from around South Asia. I was disturbed to see how the vernacular style, which had once come about to retrieve local art forms from colonial influences, was now used to give the hotels an exotic garb. To adapt to the demands of tourism, had this movement, alongside the other changes in the Fort, begun to echo refrains of the old colonial relationship?

I walked for a long time, curving my way up to an elevation where I could see more of the Fort. I was jarred by the recent changes and the repeating patterns of power unfolding within its walls. I had become so drawn to the Fort, contrary to my expectations upon entering it. There was much that it held: the thick, granite walls that rose from the grass-covered foundations and encased the Fort city, the temple and mosque near the old Dutch church, the beautiful ageing buildings, the densely woven streets with their neighborhoods, and beyond the ramparts, the sea. My pull to the place had much to do with the survival and reinvention I had stumbled upon in its streets, taken aback because I had expected to only see a foreboding fortress, a dead relic of colonialism. This regeneration had thrown a different light not just on the Fort, but also on colonialism. No doubt the colonial Fort actualized the exploits of the Dutch East India Company and the bureaucratic order of the British colonial administration. And the post-colonial Fort, with its thriving real-estate market capitalized on colonial nostalgia, generating modified versions of the structure of rule and service. Yet that was not all. Within the Rampart walls there was also something unpredictable, something creative that suggested an alternative local story alongside the old tale of conquest and the new one of gentrification. It was the beginning of a conversation in my mind about the capacity of the colonized to resist as they obeyed, to reinvent as they reproduced.

***

Four years have passed since my visit to the Galle Fort in the winter of 2006. A year and a half in Sri Lanka and several months into my fieldwork in

Galle, I remain unclear about what it means to go away and to come home. At home my attempts to bridge class divides have inevitably accentuated the differences, highlighting the difficulties of such endeavors. Perhaps this is because I haven't yet come to grips with the social forces that shaped me. I find I can no sooner disown my private school education or American degree than the local architects of the vernacular era could renounce their anglicized understandings of space, which they reproduced even as they sought alternatives to it. I still feel a longing for the Sri Lanka from which I was alienated, a desire I remember having even before I left the island. I wonder if this is also a yearning to revisit my long childhood road trips with my father, as he traveled seeking still-living indigenous craft villages, and I traveled with him, seeking his attention.

My yearning to belong in Sri Lanka is juxtaposed by a sense of displacement that's palpable. Leaving shifted the ground beneath my feet; I no longer comfortably inhabit my inherited position in the class structure. Yet, working at home as an adult has shown me the precariousness of my position. As I confront economic pressures, I'm now facing the beautiful irony of scrambling to finance the day-to-day needs fulfilled by a class status I find deeply problematic. To further the irony, I find it hard to geographically locate academic spaces in which I can thrive; just as I'm frustrated with the east's attempts to flaunt its acquired westernness, I'm also allied with western voices that use non-western thought to work against its own oppressive forces. This dislocation is the closest form of a "home" I'm making for myself. Perhaps these words can only emerge through the vitality and energy of the friction generated from the movement between Sri Lanka and North America. Maybe there's something worth claiming in this space created by what feels like a flight in two directions.

13 Three stories

A way of being in the world

Patrick Thaddeus Jackson

Whenever I sit down to try to write this, one of two things happens. Either the piece becomes a form of reflective journaling that it would be too self-indulgent to publish, or the piece gets too clever for its own good, as I pluck vignettes from my life and then force them to support a point I want to make about who I think I am as a scholar. I think that the problem comes, at least for me, from the effort to use my own biography as raw material for a piece of critical social science. I seem to have too much wrapped up in the outcome of any such effort to actually do in this case what Weber advised: be "devoted only to the subject," and let the analysis play out in surprising ways. I can surprise myself by living my life, but not when I try to social-scientifically explain my academic vocation.

So instead of trying to produce a systematic empirical account of myself as a scholar and teacher, I'm just going to tell stories. Three of them: one about *Star Wars*, one about the Catholic Church, and one about my autistic son. I'm not going to try to draw any explicit connections between those stories and my scholarly vocation, since that's where things always felt the most forced in my previous failed attempts to produce a contribution to this project. I'm telling these three stories because when I think about trying to tell other people about what drives and delights me, these are what come to mind. I don't see or experience my life as dominated by a desire to change the world; if I'm being honest with myself, my actual passions, whether as a scholar or just as a human being, involve speculative fiction, the pursuit of knowledge, and the opportunity to teach. These stories focus on those themes. It's not that I don't get pissed off at things or don't wish that the world were different sometimes – but if I'm being really honest with myself I will have to say that unlike a lot of people in this field I don't get anywhere near as impassioned about injustice and oppression and discrimination as I do about people misusing the philosophy of science to close down scholarly debates or the statement that underneath my son's autism is a "real, normal" boy who can't get out. In many ways I couldn't care less what countries do in their foreign relations, except inasmuch as it provides interesting occasions for conceptual refinement and the asking of difficult questions highlighting uncomfortable facts. Why I'm in IR is, to my mind, almost completely the result of random happenstance – except that while that makes for a defensible empirical explanation, it doesn't make for a very meaningful story.

So as I said, I'm just going to tell stories. What you do with them is up to you. Maybe they help to clarify something about my scholarly vocation; maybe they don't.

The Force will be with you

My parents tell me that the first movie I ever saw in a movie-theater was *Snow White*. They claim that they took me to see it on one of its periodic theatrical re-releases, and they claim that I was attentive and didn't disrupt the movie for anyone else. I have no idea; I was younger than five when this happened, and I have no memory of it whatsoever. I know I was younger than five because I distinctly remember seeing a film that year – 1977 – and for whatever reason I can't remember having seen a film on a big screen before that. Maybe it's because the 1977 film drove everything else from my mind for quite some time; I even started adding lightsaber duels to all of my kindergarten drawings from that point on, replacing what "they" wanted me to study with what I wanted to talk about.

The film, of course, was the original *Star Wars*, since relabeled "Star Wars Episode IV: A New Hope," but still just *Star Wars* to me (and to millions of other people). My dad was a science-fiction fan, and he'd been excited by the film's release; my mother wasn't as much of a fan of the genre, but as a student of literature and developmental psychology she found a lot to love in the film (I know this because we discussed it in later years). In 1977 I already had two younger siblings, so going to a conventional theater as a family presented logistical challenges – which, I suppose, is why we ended up seeing *Star Wars* for the first time at a drive-in movie theater. I remember helping to clip the speaker to the car door; you had to roll down the window and attach the speaker in the resulting opening, and then your whole car would be filled with the sounds of the movie. And what sounds! According to reports I sat basically motionless for the entire film, frozen in the front seat of the car and listening intently to the speaker, humming along with the theme music during the closing credits. After the film ended – it was a double feature, but I have no idea what the second film was – I climbed into the back seat of the car and fell asleep trying to reproduce the perfect lightsaber sound with my mouth.

Yes, there were spaceships and laser guns, and those figured into my games and drawings too, but what really captivated me was the lightsaber duel between Obi-Wan Kenobi and Darth Vader. The whole idea of an epic clash between good and evil, represented by two magical beings who could tap into "the Force" to do extraordinary things, completely consumed me; besides the obligatory hours that I spent trying to see things with my eyes covered (the clearest demonstration of Force-powers by the young Luke Skywalker in the film), I spent a long time trying to imagine the back-story between Vader and Obi-Wan, and the ways that they were brought to such a potent moment of crisis. Obi-Wan's hints about the Force were tantalizing – surrounds us, penetrates us, binds the galaxy together, both controls your actions and obeys your commands – and sounded suspiciously like what I was told in Catholic catechism class about God and prayer. And the Archangel Michael was always pictured with a sword in hand, so there was precedent: religious faith and *Star Wars* were compatible, even down to my immediate ambition to grow up to be a Jedi Knight. I remember having endless debates with children my age about whether Luke Skywalker or Han Solo was the cooler character, but for me there was no real ambiguity, since Luke got a lightsaber and the promise of Force-powers, and all Han had was a fast spaceship and a good blaster.

I don't think it's retrospective reconstruction to say that even at that young age what attracted me to *Star Wars* was its epic quality. Of course, I had never heard of Joseph Campbell and the archetypal myth of the hero journey; nor had I seen any of Kurosawa's films, so George Lucas' visual storytelling techniques were not conscious objects of my reflection. But I was certainly lost in the story for many years after seeing the movie and its two sequels. Luke Skywalker's journey to his ultimate realization that the only way to defeat evil was not to actively fight it but simply to remain pure – "I am a Jedi, like my father before me," he tells the evil Emperor Palpatine at the climactic moment of *Return of the Jedi* when he refuses to kill his father, Darth Vader – felt to me like a set of instructions as clear as those that Moses had received from the bush that burned and was not consumed. My own inability to levitate objects or to see the future seemed like a minor inconvenience; I was a child who had been in gifted and talented programs (some of which had basically been created by the school for me; after all, this was the 1970s and 1980s, before such programs were commonplace) for my entire life, and that seemed as distinctive a social status as being a member of a persecuted line of mystical warriors. All I needed was to find the proper Obi-Wan to instruct me in these ancient ways, and I would be all set. *Star Wars* was my template for surviving childhood – and I do mean "surviving," because I was always more comfortable with the company of adults than I was with kids my own age; this led to isolation and teasing and the occasional threat of physical violence (apparently because it's *fun* to threaten to beat up the nerd), and I often thought of childhood as a gauntlet to run and a trial to endure until I could get to college and *actually start living* – not in the least because it pointed towards greater things lurking just beyond the horizon.

I suppose that *Star Wars* also fueled my ambition to go into space one day. Even though the *Star Wars* films aren't, strictly speaking, science fiction – they take place "a long time ago in a galaxy far, far away," not in some hypothetical human future or alternate timeline – they certainly helped to cement that desire early on, especially when combined with the science fiction I consumed quite voraciously (*Star Trek*, which I used to watch with my dad on the weekends, plus the Asimov and Heinlein novels that he kept me supplied with, and the promise that one day when I was older he'd let me read *Dune*). And Carl Sagan's PBS series *Cosmos* showed me the pathway: become a space scientist and go up into space as a mission specialist. That was how I envisioned my future unfolding until that day in January 1986 when the space shuttle *Challenger* exploded – a day that I, for once, wasn't watching the televised launch because they'd almost become *routine* events, so I only heard about it when someone burst into the classroom and simply said "it blew up!" quite loudly; I ran down to the school library to sit in front of the TV screen with a few other students and teachers to watch, horrified, as they played the liftoff footage over and over and made inane comments trying to make sense of the tragedy, and all I could think was my God, am I ever going to get into space now? All of a sudden space was *dangerous*, and the danger wasn't that you'd be heroically killed by Imperial stormtroopers, but that you'd disintegrate on liftoff because of an unglamorous mechanical malfunction. And even at that early age I knew that there would be Congressional investigations, and politicians trying to make names for themselves by forcing NASA to change its way of operating: meddling, interfering, and generally raising obstacles to the great adventure of scientific discovery. I knew they wouldn't get out of the way and let the professionals figure out what went wrong and fix it – they never did – so I wondered if the space shuttle would ever fly again. I knew that it would take time to get the program running again, if it ever got running again at all; and I knew that I'd never be a part of it.

In the name of the father

I'm sure that Father Smith *had* a first name; undoubtedly he'd been baptized with one, and I'll bet that some of the adults knew what it was. But as far as we altar boys were concerned, his first name was "Father," last name "Smith," and he seemed to have been a priest forever, or at least for more years than we could imagine. I think he only knew one hymn – "How Great Thou Art" – because whenever he said mass by himself, that's what we sang. Fortunately, this was the era of the "folk group," when Catholic churches across the country started permitting small ensembles of laypersons equipped with tambourines and acoustic guitars to perform more modern music in the course of the weekly worship service. As leader of the folk group, my dad got to plan the music whenever the folk group performed, so on those Sundays we got a wider variety – including my dad's great rendition of The Beatles' "Let It Be" and his combined arrangement of two songs from *Godspell* ("Day By Day" and "Prepare Ye") that we performed at least a couple of times a year. Quite a contrast: my dad, folk group guy, and Father Smith, priest forever. And there was never any question about who ran the church and who was only there by his permission, evidenced by the fact that every time the folk group wasn't performing – like at the numerous funerals I was an altar server for, since we lived fairly close to the church and I could be called on at short notice – we went right back to a pretty traditional cycle of boring old hymnody.

That's one of the major reasons why Deacon Rich was such a breath of fresh air. For one thing, although I'm sure that he *had* a last name, I have no idea what it was. Rich was his first name, and that's how we knew him – but with the status-title of "Deacon" appended, since he was nearing the end of the process of priestly formation. For whatever reason, the wider Catholic hierarchy decided that our little church in a small New Hampshire town needed a deacon, and they sent us Rich – who was several decades younger than Father Smith, but certainly old enough to take command of the altar boys without any resistance. He was about the same age as the youngest of our Boy Scout leaders, and hip enough to make pop-cultural references when talking to us. A good youth leader, in other words – just what the corps of altar boys could use.

Altar boys (at the time only boys could be involved; these days it's altar *servers*, because girls can participate as well) play specific and well-established roles in a Catholic mass. Their job is to assist the priest at various points in the ceremony, such as carrying the Bible over so that he can read aloud from it, bringing the water that he uses to ritualistically wash his hands at the beginning of the communion litany, and ringing the bells at the point in the mass where the priest holds up the host and the chalice to consecrate them. Altar boys, like priests, wear vestments, generally a white robe; they process in and out with the priest, often carrying candles, a cross, or some other ritual implement. In a way, altar boys get closer to the mystery of the priesthood than ordinary lay members of the congregation; they are "on stage" during the mass, close witnesses to the daily miracle of transubstantiation whereby the priest invokes the Holy Spirit to transform bread and wine into the body and blood of Jesus Christ. It's a great honor, especially for special occasions, such as when the bishop visited (I got to take responsibility for his miter, or official ceremonial hat) or during the funeral of someone important or esteemed (I particularly remember serving at the funeral of my mother's Uncle Joe, and how pleased all of my relatives were to see me assisting in that role). And while it wasn't formally a "junior priesthood," serving as an altar boy was often a gateway to that vocation later on.

Deacon Rich had been an altar boy, and could therefore relate to us quite easily: he was of course closer to our own ages than Father Smith, and by virtue of the hierarchy of the Catholic church he, as a deacon, couldn't actually *perform* the communion rite, although he – like us – could assist. I remember several masses where he and I served while Father Smith said the ritual words, and of course both Deacon Rich and I (and every other member of the altar boys' corps) knew all those words by heart but we could only speak them under our breath while Father Smith *really* said them out loud. Deacon Rich took the lead in organizing some fun excursions for the altar boys, day trips to museums and the like – opportunities for the altar boys to hang out as a group away from the church. These excursions were basically youth group outings, so we'd have a prayer whenever we got wherever we were going and then just have fun, while Deacon Rich would supervise and circulate among us discussing issues of faith. Of course we always asked him what it was like to be a priest-in-training (some of the other altar boys actually referred to him as "PIT"), and sometimes he'd ask us about our own plans for the future. At least when he and I talked, the priesthood came up, since it was a sort of logical next step beyond altar service, and because I'd basically been composing homilies (Catholic sermons) on biblical texts in my head for years – sometimes because of what I will tactfully refer to as the underwhelming preaching and exegetical abilities of many of the priests I had known.

So Deacon Rich represented a sort of potential future for me. This was never clearer to me than it was one particular Easter Vigil celebration, when Deacon Rich's theatrical flair was on full display. Easter Vigil is an intriguing moment in the Catholic calendar; it takes place after sundown on the day before Easter, and involves (among other things) the blessing of the Easter fire that is used to light the Paschal candle (representing the risen Christ) that had been extinguished the previous Thursday to symbolize Jesus' death on the cross. This is high drama, especially as the Easter fire and re-lit Paschal candle are re-introduced into a completely dark church. This particular year I was serving the mass, and Deacon Rich was handling the Easter fire – which was the baptismal font filled with cotton-balls and doused with lighter fluid. Everything was dark, and we stood in the back of the church waiting for Father Smith to take his seat. Father Smith sat, Deacon Rich took out a book of matches, struck one, and muttered "*fiat lux*" – the words that God speaks in the book of Genesis when creating the world: "let there be light" – as an aside to me as he dropped the match into the flammable balls of cotton. FWOOSH. I handed him the unlit candle, and he lit it from the fire and proceeded through the rest of the service, including his chanting of the beginning of the *Exultet* in crisp Church Latin (which was unusual, since by this time most Catholic masses were celebrated in the vernacular language, not in Latin). I watched him recite the first few stanzas of the hymn and then smoothly switch to English for the call-and-response section of the hymn (Deacon: "The Lord be with you." Congregation: "And also with you." Deacon: "Lift up your hearts." Congregation: "We lift them up to the Lord." Deacon: "Let us give thinks to the Lord our God." Congregation: "It is right to give Him thanks and praise."), and then I followed him around the church swinging the incense while he recited the rest. The magical flow of the ceremony completely captivated me, and Deacon Rich walking around in his white vestments looked not a little like Obi-Wan in his Jedi robes – but where Obi-Wan had a lightsaber, Deacon Rich had only his voice as a weapon against the dark. His voice, and the candle that I had handed him a few minutes before.

Between singing in the folk group and serving more than my fair share of masses, I spent a lot of time on the stage of the front of the church. I firmly suspect that there is a parallel universe, not so different from our own actual universe, in which I stayed on that stage and followed Deacon Rich (and, I suppose, Father Smith, even though he wasn't the role-model I was looking for) into the priesthood. That I did not do so – and that I spent several years vainly trying to convince myself and everyone around me that I was a comfortable atheist, a stance performatively contradicted by my insatiable *need* to have my professed lack of belief in God affirmed by everyone I discussed the subject with – has a lot do with the fact that I went away to a boarding school for high school, and fell out of contact with Deacon Rich and the rest of that church community. The Catholic community at Phillips Academy Andover was small enough that the weekly masses were held Sunday evenings and did not use altar boys. Not being able to formally participate in the mass relegated me to "Catholic calisthenics" – stand up, sit down, stand up, kneel, sit down again, over the course of an hour where I spent most of my time pondering my schoolwork or whatever kind of crazy activity (generally involving computers, but that's another story) I was involved in with my classmates. A lot of other things happened as well, things I'm not going to talk about here because that would take us quite far down a path of therapy or confession. Suffice to say that being at boarding school exposed me to a much wider variety of people and situations than I'd experienced before, and the simple rhythms of the Catholic catechism no longer seemed adequate to make sense of them all.

Church seemed more and more like an interruption in my life, and halfway through Confirmation class – after I'd already decided that if I did confirm my Catholic faith I'd do so by taking the confirmation name "Thomas," as in "doubting Thomas" from a famous gospel story – I decided, much to my mother's regret, to drop out of church altogether. I still went to church when I was home on holiday breaks, because she insisted on it, but by then they'd moved from New Hampshire to Michigan, and even spent some time attending a Congregational church instead of a Catholic church. My father stopped playing the guitar in worship. By the time the family went back to Catholicism, I had moved off in other spiritual directions, and Father Rich – he'd been ordained before I left for school, in a ceremony that was so overwhelmingly intricate and moving that I can't possibly write about it – was reassigned someplace other than the town where we used to live. I have not seen him since.

The spectrum

We first really accepted that something was different about my son Quinn when he was three years old. I suppose that there had been signs earlier, but we and the doctor interpreted them differently: Quinn's fairly sudden loss of vocabulary and grammatically accurate speech was attributed to a blockage of the ear canals, the same sort of malady that I'd had as a child, and one that was easily remedied with minor surgery to put tubes in his ears.

Quinn had the surgery, and his pronunciation improved, but his grammar remained somewhat odd. Personal pronouns eluded him, and a lot of the things he said were quotations from television shows and videos. His third birthday party was an especially dramatic signal, since he spent most of it talking to himself in the corner instead of interacting with anyone. The contrast from his second birthday party was quite stark, and any doubts about the diagnosis quickly evaporated: Quinn was autistic.

When my wife and I started off on this particular journey we had, I think, the same misconceptions as most other people about autism: the film *Rain Man*, the prominence of fixed routines and obsessive behavior, and the idea that a future in some kind of institution loomed ahead for our son. We read everything we could get our hands on, and started working the Internet for information, contacts, clues, strategies – whatever we could do to figure out what was happening to Quinn and how we could help him. What we found, over and over again, was the declaration that "autism is a spectrum," and that there were no generally valid statements about the whole population of autistics beyond the behavioral diagnosis criteria: semantic language difficulties (grammar and vocabulary), pragmatic language difficulties (the use of appropriate words, and the sense of what is acceptable in particular social settings), and narrowly focused and obsessive interests (which often contribute to "transition issues" when an autistic is redirected from one activity to another). Some descriptions of autistic children sounded very much like Quinn, and others did not – the variety was astounding.

In fact, more than a few of the descriptions of high-functioning autistics sounded like *me*. When Quinn was formally diagnosed, his specialist asked me a few questions about when I started reading and how I navigated elementary and high school and said that I sounded like a high-functioning autistic myself – not surprising, since the parents and relatives of children diagnosed on the autism spectrum often display "shadow traits," autistic-like tendencies that in many cases are only a shade less pronounced than those of the diagnosed autistic. Narrowly focused and obsessive interests? Challenges with pragmatic language and the decoding of social codes and situations? Those descriptions rang true to my ears – I'd generally thought of it as "having been born without social antenna," and therefore being unable to pick up on whatever subtle signals everyone else was receiving that told them how to interact in social situations, plus my being interested in things that I couldn't for the life of me figure out why everyone else wasn't also obsessively interested in (like science fiction, computers, subatomic physics, the differences between the variants of the musical *Chess* or the numerous recordings of Mozart's *Requiem, et cetera*).

Those features together, I learned, constitute a subtype of borderline high-functioning autism called Asperger's Syndrome. Yes, they also describe many people in academia (and in the sciences, and in the priesthood), but maybe that's no accident: the proverbial absent-minded professor was probably on the spectrum, and the sciences and the priesthood both feature a surplus of structured behaviors and interactions that can be very comforting to an autistic. Maybe that's part of what attracted me to them in the first place: it was and is always easier for me to perform an established script or role than to work in an unstructured environment, and if things are getting too unstructured I will generally either reach for a defined social role or an appropriate quotation from one of the *Star Wars* films or some other work of speculative fiction. So Quinn's diagnosis gave me words to describe an important thread running through my entire life, and helped to put into perspective many of my own quirks and obsessions.

Quinn's diagnosis also gave me my first indication that it was inappropriate to refer to someone on the autism spectrum as a "person with autism," because that separated the person and the condition – as though there were a "me" *separate from* those tendencies and patterns and challenges. I can understand why "person with" language might be preferable for, say, advocates for disability rights, since in that context it makes sense to say that a person who can't walk and has to use a wheelchair is not defined by that condition. But autism, like many neurological conditions, is different; the spectrum, and being on the spectrum, is intimately interwoven into every aspect of your life, and it *does* define you. Autism is a form of being-in-the-world. Diagnosis gives you an expressive language, but it doesn't change who you are, or who you were before you had that language; nor does it hold out any possibility of separating who you "really" are from the behaviors and tendencies that afford the diagnosis in the first place. To put this in perhaps inappropriately analytical terms (and I say "perhaps inappropriately" for *your* benefit, not for mine; I think it's perfectly appropriate, but I'm a borderline high-functioning autistic, so my sense of "appropriate" is likely somewhat orthogonal to yours), there is no plausible counterfactual non-autistic version of someone on the autism spectrum: any me that I can imagine has these same spectrum traits, even if things that I would consider less essential-to-the-person traits (height, weight, national origin, socioeconomic class, ethnicity, gender, historical era, *et cetera*) vary quite widely. I can imagine counterfactual versions of myself by varying those things, but I *cannot* (or, perhaps, *will not?*) imagine varying autism-spectrum traits, either for myself or for my son.

Of course, these realizations didn't dawn all at once. First of all I had to figure out how to relate to this little boy who was so much like me, but whose challenges with semantic language made it almost impossible for him to have a sustained conversation with anyone. When Quinn wants to tell you something, it's more often than not a line or two of dialogue or a description of a scene from a recently viewed movie, or a recitation of his daily schedule. If you know the references then you can figure out what he's saying, but it's often just a reference: yes, that's what happens in that scene from *Cars*. Yes, it's funny when WALL-E puts his dirty tread on M-O and confuses his sensors. But all of this is a self-contained semiotic system, and is basically only about itself; it might be communication, but it's not connection.

The first shift was the cicadas. In the year 2004 the famous once-in-17-years brood of cicadas hatched all over the northeastern United States; cicadas were literally everywhere. Quinn loved it. He'd walk over to cicadas that were sitting on the ground and try to pick them up; when he succeeded he'd be surprised when they struggled, and he'd drop them and laugh. One day I was at his nursery school for some parent showcase, and we were playing on the playground; I kept putting cicadas on my arm, and he'd laugh and count them and say "put more on, Daddy!" That day he actually asked me to stay at school with him, something he never did, so I stayed – and we had a cicada fight, tossing the bugs at each other as we ran around the grounds. Later we went for a walk, stopping at every tree to look for cicadas on the trunk or the leaves. Quinn seemed to have more language at his command when he was in motion; he was still basically describing what he was seeing, but the descriptions got more elaborate and he started asking questions (like "how many cicadas are there?"). That was something like a connection.

Quinn started drawing stories about a year or two later. He'd take sheets of paper and put a scene on each one, and then tell us the story by turning the pages over as if they were part of a book. At that point, Quinn's drawings didn't have words, but they did have a script. Usually they were reproductions of a book that someone had read to him or something he'd watched on TV, but occasionally he would combine parts of several stories to produce something novel. Different characters inhabited one continuous world for Quinn, so there was no logical reason why Dora the Explorer couldn't show up with the Teletubbies and have a picnic with Thomas the Tank Engine. He'd play out these scenes with his toys too, and when they weren't right nearby, he'd use his hands or some other object to stand in for a character. Sometimes I would intervene, breaking up the flow by moving a character or introducing a new plot element ("And then Po decided to go for a walk.") to see what he'd do. Sometimes he just got frustrated and corrected me ("No, Daddy, Po rides a scooter!"), but sometimes he'd incorporate what I'd done and try to make it fit with the rest of the story. That was something I remembered doing in kindergarten when we'd play Batman and Robin on the playground and I was always the master storyteller; something I did all through middle school as the Dungeon Master for our Dungeons&Dragons group; something I did all through high school and college in a set of notebooks in which I laid out the contours of a post-apocalyptic world through which a series of characters journeyed. The topics of Quinn's stories evolved, and the plots got more elaborate, much like mine had over the years; eventually he moved into drawing guidebooks containing the animals of Africa or the major types of shark, but he still had stories to go along with each.

Then, a few months ago, something clicked for Quinn and he started to be very interested in having me do things with him. He invited me to play with his plastic animals, to watch his then-favorite Animal Planet program with him, and just generally to be around him. He wasn't exactly ignoring me before, but he would spend most of his time in his own world; now he was actively reaching out. One day when I was clicking through the programs that we had archived on the DVR I decided to try something new, and put on an episode of the animated series *Star Wars: The Clone Wars*. We'd watched most of the films once before, but he didn't seem to have much interest at that point. He was older now, and he was also more of a fan of animation than of live human action, which made perfect sense in terms of the autistic difficulty with interpreting facial expressions and other non-verbal signals – animated faces and figures have less dynamism to them, so many autistics prefer animation. Quinn was transfixed, although he didn't sit still – he rarely sits still when he's paying attention to something on the television, as he prefers to move around or jump on his trampoline – and he kept peppering me with questions: Who is that shooting? Why does that man have a sword? Are the clones good guys or bad guys? Is R2-D2 okay? (The droid R2-D2 is far and away Quinn's favorite character; he likes Anakin and Obi-Wan, but always comes back to R2-D2.) After the show ended he went up into his room and arranged his toys to act out what we'd just watched; not having any specific Star Wars characters, he impressed other toys into service. And then he invited me in and insisted that I watch him re-enact the episode, which he did pretty well. "Would you like us to buy you some Star Wars toys, Quinn?" I asked.

"Oh, Daddy, that would be wonderful!" All smiles, and a huge hug. "Can we buy an R2-D2?"

"Of course we can."

Some day when he's older I'll open my boxes of Star Wars figures and accessories, and let him take the pieces he needs to assemble whatever story he's presently in the middle of. At this point he says that he wants to be a movie director, a writer of stories to be staged on the big screen. Everything precise and measured, unfolding according to the script, practicing a narrative that hums along to its own inner logic. Perhaps that's his future.

In any event, he'll need help, someone to equip him to deal with a world that doesn't really think like he thinks, but a world that needs what he has to offer even if it doesn't know it yet, and even if he's not quite sure what he has to offer yet. He'll need training, so that he's able to unlock the potential that runs in his bloodline, and discern his true calling. But most of all he'll need to have the tradition handed down to him, the tradition that contains all the stories humans have told each other over the millennia, and the tradition the contains the broken bits of philosophy and narrative and ethical commitment out of which we create new things. Quinn is, in short, a student not unlike my other students, and I thank God that I may be able to serve as one of his teachers. The Force is with him, too.

****

If this were a *Star Wars* movie, that last paragraph would be the final scene before the inevitable flourish of instrumentation and the start of the closing credits, accompanied by the soaring melody of the basic *Star Wars* theme – "Luke's Theme" – and rolling against a black background punctuated by stars. Even the *Star Wars* films that end ambiguously, the middle components of each trilogy, feature that kind of grandiose, even operatic send-off, as the camera pulls away and our visit to that galaxy far, far away draws to a close. Of course there are unresolved tensions being glossed over. Of course there are avenues left unexplored. Of course the whole illusion of an epic narrative depends on the conceit – shared and sustained by the author and the readers – that it wraps up neatly, or at least comprehensibly. I don't know what these stories mean; I don't know just what kind of work they do, either for you or for me. I do know that they feel in some difficult-to-define sense like *authentic* expressions, much more authentic than my earlier forced attempts to connect my biography with my life as an academic. So I have ignored that subject, at least explicitly, and instead tried to convey some sense of the vocational shape of my life out of which other things somewhat contingently grow. I can relatively easily imagine a counterfactual me who is not an IR scholar, but I cannot (or will not?) imagine a counterfactual me without the autism spectrum, a priestly disposition, and a sense of being one of the last of the Jedi.

Even now I'm trying not to wrap this all into a seamless whole, I'm trying to leave the threads dangling, and I *just can't leave it alone*: the story, unlike the messy and contingent happenstances of actual life, needs an ending. Or maybe I need it to end. Regardless, there has to be closure in order for me to let even these admittedly incomplete stories go. So close your eyes and imagine the end of my favorite of the *Star Wars* films, the original 1977 release: Han and Chewbacca and Luke standing on the altar-like stage, having ceremoniously received medals from the radiant Princess Leia for a well-struck blow against the evil Empire, and the assembled throng of soldiers exploding in applause to celebrate both what has been and what may yet be. There are sequels and prequels to come, but for the moment, there is just this much of a perfectly balanced resolution, accompanied by majestic music. The stable closure of the tale is only false in the sense that all stories are false, because they only selectively mimic – re-present – the events that they are about. The important thing is that they be good enough for the moment, that they allow us to keep on living into the senselessness of actual life and somehow, miraculously, transubstantiate it into something meaningful.

14 G(r)azing the fields of IR
Romping buffaloes, festive villagers

Quỳnh Phạm and Himadeep Muppidi

Jis gaon nahin jaana, uska raasta mat poocho.
Don't ask the way to a village if you don't want to get there.
Indian Minister of External Affairs[1]

Görünen köy kılavuz istemez.
The village that one can see requires no guide.
Turkish proverb

Affairs international

"Are you having an affair?" she asked me dead seriously in the middle of a surprise birthday party. An affair? I couldn't but smile! The affairs I knew about most intimately were all international.

But the way she mouthed that word, her conspiratorial tone, made an affair seem full of promise and excitement. It evoked a daring transgression of the domestic, some secret insurgency against the status quo. Though taken aback, I was struck by what that query sidelined even as it emerged: the prospect of intimacies more meaningful than affairs. Did concerns about affairs betray a lack of curiosity about other possible social relations? Did it say something about the sorts of convivial communities we can or cannot imagine in our worlds? What if the sense of danger and excitement one felt was not from affairs but from something far riskier? What if it was about the instability of the legal signs fencing home from the neighborhood, the arbitrariness of the lines slicing the domestic from the ostensibly foreign?

I teach international affairs/relations/studies/politics. But how well did I know the distinctions between those various relations of intimacy and estrangement? Could I imagine possibilities other than these, beyond what I already knew, or thought I knew, about reading the international?

What about loving the international and not merely having affairs with it? What would it mean to embed international political theory in the day-to-day realities of life and love, of *ishq* and *muhabbat*?[2] As it often happens when

I ask too many questions, rhetorical or otherwise, a song from a Hindi movie wafts through me:

Ishq bina kya marna, yaara?
Ishq bina kya jeena[3]

The I(shq) of IR

My spoon glided thinly under the soft, pure, milky surface of the dessert. I raised the delicate layer to my eager lips and felt, at first touch, its coolness liberating my mouth from the swelter of June. The creamy base was just sweet enough to please my tongue and yet it retained a tender sourness to pull my taste buds in a different direction. The foundation was neither too thick nor too lax, but held together just the right looseness of texture to melt in my mouth with heavenly bliss. It was the perfect yogurt, and that was how I knew to eat it best – little bit by bit to savor the smoothness, the softness, the exquisite milk and cream that went into such a delightful making.

The magic of Ba Vì yogurt is not a private secret: Ba Vì cows give the best milk in the northern region of Việt Nam. But where do these cows come from? How are they raised? Only this past summer did I hear the story of their special ancestry.

Our car was running through Ba Vì's roadsides of rice and corn fields, whose view from my seat was intermittently suspended by farm houses, fruit stops, dogs napping in the shade, and the familiar miscellany of street signs: *Phở, Cháo, Sửa chữa* (which means vehicle repair, but funnily enough, my sister almost always mixes it up with *Sữa chua*, which is yogurt), *Tổng Đại Lý Bánh Sữa, Hồ Giáo...*

"Ah, the 'Hero of Labor' Hồ Giáo, do you know who he is, dear?" my mom turned to me only to see my face drawing a complete blank. "He was entrusted with raising the milk cows that Cuba gifted us after the war. It was very difficult, as you can imagine, to foster a foreign breed, but he tended the cows like he did his own children, so the herd thrived to everyone's joy."

Before I could utter my admiration for uncle Hồ Giáo, along with my belated gratitude for the gracious support from our dear *compañeros*, my dad was searching his memory out loud, "Was it Cuba or India? I remember India sent us 502 buffaloes." Cuba or India? People so far away could be as close as kin! Flashes of my recent trips to Oaxaca, Mexico and Hyderabad, India brought colors to my mind and smiles to my heart. How timid and awkward I was when I found myself, a stranger, stumbling into the middle of a fiesta in San Agustin Yatareni ... until uncles and aunties at the village brushed away my silly worry of intrusion and truly made me feel that *su casa era mi casa*. Their huge baskets of bread along with hot pots of Oaxacan chocolate milk stayed bottomless for any newcomer, just as their tireless musical orchestra would spring any feet to dance no matter how old or young, how shy or bold. My stay in Hyderabad was familial in another ("same same but different") way.

I kept wondering which previous lifetime I was born there as I relished hot chai and poori in the morning while commingling with buffaloes (and even a camel) later in the day. Some of these lovelies were strolling leisurely across traffic-thronged streets, while others held court mid-road wiggling their tails, their brown eyes winking at impatient drivers, *"Jaana jaana jaldi kya hai?"*

"Jaldi kya hai" indeed! Why not take some moments to soak in all the ambrosial and colorful *aanandam* of life around you: the kaleidoscope of *sarees, salwar kameezes,* and garlands, the golden spectrum of *gulab jamoon, ras malai, ladoo, soan papdi,* the mouthwatering heaps of papayas, pomegranates, jackfruits, mosambis, mangoes … Ahhh, the sweet, gushing succulence that was *rasalu* mango!

My face must have brightened as these precious times in Oaxaca and Hyderabad flooded back: how mothers and fathers in all these homes, from the very first day, had embraced me, a foreign breed, as one of their own children. But reading my lit-up eyebrows as being perplexed by "502," my dad chuckled, "You know why the extra two, darling? Those were Indira Gandhi's special gift to our PM. And when our PM trusted Hồ Giáo to raise the buffaloes well, he could not have put the country's hope in a more dedicated person." The weight of the word "hope," for a moment, made my stomach churn to think of all of our decimated buffaloes, cows, dogs, and fowl under US bombings. "Hero Hồ Giáo showered these buffaloes with so much affection that they were remarkably well-nourished – some weighed as much as a thousand kilos – and smitten with their guardian father. Some, I heard, after ten years apart, still recognized him when he came back to visit them, wagging their joyous tails and tilting their heads snugly into the warm hands that had fed and fondled them years before."

"Not only that, he named each one in his herd intimately after a beloved location in his hometown, and imagine this, dear, when it came time to weigh the buffaloes, he'd call their names and they would each step on the scale by themselves. By themselves! How much love it must've taken for those giants to turn out so amenable! Surely buffaloes are not your most tractable animals … ," guffawed my dad, "even the Indian experts were impressed."

Amazed, I laughed along. But I was also not completely astounded. Such is the beauty of our life-world (I thought to myself): Nothing is plainly what it is. Animals are never *just* animals; gifts are never just gifts; even cow milk is never just cow milk.[4] Who knew that a small cup of yogurt could be fermented with so much history, so much *ishq*, so much IR!

The Indian buffaloes that my dad was recalling, I later discovered, actually resided in the southern and central regions of the country. So extraordinary were those Murrahs that not only did they yield nutritious milk and plough with twice the might of the Vietnamese buffaloes, but better still, they pulled better than any tractor could: "Tractors get mired in the mud," Hồ Giáo shared with pride, "but these buffaloes get out of it as easily as one-two-three" (Hoàng 2008). I was wonderstruck to find out that four of our precious friends are still being personally tended by our hero, who is as attached to them at the age of 81 as he was 35 years ago. Every morning, no matter what day or what weather, villagers would see their elder Hồ Giáo walk six kilometers from his home to the cowshed, to cut at least a hundred and fifty kilograms of fresh elephant grass – the tall, thick, bulky, and awfully heavy kind – to feed his remaining children and take full care of them, before treading another six kilometers back home.

In 20 years, the herd that he helped raise to a flourishing 1,404 has diminished to a few dozen nationwide. Their milk is not in demand. Their bodies have been displaced by machines. Yet cow-herd Hồ Giáo is devoted to them all the same. I am deeply touched by his fidelity, since the villager in me does not want to let go of them either. The Murrahs are not only our *com-pan-eros* in the fields, literally those who share our *"pan"* (bread) and our pain,[5] but they also carry our decades-old familial ties with *compañeros* from villages afar.

I am happy that villagers in Mộc Châu, the other famous milk area in the North, share the same sentiments. Mrs. Lịch, a local and global farmer, pointed out that the walls of their farms, home to the thousand cows that Cuba sent us, still honor a fraternity inscribed in deep red, *"Viva La Amistad Entre Vietnam Y Cu Ba."* Even though our friends had written that in the 1980s, aunty Lịch beamed, "we've never had any intention to erase it."

So contrary to my parents' impression, none of the gifted buffaloes or cows reside in Mount Ba Vì today (though the Moncada cow-breeding farm and the Leghorn-chicken farm, both of which were sponsored and co-initiated by Cuba, are still standing there). I would not be surprised, however, if my sister told me tomorrow that some of our Ba Vì cows were descendents of those that had crossed borders all the way from Algeria, or that they were cords of kinship extended from nonaligned countries in the 1960s – the (k)in-ternational as we know it.

"Naturally," as a Kiều verse goes, "when kin spirits meet/One tie binds them in a knot none can yank loose."[6] The kin-ternational as we know it – aunty Lịch understands this well – is an inerasable village bond, a knot none can yank loose, and a promise to be learnt and kept, continually.

> *Ishq bina kya marna, yaara?*
> *Ishq bina kya jeena*
> *Gur se meetha, ishq ishq*
> *Imli se khatta, ishq ishq*
> *Vaada ya pakka ishq ishq*
> *Dhaaga ye kachcha ishq ishq.*[7]

World literatures

> Once upon a time …
> *Anaganaga …*

Once upon a time, English brought foreign adventure and mystery into my school life: the Secret Seven, Famous Five, Hardy Boys, and Nancy Drew.

I remember the first Enid Blyton I read, with penguins and puffins marking age appropriateness. Inspired, we formed our own club of seven, came up with a secret password (knowing this would initiate you into the club) and resolved, as our very first mission, to rid our school sidewalk of *bandi-wallahs* such as Rahim. Rahim's crime, in our puffin-minds, was peddling "unhealthy" food. I see Rahim very clearly, his hands ceaselessly shaving ice from a gunny wrapped block, his face intent, his thin body barely covered in an always brown, half-open shirt, mobbed by kids in well-pressed white and khaki school uniforms, with blue and gold ties, clamoring for flavored ice on hot afternoons. Hungry and thirsty boys sucking coolness from his hands; hungry and thirsty boys willing to betray him for an idea from an English book.

We were posturing and, now, I am grateful it didn't go beyond that. But the ease with which we picked on Rahim as the object of our foreign-inspired cleaning-up was disturbing. He offered us what we desired but also what we had somehow learnt was bad for us. Your body wanted it. Your senses desired it. But the voice of science and nutrition warned you to step away from the *bandi*: Resist your desire. We seemed to have resolved this tension by turning him, instead of ourselves, into the object of our policing. Did we need him off the streets so that we didn't have to face our street-level desires? Lurking in the shadows here were the portents of other developmental projects: slum-clearance, urban renewal, communal cleansing. In the end, our lack of power and lack of commitment to ideas from abroad saved us from ourselves.

The image is still fresh in my eyes: My Dad driving me on his red *Jawa* to A.A. Hussain in Abids, that treasure trove of all that was delightful in English, all that was foreign and generally unaffordable, and I got to pick the books I wanted. A.A. Hussain was one of those small and packed booksellers on Abid Road, one that I would frequently stop by on my way from school but could rarely buy anything. The children's section was upstairs and there, in that space tightly decorated with books, you finally met the international lit set: Enid Blyton, Asterix, Lucky Luke, Sudden, Tintin – glossy, colorful, and glamorous beings. I knew that their world of dollars and pounds was not traversable easily from my world of rupees. I would go up anyway, shyly sneaking past one of the Hussains below to spend time in those nooks and crannies before heading home. But that day with my Dad was different. That day I crossed the border openly and brought many of my glossy friends home.

I recollect my Dad ordering for us Arthur Mee's *Children's Encyclopedia*, all ten volumes of it. It came accompanied by three additional volumes of an English Dictionary (Grolier's) and two year-books. Most of my devotion was reserved for those ten brown volumes. Ten brown volumes, with golden titles on their spines and a picture of a bespectacled and very pink Mr. Mee inside. Ten brown volumes that I would leaf through all the time, show off to cousins and aunts, lug to school to illustrate some principle to my teachers, taking care, all the while, to not crumple or hurt the pages in any fashion. Ten brown volumes redolent of foreign fields, furrowed well. What did my cousins and teachers think as I toted and touted these foreigners around? Were they pulled in by the prospect of other solidarities and affinities? Or did they wonder what I was missing among my local friends?

Ten brown volumes neatly partitioned the world into philosophy, botany, zoology, and so on and left me with the comforting illusion that everything knowable was available within. This was my first glimpse into the global ambitions of knowledge: a knowledge that desires to grasp the world comprehensively, systemically, and instantaneously. Yet these thick volumes, these resident aliens, had little to say on *ishq*, *muhabbat*, or other corporeal passions. The passions they embraced were sublime, artistic, or religious but few connected me to the calls of my newly rebellious body. The world of encyclopedic knowledge was estranged somehow from the world of my more earthy desires.

>Another once upon a time ...
>Ngày xưa ngày xưa ...

"Lev Tolstoy is marvelous, but *War and Peace* might be a bit beyond your age. Why don't you start with Hector Malot's *Without Family*, my love? Your sis adored it and she read it when she was even younger than you are!" – That was how my mom used to invite me, tirelessly, to explore our humble library. She was sure that once I started my first novel, I would gravitate toward the second and the third, the way she herself and my sister got into reading as children. So at some point, maybe when I was 12, I finally gave *Without Family* a try to make my mom smile. I lasted through the four hundred or so pages, liked the story somewhat, but never moved on, as my mom had so eagerly expected, to other great works of literature in my parents' collection.

I was the only one in my family who found no interest in reading. My mom and dad would frequently rehearse with amusing delight how passionately my sister Quyên used to bury herself in tales of all sorts when she was my age: how she would hide under school tables to escape boring lessons and find refuge in the magical world of stories from around the globe; how when bedtime came, she would pretend to sleep soundly under the camouflage of a head-to-toe blanket, while dexterously holding a small flashlight underneath, gluing her eyes to the sandy paper printed in almost illegibly coarse ink, and masterfully turning page after page without producing the slightest sound. These were the tricky conditions under which my sister had journeyed from Nguyễn Công Hoan's short stories to Pushkin's love poems, to Greek mythology, to *One Thousand and One Nights*, to Victor Hugo's *Les Misérables*, to Dostoevsky's *The Idiot*, to Guy de Maupassant's *Boule de Suif*, to name only a few of her favorites. I missed all these gems by simply never nearing our family's bookshelves.

I was too busy immersing myself in unending series of Chinese martial arts movies. Each film series consisted of at least 20 or 30 videos, and I would sit through one set after another, month after month, leisurely following the journeys of different folk heroes, mesmerized by their breathtakingly defiant sweeps and leaps and kicks and strikes. My inherited distrust of anything Chinese dissolved in that moment and gave way to a thrilled absorption of their beautiful văn võ (literary and martial) philosophies. I remember meticulously scribing a notebook full of imaginary calligraphic Chinese characters (I did not know an iota of Mandarin) just because I was so fascinated by the venerable ways in which learned men delivered gracious strokes and weaved various combinations of lines and dots into such profound layers of meanings. I was most engrossed in episodes where the dharma of the folk heroes was put on trial: when they were torn between family and king, between invincibility and vulnerability, among lovers, among debts, and so on. Perhaps I did not associate these movies with the China that had dominated our people for more than a thousand years precisely because of this shared humanity: the everyday dharma that makes up the dramas of our lives.

Sringara[8]

Pulpitations

Placating the desires of my restive body meant reaching for the English on the street. On the way from my Roman Catholic School to my house lay Koti, the British Residency. Postcolonial India had converted this erstwhile home of the British Ambassador to the Nizam of Hyderabad into the Osmania University College for Women. Now this Palace, once home to the international intrigues of the East India Company as well as the domestic scandals/affairs of British Residents and Muslim nobility, was ringed on its outside by a series of pavement shops, selling pirated novels and cheap textbooks.

Spread-eagled English pages introduced me, on these pavements, to a new nectar of desire, a fruity concoction of peaches, plums, and cherries. Love mutated into Sex through alien presses. And sex was a textual act shared and felt between the sheets of English fiction. James Hadley Chase, Nick Carter, Harold Robbins, Anonymous, Sidney Sheldon were the pimps, pirated and peddled. Incidentally, these street stalls did more for my grammar than the dry strictures of Wren and Martin. Still, the garden of my earthly desires bore only foreign fruit while what I could actually touch and taste were the local ones: *aam, jaam, anaar, jaamun, sharifa, karbuza.*

That disconnect shaped my desire to learn French rather than Sanskrit in high school. I associated the former, vaguely but positively, with a certain cosmopolitan modernity and cultural openness in matters of sex and love. The French had given their name to kissing. How bad could it be then, or so I thought, as I chose to enroll in French in high school. It wasn't that big a risk anyway. A foreign language was not a serious affair. One was already learning English, Telugu, and Hindi in a context in which the only subjects that mattered academically were the sciences.

One dabbled in French, knowing it was not meant to last long, maybe only long enough to make a few semesters interesting. Akin to a fling before getting back to the serious grind of Biology, Physics, Chemistry (BPC), or Math, Physics, Chemistry (MPC), your true mates. Approved by your family, these companions would stabilize you in Life and help you settle down. If you were (or were thought to be) smart, you opted for MPC or BPC. The reverse was also true. If you chose other pursuits, your smartness was in doubt. Such was the ordaining of our postcolonial tradition. Your marriage to the sciences (the perfect combination of caste and class) had already been arranged – a match made in the haven of our imagined modernity.

Our French teacher, an Indian, embodied the attractiveness of the foreign, the unexpected, the unarranged and the utterly irrelevant! Young, pretty, with beautifully shaped specs and a vibrant smile, she embodied the flashy and not easily traversable appeal of the international. Was desire for the international not desire for what was out of one's immediate territorial and cognitive reach? Was it not that which, in its appearance and disappearance, could blind you momentarily?

My desires notwithstanding, the French were already in decline. *Alliance Francaise* occurred on the ascetic lawns of a Hindu Monastery, the Ramakrishna Math. Their kisses, as we gathered from our textbooks, were sterile good-byes in decrepit railway stations. And French wine never quite replaced the fullness of English smoothies.

Meanwhile, in classrooms not too far from where we read French, others from our cohort were feverishly reciting Sanskrit poetry. Those whom we had taken to be provincial, who, in our ill-educated view, had dared not to aspire to the cosmopolitan, that is our classmates who had chosen Sanskrit, were regaling each other, class after class, with erotic poems that they *had* to study. English fruit and French kisses were irrelevant in their search for the *sringara* of life. Their language, my language, from which I had estranged myself to achieve a seeming internationality, resonated with the joy and pleasure of *kama* and *rati*. The translated verses our classmates occasionally threw at us were scandalous to my ears and shockingly welcome to my other senses.

So much passion and desire vested not in the foreign but in locally divine(d) tongues (the language of one's own goddesses and gods) so close to home? This was not my map of the international and intellectual distribution of knowledge and pleasure in the world. But what was I mapping when I thought I was mapping the cosmopolitan international? Whose mission,[9] in retrospect, was I following and whose was I betraying?

Tàijí mission

How enchanted was my ten-year-old world by the art of *tàijí quán*, as I was helplessly falling in love with Zhang Sanfeng, the founding father of *Wutang* kung fu. "Động trung cầu tịnh, khúc trung cầu thực" – I used to wrack my brain trying to comprehend his counterintuitive principles of martial practice: How can one seek quietude in motion? How can one find straightness in bending? But even before I could grasp the concept myself – maybe it was not meant to be "grasped," comprehensively, instantaneously, or otherwise – Sanfeng's powerful performance of *tàijí* on screen swept me off my feet, literally. Rewinding his moves in my head over and over, I took a deep breath, raised my arms slowly in the air with muscles as loose as I could let go, and twirled them around in balanced coordination with my swaying torso and shifting legs, all the while not forgetting to orate a moral-philosophical speech before flying off my bed to the floor in the most dignified manner. I was especially entranced by the calm way in which Sanfeng would take his opponent's hammering punch in his palm, fluidly concede to be pressed along the momentum of the initial attack and yet unpredictably motion his body and circulate his inner energy so as to fully reverse the very force of aggression back to his opponent. The power of *tàijí*, as I gradually took in, does not lie in "hard" force – in either its magnitude, its accumulation, or its raw application – but draws on the thousand and one formations that flexibly divert, confuse, shuffle, and ultimately return the force to its originator. It challenges those less physically robust to be more creative in communication, more resourceful in resistance, and more resilient in spirits. Perhaps I was intuitively drawn to this subaltern tenacity for I was born into a tiny country that has endured and resisted, for centuries, the yoke of domination from more than one invader who predicated themselves on "hard force."

Above all, the beauty of *tàijí* culminates in its gentleness, in the soft – almost tantalizing – manner in which one's muscles do not tense up when assaulted but, against all instincts, relax and adapt to the opponent's movements of extension and contraction. What I respect most about Zhang Sanfeng's martial arts is that his yielding pulls and seamless counter-pushes seek to unbalance and restrain – rather than inflict harm upon – his assailants, but if need be, he would turn every grab, wrench, bend, or twist upon the aggressors themselves, using their own brute force to crack their elbows, dislocate their shoulders, or fracture their knees. His tender, albeit resolute, composure triumphs over his opponent's militaristic masculinity not because he out-muscles the latter, but precisely because he rejects machismo altogether. Adversaries who fail to appreciate Sanfeng's humaneness and mistakenly take it as his weakness, who continue to exert crude strength, in vain, are simply exposed to be, in actuality, piteously weak. They are defeated, I have no doubt, from the very beginning of such an engagement.

Cultivating *tàijí*, as well as any other martial arts, I soon learned, is not just a matter of honing one's strength. It teaches practitioners from how to breathe, to how to exercise their (bodily/intellectual) energy – there is no separation between the bodily and the intellectual – to how one ought to relate and respond to others. Though I never seriously learned *tàijí* (something I have always desired to do) and only went so far as mimicking Zhang Sanfeng's cool moves in our living room, I was captivated by his *đạo*, his path of living and teaching, of nurturing oneself, of being human.

I was immersed in a charming life-world and I was enthralled. Chinese kung fu series did for me what literature must have done for my mom and my sister. Only when I encountered Chinua Achebe, Earl Lovelace, Ghassan Kanafani, Eduardo Galeano, Amin Maalouf, and Mahmoud Darwish later in college, did I realize that literature, like martial arts films, also teaches ways of being in the world, ways that can be so villagely close to home. Only then did my eyes open to how literature could perform *tàijí* to counter the omni(-social-)science of colonial power/knowledge. Arrested by Assia Djebar's and Amitav Ghosh's humane appropriation of the colonizer's tongue, by one's ferocity and the other's gentleness, perhaps I finally understand how to seek tranquility in the petrifying motion of a "foreign lan lan lang language l/anguish anguish – a foreign anguish" (Philip 1989: 56), how to find straightness in bending myself to engage with the omni-science that is contemporary IR.

When I&I get muddy

I remember Ashis Nandy coming to JNU when I was a student at the School of International Studies. Sudipta Kaviraj, my favorite political theorist, introduced him as a dear friend but also as one with whose views he had some strong disagreements. That was understandable because Kaviraj had a reputation as a Marxist and Nandy was a radical but, somewhat unusually in India then, not of the left variety. I don't remember what he spoke on that occasion but, like his op-ed pieces in *The Times of India*, I remember it "made sense" because it drew upon the experiences and categories of my world. This was the very same feeling I had when I randomly picked up Sudhir Kakar's book, *Shamans, Mystics and Doctors*, and had the sense of listening to a social scientist theorizing the world around me (of people visiting temples, mosques, and sufi shrines, of women being possessed, of gods and goddesses and of saints, fakirs, and scoundrels).

I am not saying that, as a student of politics and economics, I was somehow deeply alienated from the world of social science scholarship. Hans Morgenthau and Paul Samuelson were compelling in their own ways. *Politics among Nations* gave you the key to the West's seemingly special place out there. It was not about modernity, progress, civilizing missions, your backward culture and all that stuff. Even *they* were telling *you* that it was about power, their power to force you, to kill you, to annihilate you en masse, rationally, in their self-interest. We had suspected this but now, with enough effort and access to the realm of the international, we knew. Samuelson's *Economics* was an alluring text, pleasing to look at, nicely inlaid with charts, graphs, and colorful curves. It embodied all the elegance of a foreign language: Thinness/Parsimony. Method. Freedom. Learn the Techniques and you have a way of reaching the treasures of the West, the secret of its continual accumulation. In this world, Politics and Economics mutated into Power and Money. Value-free and method-driven social sciences were the secret passwords to powerful clubs (G-7, P-5, the Revolutionary Vanguard, or the New International).

When translated with an eye to the domestic constraints and possibilities, the explanatory power of realism (in the writings of K. Subrahmanyam) and the elegance of Amartya Sen's integration of politics, economics, and philosophy weighed profoundly on my thinking of international relations. In Kaviraj's lectures, political theory finally came together like a beautiful landscape, while Ashok Guha's precise and deliciously slow rendering of the logic of development economics left me wanting more, not less. But the world they portrayed was distinctly out there, outside the immediate reach of those in the classroom, outside of our day-to-day relations and sensibilities, an international system to be learnt, understood, and adapted to. It was not the world I lived in. But it was definitely the world I wanted to soon inhabit.

So I learned a new language – power, self-interest, utility, preferences, social choice, possessive individualism – getting a passport to facilitate my entry and membership into that international. But these were not words that made sense of what happened on my streets or at home. And when I sought to use them in places close to me, some part of me knew I was posturing. What did it mean, in family debates about mutual responsibility, to argue that everyone was selfish and responsible primarily to themselves? Or to talk about devotion and prayer as superstitious rituals while continuing to accept *aarthi* from your mother? In traipsing past the everyday dramas, I suspected I was trampling on multiple dharmas. And I would, sometimes, hide the thinness of my performance by over-asserting the textual and institutional authority of my new learning. That was what my modernity was about, after all, wasn't it? The desire and dare to know. The boldness to question that which, I assumed, had never been questioned. That was what made my education, and education in general, worthwhile. Of what use was access to the wisdom of the international, of the Great Powers and Greater Minds, if it did not allow you to challenge and change the domestic with nerve and verve?

And what were those subject to my performances thinking? Was it like suddenly hearing proper British pronunciation or a perfected American accent at an Indian school? Did everyone know instinctively that something was off key? In a world of multiple languages layered over each other by histories of commingling, how does one produce a perfectly "pure" accent from abroad? Weren't these the truly suspicious ones, and hence, the butt of mutual mockery and fun? You didn't have to be a Foucauldian to see through this one.

I remember being among those pure wanna-bes. Eagerly registering ourselves for an "accent clinic," we were sanitizing our internal Rahims – though we must have denied it – not knowing that we were performing somebody else's cleaning-up operations, somebody else's idea of adventures and mysteries, of social science and societal nutrition. Not quite seeing the Secret – or not so secret – Seven in well-pressed uniforms, we were ultra confident in our "individual preference" of mastering the foreign tongue, of tidying up our accent. But before "choosing" to take the cleansing shower of modern civilization, we first had to strip ourselves of our always brown – mud-browned, earth-browned, dung-browned – village shirts. Drilled into our heads, along with lessons on what were the "correct" pronunciations, intonations, and liaisons, were what else but sophisticated lectures on "(which) culture matters": US culture – defined as self-reliance, individual achievement, efficiency, and future-orientedness – was part of our/*the* education and development, while our culture, we were told, remained pathetically resistant to change, like a Murrah stubbornly refusing to be discharged by a machine (which, we were not told, *looked* advanced but could not even deal with mud).

"Culture" matters, indeed. Isn't that why the literature that my parents collected from different places, no matter how poetically they were written and how worldly they professed to be, never appealed to my senses of sight, smell, taste, and touch? I was certainly moved when Remi (in *Without Family*) reunited with his long lost brother at the end of the novel, but how awed could I be by the magnificent castle and fortune that he came to inherit when the most endearing form of a home with which I had grown up, in images as well as in melodies, was a thatched hut?

Perhaps culture matters too much for us to let go of it, for songs, proverbs, legends, epics, folk poetry, and vernacular stories of all kinds not only cultivate in us different seeds of dharma, but they also give us our world in its wholeness: Literature is history is politics is culture is life. Our (childhood and lifehood) stories constituted more than one "I" (I's R, not I am): "I" followed *shī fu* with Sūn Wùkōng in a *Journey to the West* filled with adventures and challenges blessed by Buddhas and deities; "I" rode on the trail of Trường Sơn in the lorry without windows "not because it had no windows, but because bombs had shocked and shaken them broken";[10] "I" grew up watching grandmothers preparing *pidakalu* and grandfathers distilling *rượu thuốc*; "I" was not only born in the cities of Hyderabad and Hà Nội but "I" was also cradled next to the rivers where *câu hò quan họ* were exchanged, near the rice paddies of flute-playing Krishnas and kite-flying bare-feet children, in the villages that are home to our thousands-of-year folk idioms

> *Trâu ơi ta bảo trâu này,*
> *Trâu ra ngoài ruộng, trâu cày với ta.*
> *Cấy cày vốn nghiệp nông gia,*
> *Ta đây trâu đấy ai mà quản công.*
> *Bao giờ cây lúa còn bông,*
> *Thời còn ngọn cỏ ngoài đồng trâu ăn.*
> O buffalo, I am telling you dear buffalo
> Come to the field and plough with me
> Sowing and plowing is the trade of a farming family
> Me here, you there, who needs to count the labor?
> For as long as the rice plant has grain
> There is grass for you to eat dear buffalo

When I&I write I('s)R, are there ways to write that serve neither Killing nor Knowledge? Are there ways not to gossip[11] about international/external affairs, but to write the *ishq*, *sringara* and *muhabbat* of our everyday lives while honoring Kin-ternational secrets[12] and solidarities?

Are there ways to enunciate the villages in our world and the worlds in our village?

Kaisa yeh ishq hai
Kaisa yeh khwab hai
Kaise jazbaat ka umda salab hai
Din badle, raatein badli, baathein badli
Jeene ke aandaz hi badlein hai
In lamhon ke daaman mein
Pakiza se riste hain.[13]

Notes

1 Jaswant Singh quoted in Talbott (2004: 87, 244).
2 *Ishq* can be translated as love; *muhabbat* as "the inclining of the heart towards something which gives it pleasure".
3 See www.youtube.com/watch?v=k9CuCKJopds (accessed 19 September, 2010): "If not for love, what is left to die for? / If not for love, what is left to live for?"
4 As Mbembe has noted on the postcolony:

> That the sign should be in conformity with the thing was, at the extreme, a matter of secondary importance. What was important was the capacity of the thing represented to mirror resemblances and, through the interplay of bewitchment and enchantment – and, if need be, extravagance and excess – to make the signs speak. It was to this extent that the world of images – that is, the other side of things, language, and life – belonged to the world of charms. For having the power to represent reality (to make images, carve masks, and so on) implied that one had recourse to the sort of magic and double sight, imagination, even fabrication, that consisted in clothing the signs with appearances of the thing for which they were the metaphor.
>
> (Mbembe 2001: 145)

5 See Blaga Dimitrova's poem "The Water Buffalo" (Ha Noi, 1972) in Schley (1985).
6 "*Lạ gì thanh khí lẽ hằng/Một dây một buộc ai giằng cho ra.*" This is a popular verse from Nguyễn Du's *The Tale of Kiều*, a Vietnamese epical classic. For a wonderful English translation of the whole text, see Huỳnh Sanh Thông (1987).
7 See www.youtube.com/watch?v=k9CuCKJopds (accessed 19 September, 2010):

> If not for love, what is left to die for?
> If not for love, what is left to live for?
> Love is sweeter than raw sugar
> Love is more bitter than tamarind
> This love is a solemn promise
> This love is an elemental bond.

8 http://en.wikipedia.org/wiki/Sringara (accessed 19 September, 2010)

9 "Each generation must discover its mission, fulfill it or betray it, in relative opacity." See Fanon (2004: 145).
10 This refers to "*Bài Thơ Về Tiểu Đội Xe Không Kính*" ("A Poem about Drivers of Lorries Without Windows") by Phạm Tiến Duật.
11 See Trinh T. Minh-ha's critique of "scientific gossip" (Minh-ha 1989: 47–76).
12

> [W]e must also attend to Menchú, reading her too against the grain of her necessarily identity-political idiom, borrowing from a much older collective tactic against colonial conquest: "Of course, I'd need a lot of time to tell you about all my people, because it's not easy to understand just like that. And I think I've given some idea of that in my account. Nevertheless, I'm still keeping my Indian identity a secret. I'm still keeping secret what I think no-one should know. Not even anthropologists or intellectuals, no matter how many books they have, can find out all our secrets." (p. 247) That text is not in books, and *the secret keeps us, not the other way around*.
>
> (See footnote in Spivak 1999: 245. Our emphasis)

13 See www.youtube.com/watch?v=4EsV0anEqq0

> What kind of love is this?
> What kind of dream is this?
> What kind of emotions have flooded in here?
> The days have changed, the nights have changed, the conversations have changed.
> Indeed, the very basis of life has changed too.
> Beyond the intimacy of these moments
> There is a holier than holy relationship.

References

Fanon, F. (2004) *The Wretched of the Earth*, New York: Grove Press.
Hoàng, V.H. (2008) "Chiêm ngưỡng anh Hồ Giáo (2)," *Thanh Niên Daily*, January 28, 2008 ("Admiring Hồ Giáo – Part II").
Huỳnh, T.S. (1987) *The Tale of Kiều: A Bilingual Translation of Nguyễn Du's Truyện Kiều*, New Haven, CT: Yale University Press.
Mbembe, A. (2001) *On the Postcolony*, Berkeley, CA: University of California Press.
Menchú, R. (1984) *I, Rigoberta Menchú: An Indian Woman in Guatemala*, translated by Ann Wright, London: Verso.
Minh-ha, T.T. (1989) *Women, Native, Other: Writing Postcoloniality and Feminism*, Bloomington: Indiana University Press.
Philip, M.N. (1989) *She Tries Her Tongue, Her Silence Softly Breaks*, Charlottetown, PEI, Ragweed Press.
Schley, J. (1985) *Writing in a Nuclear Age*, Hanover, NH: University Press of New England.
Spivak, G.C. (1999) *A Critique of Postcolonial Reason: Toward a History of the Vanishing Present*, Cambridge, MA: Harvard University Press.
Talbott, S. (2004) *Engaging India: Diplomacy, Democracy, and the Bomb*, Washington DC: Brookings Institution Press.

15 The sound of conversation

Sorayya Khan

The ancient Miani Sahib graveyard rises and falls in mounds, and we stumble along as if wandering among the crevices of a Lahore topographical map. It has been three years since we've visited, but my teenaged son is first to find my father's grave. He and his brother hang garlands of rose petals on side by side marble headstones, my father's rectangle the far corner in a line of brothers, great uncles my children have never known. A caretaker pours water from a mashak, and with the cup of his palm, he lovingly cleans the 99 names of God bracing my father's grave, and I pretend he's offered such attention each day in the long, almost ten years since my father was swallowed into the belly of the graveyard. A man in a crisp white shalwar settles near where I picture my father's shoulder and sings verses from the Holy Quran. My cousin, partner in prayer, stands solemnly beside me before gently translating headstone inscriptions, a doctor transforming the Arabic numerals of birth dates and death dates into life spans. I try to concentrate on the warmth of his voice, the singsong ages of the dead, but I am distracted by my children. They shuffle their feet, kicking up fine winter dust with their white sneakers. Their mesh T-shirts are loose on their skinny bodies, pointy shoulder blades emerging each time they bend to drop strings of rose petals on the headstones meeting their hands.

The graveyard, a hundred acres in the center of the crowded city of ten million people, is my pilgrimage site. As a child, I routinely accompanied my father to the bursting family plot where over a lifetime he buried his grandparents, parents, brothers, uncles, aunts, cousins, and countless more distant relatives. Each visit, he'd recite their names, how and when they died, and elaborate on the stories that defined the dead. I recall one visit when I was in college and death started to feel real. My father paused for me as I tried to sketch rows of graves with a dull pencil on a yellow legal pad. I filled sloppy rectangles with misspelled names and inaccurate dates until I'd contrived a crude map I quickly misplaced.

Now, as an adult and without my father, I replicate the pilgrimage with my husband and children whenever we visit Pakistan. Instead of my father, one of my favorite cousins who is a few years older than I am, is recounting the names of the dead, and I don't contradict him when a detail challenges one shared by my father. Our sons squeeze between graves, and I'm relieved they are old enough to know not to step on them. By the end of our visit, our older son has the look of an adolescent barely tolerating his surroundings. Our younger son stands at a distance from us, and I think this right. He is only partially with us, anyway, his mind already taken up with the next day's prospect of visiting his cousin, six weeks older than he, a brother he wishes was also his. As we walk back to the car, our older son rests an elbow on my shoulder, enough weight to slow me down. His mind is sanitized by perfect gardens of the dead, uniform graves in pristinely manicured rows flanking some of Ithaca's lovely roads. He declares the Lahore graveyard a terrible place. My cousin steers us through a maze of narrow lanes scattered with garbage and refuse, and rose petals, too, and I sadly marvel that my refuge is the opposite for my child.

It is my refuge because I imagine I might come from that crowded plot in Miani Sahib graveyard in the middle of Lahore, gnarly trees raising stunted limbs into the perfect sky, as if in adulation. I inhale the winter's dust and muezzin's song, absorb the chaotic jumble of the dead, the disordered mounds of mud graves sprouting from every cranny, and in the distance, I notice dwellings infringing upon the dead as the city refuses to be contained. The web of my life – the paths and the journeys of who I am and where I've been – grows outward from this center. A spider's thread is spun to Islamabad where I grew up, other threads reach elsewhere: Maastricht where my mother endured a part of her war, Amritsar where my grandfather had a flower garden, Rudolfienerhaus, the hospital in Vienna where I was born, Dhaka where half of Pakistan was surrendered, and many other places, including New York state, my home for the last 22 years, a place in the midst of all others remarkable only for its silence. The more I think about it, the wider the web gets, the looser the weave, the more slippery the links.

Lying awake that night, listening to the sounds of my sleeping family in my cousin's beautiful guest bedroom, I try not to fault my son for his discomfort. I felt the same way as a 16 year old and had since conveniently forgotten. Miani Sahib graveyard is filthy and chaotic, it has a foul smell and is impossible to navigate. Yet when I imagine the center of my web, the family burial plot comes to mind. This fact is filled with irony and contradictions. More often than not, I was unable to communicate with family members buried there. I do not read or speak Urdu fluently, am dependent on my cousins and others in Pakistan to translate for me, three whole years have passed since my last trip to Pakistan, and I don't know when I'll visit again. I live in the United States, and despite a Pakistan that sports chic indoor malls, Nike stores, GNC branches, internet cafes, and frequent signs for Kentucky Fried Chicken and McDonalds, I cannot conceive of a more disparate reality.

My web, I think, is not formed by a spider's silk. I write my web. The more I write, the tighter it gets and the more certain I am that it is there.

****

I didn't intend to write. I hadn't even known writing claimed me until my other goals came crashing down. I can't remember what I wanted to be in elementary school, but in high school I had specific goals. I would study Political Science and land a job with a United Nations' organization. I would travel the world and solve refugee crises, I would dig my heels in disaster zones and hand out bottles of water, I would arrive in war zones and negotiate peace. I went through college collecting relevant courses and I traveled to graduate school to hone my skills. I wrote papers on Human Rights, the Soviets in Afghanistan, the miracle of NICS like South Korea. I didn't doubt my calling or ever question my trajectory. I rushed to graduate early after friends helped me secure a job offer from the World Bank. When I brought in my green Pakistani passport on my first day of work and presented it to the person who handled such matters, I was told that if I left the World Bank, the institution would not assist me in adjusting my visa status in the US. It did not occur to me that I would ever be in such a situation. Some months later, on my own volition, I was back in the personnel office, my passport stamped to indicate I was no longer an employee. It hadn't taken long for the imagined reality of my work to crumble. The work wasn't meaningful and I didn't believe (or maybe I did for the first few days) that I might positively affect any injustice in the world. I was a low level research assistant working on an education and training project. My statistical analysis demonstrated that in a certain time period in one part of the world, the World Bank's sector loans were more successful than project loans. The people I was working with hoped the analysis would show otherwise. All around me, the prevailing mindset was certain of how to "develop" the world and how to "provide" for the needy. I quickly decided I wanted neither to "develop" anyone, nor "provide." But it took me getting physically sick, the lining of my stomach following my dreams into the toilet, to find the courage to extract myself and enter a frightening void – the first time in my adult life not knowing what I wanted to be.

I tried a few different things. At my graduate institution, I was hired as an assistant foreign student advisor. I quickly learned about student immigration rules and official forms, emergency resources for the most distraught students, the ones who insisted on listing "Palestine" for their country of origin when, in fact, Palestine was not then, as it is not now, a recognized country in the eyes of the United States immigration authorities. I contemplated pursuing a computer degree in a new and special program for women designed at the university, and my father, rebounding from his disappointment at my departure from the World Bank, offered to bankroll such a sensible decision. Based on my Master's degree work in International Studies, I was accepted into the department's PhD program. I formed a committee, compiled reading lists and began studying for exams in my stated fields of interest, before eventually concluding it was wisest not to pursue further graduate studies simply because I could not think of what else to do.

Then one morning somewhere along the way, I sat down in front of my friend's borrowed Otrona computer, blinking green cursor beckoning, and shook out the image inside my head onto the black screen. The picture was a corner of Five Queen's Road, my grandparents' dilapidated house in Lahore, a place where bird droppings fell from ceiling-high windows and paint and plaster fell in joined clumps to the floor. Although we'd never seen it as such, it was the once-upon-a-time, pre-Partition, astonishingly grand home of an Englishman whose terraced perennials I fantasized were famous throughout the city. The image came out whole, as if it had been germinating for years, and it was a place I could see, feel, hear, smell, and touch in one paragraph. With that rare moment when muse and words arrive seamlessly as one, it was as if a plug had been released in my mind. I could not stop. Over the next years, the lone image led to countless others, the Otrona became an Apple computer, my home moved from Denver to Syracuse where the Colorado blue skies were replaced with gray. I received firm assurances from an amazing teacher, the novelist Douglas Unger, that Syracuse, the dying city in the rust belt, was an excellent place to accomplish work. Years later, I don't remember exactly when, with several rough drafts of my first novel tucked into boxes and desk drawers and a few publications to my name, I began calling myself a writer.

****

My mother is from the Netherlands and was a child in Maastricht and Amsterdam during World War. My father was born in Kasur, a city in what would become Pakistan's Punjab, and lived with his parents and six siblings in Lahore during Partition. In the Lahore Museum, there is a photograph of a gathering with Mohammed Ali Jinnah, the "father" of Pakistan during the summer of Partition, and my father's brother is clearly visible, the plaid scarf around my uncle's neck caught in a rare gust of wind. My parents met in Chicago, Illinois, where they were both studying and working, and married in the new mosque in Washington, DC, an Egyptian Imam conducting the service, overseeing the ring slipped onto my mother's finger underneath a white scarf. They could not marry in North Carolina where my father's host family lived because miscegany laws forbade their mixed marriage.

My brother was born in Amsterdam, a gift to my mother's mother who was already dying by then, and my sister and I were born in the same hospital in Vienna, Austria, the city in which my father worked for years and where, eventually, he would come to die. When I was ten, the summer after the 1971 war which Pakistan lost and from which Bangladesh was born, my father moved us, kicking and screaming, to Islamabad.

In those days, Islamabad was nothing but a sleepy city of a handful of wide and empty roads, a place where nothing ever happened and time, in a version particular to place and adolescence, stood still. It was as far away as possible from what it has become today, a miniature version of Beirut in the 1970s. Armed police units sport cocked semi-automatic rifles and are holed up in sandbagged bunkers guarding embassies. Zigzagging roadblocks interrupt the familiar route from my old house to the neighborhood market. Adjacent to a road no longer accessible to traffic, grounds the size of football fields still harbor debris from the Marriott Hotel bombing. My in-laws' dead end street abuts the site of last weekend's suicide bombing. Unlike the city of my adolescence, Islamabad is now a place that is living time, filling its once deserted roads, hosting every imaginable facet of humanity – from guns, killing, and checkpoints to the bustle of weddings, the evening smells of chicken tikka grilling in bazaars, and the mesmerizing vocals of the Qawwals. It is a city, I am sure, on the lips of current students in the tiny liberal arts college I attended in Pennsylvania, my first port of arrival in the United States in 1979, where no student I met in my first few weeks knew where Pakistan, let alone Islamabad, was.

My story, my history, if this is what it is, is a mouthful. I have yet to settle on a proper response when asked "Where do you come from?" And even if I can settle on a country, do I belong to the place it has become or the place it is in my memory or the place it was long ago?

Or is the place not a tangible, concrete reality at all? Is it the reality I imagine in my writing? Do I claim my home with my own words, my stories, my characters? Is that why I bury myself, for years at a time, in the home I create in my novels?

To see my web, to tighten it and draw it near, I compose universes for imaginary people living imaginary lives. I dream my home. Long, continuous, multi-colored dreams of words that others, and therefore I, live.

****

I know that what *I* try to do in my writing, explore the relationship between the personal and the political, I cannot accomplish meaningfully in any other format. But there are those who write in multiple forms, swinging back and forth as if one nurtures the other. On a given day, the lucky writer might choose a poem for his conveyance, rather than a play or a film treatment. Subject matter in the most abstract sense – a moment of colonialism, say – can be delivered in a movie, a newspaper article, an academic article, a poem, or any of an endless variety of other prose possibilities. In fact, words are not even required. The moment could just as well be captured in another art form, a photograph, a sculpture, a painting. I suspect that subject matter determines form, and I wonder what it is about the form of fiction that lends itself to my subject matter.

What I liked most about graduate school was how it connected the world for me. Dependency theory allowed for the center of the center to be linked to the center of the periphery (which is where I imagined I fit in), political economy accounted for relationships between different parts of a society, and world systems theory offered, at least for me, a visual way of imagining the family of nation states. The world as I had known it inside my mind, suddenly had form and structure. It had a way of being seen, a way of being, and over the two years of my study, I felt as if a puzzle was slowly falling into place inside my head, as if the black and white had finally found color.

As exciting as it was then to discover the lens of structure, in retrospect, I can see my focus slowly shift to the life lived inside of it. Who are the *people* who inhabit structures? How do structures define them? Their families? How do structures dictate their decisions and circumscribe their lives? I didn't turn to fiction knowing the terrain would allow me to explore the relationship between individual and structure or between the personal and the political. I don't think I was conscious that the moments when such categories met or overlapped would be my subject matter. But my graduate school education gave me tools to re-imagine the world I had come from. I found it natural to re-imagine my world in writing (*writing* because it wasn't quite *fiction* yet). And when I came up for air, I saw what had happened. The Englishman's dilapidated house my grandparents inhabited became a metaphor for colonialism. The American boys on yellow school buses spitting on Pakistani bicyclists in Islamabad became an act of imperialism, and my silence on those buses became not just discomfort and fear, but complicity, a sad but crucial ingredient in the machinery of subjugation. Fiction, it turned out, was a safe place to consider the way structures had shaped my life, my geography, and the more I wrote (unconnected blocks, sometimes only images), the more certain I was I had found my form.

Years later, from the vantage point of having written two novels, I can see my subject matter and form almost as one. For in writing fiction, we create the universes, the structures, in which our characters survive, from countries and historical time periods to families and their kitchens. Until they come to life and dictate their own terms, we circumscribe our characters' lives through any variety of variables (for example, time, place, relationships), the perfect set of which brings them to life and allows the reader to see her reflection in them. Fiction, as a form, *is* the relationship between structure and people.

There is relief, for me, in a mundane fact: fiction is not about numbers. While my graduate studies were not quantitative, the application of my education in a professional setting was just that. How can I convey my discomfort with numbers? When the most recent Iraq War began, a neighbor situated at a well traveled intersection displayed handmade signs meant to provoke. He was anti-war, and his signs were never desecrated when he simply indicated the accumulating number of United States' soldiers killed. The first number I remember was 175, the last I saw, before he relinquished the enterprise and shifted his attention to the upcoming elections, was almost 3,000. Shortly after the war began, I read an interview by a Pakistani woman writer who talked about fiction as a process of redeeming loss. I thought of this every time I saw the number of dead on the neighbor's sign. Numbers belie humanity. They tell us nothing unless they are in relation to each other, and even then, they don't contain the essence of what has been lost, why it has been lost, or how it has been lost. Numbers are sterile, they report facts, if there are such things, they do not engage with ambiguity. It is the job of artists to redeem loss, to describe what it looks like, the sounds it makes, the tastes it embodies, the way it smells, the textures in which it arrives. The job of the artist is to make loss comprehensible to others, to discover in the loss what is shared by the audience, and therefore, to explore the shared loss in all of us.

****

I am both most interested in and have the most difficulty with structure in my fiction. I have discovered that the possibilities in fiction are endless. The same story can be written from multiple perspectives and in multiple voices, suggest all kinds of truths, paint infinite emotional landscapes, capture any essence of life's topography. There is, in fact, no pre-determined moment when a novel is complete, because the writer can always re-write the narrative, yet again, to incorporate a different possibility. Often, novels are revised this way, until the "right" set of factors, the most consistent set, is settled upon. But because I am interested in the relationship between the personal and the political, especially in Pakistan, I need to lay the groundwork, do the research, to determine what the possibilities are regarding the scope of my subject matter.

My family moved to Pakistan after the 1971 war, a war in which general estimates claim one million people died and a new country, Bangladesh, was born. Even as a ten-year-old, the silence surrounding what had happened was striking. No one talked about the war, despite the few, but glaring signs that it had happened. There were red banners, *Bring our POWs Home!*, taut above the Lahore roads, hailing the 90,000 prisoners of war. With this silence and forgetting planted in my head as a child, I found my fiction eventually veering toward it. Given that novels represent possibilities inherent in life, I was unprepared to write a novel about 1971 before discovering the narrative of what had actually happened. As if education was about receiving answers to questions on a questionnaire, I set about conducting my research. I spent six months in Pakistan in 1999 interviewing soldiers who'd been posted in what was then East Pakistan during the turbulent nine months of the 1971 conflict. My most successful interviews were conducted with a group of friends who had, for the most part, stayed in contact over the years. Their stories were filled with vivid detail, astonishing clarity, incredible cinematography. Some admitted to killing, all admitted to being attacked, none admitted to raping, the most grievous of atrocities conducted by the West Pakistanis in East Pakistan during the nine month conflict. The most astonishing truth I discovered was that the soldiers I spoke to, each and every one, sported an incredible sense of humor and in between miserable details and matter-of-fact cruelty, we laughed and joked while we drank tea together.

Prior to engaging in research in Pakistan, my plan was to write a novel about the war. I had decided – as if one can do such a thing before the arc of a story is known – to tell a story in alternating points of view, one through the soldier's eyes, and the other, through the "adopted" young girl he raises as his own in Islamabad. But already, after hearing the soldier's stories, I suspected the structure would have to change. No matter how much research I did, how much I tried to learn about infantry formations and other tactics of war, I feared I would not be able to master the battlefield theater of war. The stories I was hearing began affecting my narrative structure in an unexpected way.

Then I arrived in Bangladesh, set to embark on a research plan I'd designed months earlier, only to stumble again. I thought I would interview victims of the war and detail their stories. It took me all of two days of sharing this with Bangladeshis who were assisting me in acclimating to Dhaka before accepting that I could not, in good faith, do such a thing. Chronicling misery (*How does it feel to be raped?*), especially by someone who might symbolize the enemy, suddenly seemed absurd. So I fell back on the landscape, the topography of the country and the stories I'd been told. I would travel to Narayanganj where a soldier had described for me a boat on which women and children were terrorized. I would walk the grounds of Dhaka University where on the night of March 25, 1971, a number of intellectuals were brutally murdered and are today memorialized in busts. I pulled out the notes from my interviews with soldiers and, for the most part, I spent two months trying to physically absorb the places of the soldier's memories.

By the time I returned to writing my manuscript several months later, I was no longer locked into a pre-determined structure. As I wrote draft after draft, the structure finally emerged, a universe of time, characters, emotions, circumstances, and action drawn from every aspect of my research. I had conducted research to discover the *possibilities* for my narrative rather than the novel's final narrative. I used stories soldiers had shared with me to shape my narrative because the framework of what had happened allowed me to imagine what might have been possible. Their stories formed a web, and I wrote *Noor* in the tiny gaps between the weave.

****

Writing, for me, is like trying to draw spider's threads between the progressively wider images in an old science documentary meant to convey how small we are in the world. A frame of a couple in a park is replaced by an image of the same two people on a map in the city, their dot in the world becoming progressively smaller until they, the park, the nation, the continent, are not even specks being looked down upon from space. In a similar way, I think of my writing as directed endlessly outwards in infinite trajectories, from my life in tiny Ithaca, to Syracuse where both our children were born, to Denver where I went to graduate school, to the apartment in Vienna, Austria, where my Dutch mother now lives, to Banda Aceh which I recently visited, to the village outside of Muzaffarabad, Pakistan, during the earthquake when a family friend fell to her knees in a field watching her house slide off the side of a mountain, to a mile or two inland from the edge of the ocean in Karachi where my sister and her family live, to Miani Sahib graveyard where my father now lies.

But then I realize I'm not really looking across the world at who I have become, but inside myself, exploring how these places might have found a home inside of me. The sound of their conversation is my writing.

Cosmography recapitulates biography
An epilogue

Peter Mandaville

I hate IR, but it's where a lot of my favorite people live... so I keep coming back to it, even though I stopped doing anything that corresponds even vaguely to the fringes of its canon almost a decade ago. I keep coming back for the people, not for the theories. These tend to be folks who also have, shall we say, a "complicated" relationship with IR. They are variously political economists, critical social theorists, scions of deracinated philosophies, and postcolonial warrior-monks. What unites us all, I think, is a shared sense of IR as an *epiphenomenon* masquerading as an *episteme*. That's what Stephen Chan (himself the commensurate postcolonial warrior-monk) was referring to above when he spoke about his shift from international civil service to academia as "leaving one set of lies for another." So then it begins to be all about how we live the lie and how we position and style ourselves in relation to it. For some of us, IR becomes a strategic choice: a vantage point from which to tell a deeper, underlying story. Or IR as a laboratory, a collection of agents and structures through which we are permitted to entertain philosophies from other academic worlds. Both of these approaches involve performing certain kinds of de-exceptionalizing maneuvers on IR – intricate techniques designed to recursively render banal the omnipotent claims of discipline's imperial/ empirical center.

But it's also about how we live with ourselves once we know the lie to be a lie. So at some point we need to stop asking questions about how and what we do in/to IR, and start asking what IR does for/to us. On this account, nothing is truer than Joel Dinerstein's advice to his students: "If you're passionate about your research, at some point you'll recognize that it's meaningful on a personal level because you're researching yourself. Only you've externalized the questions." But to reinternalize these questions – as has been the chief task of these collected essays – is not always an easy thing to do. Witness how many of the preceding chapters open with testimony to the angst and procrastination associated with trying to write this very different kind of IR. I have suffered it myself, having originally been slotted to contribute a full chapter. Rather than essay an account of this IR's "I," I took the easier route and bid myself down to a more familiar role as a commentator and one that would allow me to speak in a safer, secondary voice. Given the nature of these chapters – there's a lot of very personal stuff here – this role also entails, I realize, a certain amount of voyeurism. Or perhaps I see it that way only because many of these authors, while known to me personally and in some cases over extended periods of time, appear here anew without the armatures of theory and discipline, or the designation "panel discussant." Jenny Edkins, for instance, has always been for me the Derridean par excellence, never someone's daughter.

Inevitably however, even in contributing some short reflections by way of an epilogue, I find myself having to drop into an autobiographical mode in order to interpolate between the friends, colleagues, and fellow travelers who reveal themselves in these pages, and our common mooring in something called IR. Besides, with everyone skinny-dipping around me, it doesn't seem fair to wear clothes.

Featuring early global labor migrants from California and faux Nazis

I was born and raised in Dhahran, Saudi Arabia – headquarters of what was still at the time the Arabian-American Oil Company (ARAMCO). My father, who worked in the company's Government Affairs division, also lived in Arabia as a young man. His father had left southern California as a global labor migrant of sorts. Having caught word of the burgeoning oil industry in the Arab Gulf, he headed to Arabia at the tail end of World War II, hitching a lift across the Atlantic on a US naval frigate. His first job involved traveling to southern Iraq to recruit oil workers from Basra and its environs. After several years he sent for his family to join him from California, bringing my father – then 13 years old – to the desert kingdom in 1948. After attending boarding schools in India, Italy, and Lebanon, my father began studying Arabic at the American University of Beirut, only to have the final year of his studies interrupted by the first rumblings of sectarian unrest that some 20 years later would eventually manifest as the Lebanese civil war. He finished out his studies at Georgetown University in Washington DC.

There he met my mother, herself another transfer student. She was born in Havana, Cuba, the daughter of a German diplomat who had spent much of his career on various postings to the United States. During World War II, he had run the Third Reich's chancery in Athens, arranging – unbeknownst to Berlin – for Greek Jews to be smuggled to safety. The Allied victory saved him from Nazi retribution and his prior diplomatic experience in the US saw him dispatched by Germany's post-war government to re-open the embassy in Washington DC – the city in which he eventually retired and lived out the rest of his years. This made Washington, where I now reside, the only American city with which I had any regular contact growing up.

My father was drafted into the US Army out of college, narrowly missing the end of the Korean War. After his military service he immediately took a job with the Arabian-American Oil Company and moved with my mother to Saudi Arabia. His first position with the company was in its

"Arabian Research Division," a special office devoted to the production of knowledge about the physical and human terrain of Saudi Arabia. This was, after all, two and a quarter million square kilometers of desert about to be repurposed as a giant hydrocarbon fuel production facility, and its topographies needed to be rendered legible to infrastructure. Processes remarkably similar to those described by James Scott in *Seeing Like a State* played out across the Arabian Peninsula. For example, needing to regulate the rhythm of seasonal nomadic migrations so that they would not interfere with the construction of pipelines and oil facilities, the Company built strategically placed water wells to draw herdsmen away from sensitive areas during particular times of the year.

Even after joining the division of ARAMCO whose role was to liaise with the Saudi government, my father continued to spend as much time as possible "off camp." A keen botanist with a particular interest in the socio-cultural function of plants in arid zones, he spent weeks at a time in the desert collecting plant samples and interviewing Bedouin (culminating in the publication, in 1990, of his *Flora of Eastern Arabia*). An avid collector of late colonial travelogues, he retraced many of the routes followed by explorers such as Charles Doughty, St. John Philby, and particularly Wilfred Thesiger (years later I would make a vain effort to participate in this story myself by seeking out and spending an afternoon with Thesiger – who by then had become something of a quasi-touristic curiosity – in northern Kenya while working as a UN intern in Nairobi). For my mother, having lived through wars and used to being uprooted and dragged somewhere new every few years, the experience of moving to Saudi Arabia was not in and of itself foreign. Thoroughly adaptable (yet simultaneously thoroughly stubborn and unyielding), she crafted all manner of techniques and methods that should be studied by everybody trying to navigate the confinements of so conservative a society. By knowing just when to flatter, when to play dumb, and when to just go ahead and do it (even when you really weren't supposed to, e.g. drive a car outside the boundaries of the ARAMCO compound), she perfected the art of micro-resisting Wahhabism.

The youngest (by some years) of three boys, I grew up in what was essentially a transplanted simulacrum of suburban America. There were baseball fields and golf courses (featuring "browns" instead of greens), snack bars and youth centers. While many of my friends and peers had moved to Saudi Arabia as children and still considered the United States to be their home, my overwhelming sense growing up was one of being "from" Saudi Arabia – or at least rooted there – while also keenly aware that I was not *of* the country. Our annual "repatriation" vacations (as they were termed) for me were never about returning somewhere to which I had emotive attachments. They were primarily shopping expeditions.

I recall being aware from a very young age that there were other "others" living there in Saudi Arabia, other people who, like me, did not belong. But it was also clear to me that their experience of life in the Kingdom was very different from mine. By the 1980s, migrant laborers from South and Southeast Asia occupied almost every sector of low skilled work in the country (with the exception of the few jobs given to Saudi Shi'a, others in their own right). Long before I was able to analyze what was going on in terms of social stratification and class, it was apparent to me that there was a very clear system of hierarchy – bordering at times on apartheid – in effect. The household servants who worked in American homes, most of whom came from India, Bangladesh, and Sri Lanka, lived in a wired off compound-within-a-compound (a system of nested alterity, in other words) called Domestic Camp. Our "house boy" – although he was in his 50s – John D'Souza, came from Goa, India. Early every morning he would bike to our house from Domestic Camp, and back again in the late evening. On occasional weekends, domestic employees could take trips to neighboring "off camp" towns. They were barred, however, from ever entering or using any of the compound facilities reserved for those categorized "Grade Code 11+" according to the Company's system of hierarchical ascription (which was based on the nature of one's job). In practice, Grade Code 11+ meant you were white, or had an engineering degree from a Western university. And then there were the street sweepers – mostly Bangladeshis – pushing plastic rubbish carts up and down the compound's sidewalks. They wore orange jumpsuits to remain visible in the burning haze, an image I would not see again until the same garb cropped up years later as the garment of choice for Guantanamo Bay detainees in the aftermath of 9/11.

Saudi Arabia was a curious sort of Never-Never land. There were a lot of things the few available sources of officially sanctioned information desperately wanted us to believe just never happened there. Newspapers reported nothing but exciting new production facilities coming on stream and prize ceremonies for superior management performance. The majority of the evening television news broadcast was devoted to footage of Gulf Cooperation Council (GCC) royals meeting each other on airport tarmacs, reviewing honor guards, and sitting together in gilded lounge rooms equipped with rococo style tissue dispensing devices. Which is not to say that we were unaware of the regional upheaval that surrounded us. Its geopolitical traces and corollary sonic booms – in the form of combat air patrols flown by the Royal Saudi Air Force's shining new fleet of F-15 fighters – also resounded daily in Arabia's Eastern Province. The nearly simultaneous triple whammy of Iran's Islamic Revolution, the seizure of the Grande Mosque in Mecca, and Shi'i unrest in the towns surrounding Dhahran had led to some visible cracks in the façade of Never-Never land – particularly as the Iran–Iraq war, having killed all of its terrestrial participants, moved out over open water and caught the Saudis' attention by focusing anew on oil tanker traffic. This gave us a greater National Police presence on the streets, classroom conversations about possible air raids, and – rather cryptically – the assignment of a Saudi intelligence officer to the Company school "for our protection." Protection from what exactly, we were never sure: restless Shi'a from neighboring towns?

Grand Mosque Siege sympathizers? An auto-immune response from the country's official Wahhabi establishment? With hindsight, the latter probably makes the most sense. On other occasions we certainly had felt repercussions from the intricate dance in which the Saudi government bureaucracy, the royal family, and the religious establishment squared off with each other. We knew when the latter had the upper hand because dress codes, even for men, would come into effect on the compound: no short pants above the knee.

Despite the censorship, I should note, we were never in anything even approaching an information bubble. *Time* and *Newsweek*, judiciously treated with the black ink of censorship, gave us the lion's share of world happenings. Radio, however, was our informational technology of choice. The ambiguous coloniality of the situation was confirmed in our reliance on the BBC World Service, where the chimes of Big Ben preceding the news signaled the onset of something at least vaguely approaching truth.

This is me in Grade 9, baby

In the eyes of the Saudis, Western progeny becomes dangerous at age 15. With a firm desire to see the awkward years of teenage drama, angst, and hormonal convulsion play out as far away as humanly possible, we were all packed off to subsidized places at various boarding schools in the US and Europe. I ended up at a small prep school in rural northwestern New Jersey, about an hour and a half's drive from New York City. There I encountered for the first time pay phones, newspapers that actually reported news (not to mention magazines without pages ripped out by government censors), and bagels – which, labeled a "Jewish food," had not been available in Saudi Arabia. In Dr. Marty Miller's 'Soviet Studies' class, I was given the opportunity to entertain my anti-establishment flirtation with the Communist jihad while simultaneously confronting the first inklings of a fundamental shift in world order. I learned the discourse of the *stakhanovite*, the "hero-worker," alongside Francis Fukuyama's claims that laboring subjectivity was being erased by a universal neoliberalism. The first "IR" piece I ever wrote was a 1989 critique of Fukuyama claiming that he wasn't paying enough attention to the geopolitical resonance of Islam. Everything I've written since has declined significantly in predictive value.

College applications posed a dilemma. I ended up choosing between the School of Foreign Service at Georgetown University in Washington DC, my parents' *alma mater*, and St. Andrews University in Scotland. By this point, I had developed a certain reactionary, default anti-Americaness that led me back east across the Atlantic. A large part of this decision lay in the fact that my teenage popular culture compass points had been shaped by radio signals from Radio Bahrain, the relatively liberal sheikhdom laying a mere 20 miles off the coast of Saudi Arabia. It didn't so much articulate explicitly anti-American views as give voice to certain postcolonial, anti-Thatcherite voices that circulated in the interstices of British pop music in the 1980s. I had had an unwitting activist moment in 1982 when, visiting the Edinburgh Botanical Gardens to confirm my father's discovery of a new species of Arabian salt bush (*Salsola mandavilla*), he insisted that we join a protest against the Falklands War.

Everything at St. Andrews (and beyond) quickly became variations on a theme: analysis of Islam and world politics coupled with suspicion bordering on conviction that global neoliberalism was ignoring some tough questions about the circumstances surrounding its origins and the possibility that there might be another set of stories to tell about world order and the ordering of worlds. The choice of the UK over the US – though I couldn't have known it at the moment of decision – also proved to be the difference between exposure to a curriculum in which critical social theory was viewed as a perfectly acceptable modality through which to pose the aforementioned questions (in the UK) vs. the very real (US-ian) possibility that I might never have encountered such ideas because they would have been dismissed as thoroughly heterodox in the latter stages of my graduate career.

More recently, my life has been dominated by 9/11 and its aftermath. Initially, I experienced this as a moment of crisis. The crisis in question stemmed from the disjuncture between my anticipated US response (which would have dismissed 9/11 as an exceptional event, strategically aspirational in nature) and the actual response which – in catering to those same aspirations – proceeded to play directly into the narrative that Usama bin Laden and his associates had been hoping for: namely to prompt an equally aspirational project on the part of the United States to project a particular order on to "problematic" world regions (rogue states/states of concern/Axis of Evil), of which the Middle East – namely Iraq – seemingly provided the least risky point of engagement. My first reactions to the global US muscularity of the last decade was therefore one of denial. Bizarrely, this was that much easier in Washington DC – nerve center of empire – where the feedback loops that define policy discourse quickly converted this project into the *sine qua non* of national security.

It's in watching the personalities and biographies that entered the early spaces of post-9/11 "expert testimony" that I became re-sensitized to the power of personal narratives. Many came forward to speak on behalf of the significance of this event and its attendant requirements in terms of US national security policy. Many were also culpable here in terms of the course of US commitments: the Egyptian government lied about ongoing linkages between its chief political rival the Muslim Brotherhood and Islamist militants while Israel – along with its domesticated US formations – sought an expedient conflation of HAMAS with Al-Qaeda.

In more recent years I have found it difficult, particularly living in Washington DC, to maintain a complete separation between the exercise of power and its critique. At some point I made the calculation that it was better to be in Grand Central as the trains collided (and to be some small part of the post-crisis unpacking and decoupling) than to be absent from the ensuing conversation. But being in Grand Central also socializes you to a very particular system of prioritization and scheduling that proceeds with a merciless conviction...

Something like reconciliation and conclusion

More than a decade ago, Fred Halliday and Justin Rosenberg engaged a form of "biography as IR" by conducting an interview with no less than Kenneth Waltz between the covers of the *Review of International Studies*. The most revealing aspect of this biography, I think, was its disclosure that, to Waltz, IR was something of an afterthought. After reading the interview, and beyond certain pragmatic choices that all graduate students have to make, one is left searching for the "I" in Waltz's IR – a meaningful coincidence between the world he lived in and the world he wrote.

It is tempting to read (and dismiss) Waltz as representative of a "tinkering with units" approach to IR rather than as someone who produced a body of work that resonated with a normative internationalism. We read this interview and leave with little insight as to what, as Naeem Inayatullah would ask, makes Kenneth Waltz angry. Without this information we cannot do IR. To say this is of course to make claims on IR as representing a kind of identity politics – reinterpreting that latter term to refer, quite literally, to a strategic engagement with the self. This volume, then, has been about recognizing and arguing for the value to be found in unpacking the latter. By asking about how we do IR in relation to the self, we not only render contingent (and that much more personable and human) the claims to knowledge produced by the discipline, but we also enable forms of empathetic knowing and solidarity that transcend disciplinary debate. The "disciplinary" IR of Patrick Thaddeus Jackson, for instance, involves conceptual acrobatics the likes of which I could never reproduce (I simply don't possess his theoretical chops), and yet no story of my engagement with the world would be complete without a firm anchor in *Star Wars* (not to mention *Chess: the Musical*) plus Quinn's über-sophisticated appreciation of that most ironically cosmopolitan of droids, R2D2.

The more we insert the "I" into the lie that is disciplinary IR, the more we enable and reveal crucially important conversations about why and how we do International Relations in particular ways. Better social science, as one might be led to believe, is not so much the negation of self as it is the thorough interrogation of self from a positionality that crafts a world at the same time as it engages in an auto-critique that lays bare the self-generated conditions of possibility that articulate the limits of that world.

But the limits of a world can feel constraining. So I also harbor some considerable ambivalence towards a biography that compels me to relate internationally in very particular ways. It has afforded many thoroughly unique opportunities and perspectives to be sure, and yet sometimes I also feel as if it has condemned me to play a role scripted not by unfettered scholarly agency (a fantasy we have just spent an entire volume debunking in any case), but by the happenstance of where I was born. Saudi Arabia could have pushed me towards the global political economy of energy, but for some reason I opted for Muslim politics (anthropology triumphing over macroeconomics?). I invested in that line of analysis and, even after the questions I needed answering got answered, equities were accumulated and preserved. Once we begin to trade professionally in a particular kind of self, we become to some extent a function, or factor, of the economy it creates. All that by way of pointing out that biography both enables and disables certain kinds of IR. Part of the reason "I hate IR," then, is because it constantly brings me face to face with elements of biography I would just as soon avoid or conveniently forget. And yet I would not have it any other way. While I may have serious misgivings about disciplinary IR, I also recognize that it provides certain kinds of artifices and platforms for packing and channeling the raw stuff of the international: anger, confession, incoherence, hope. But IR can't actually generate the latter, and that is why an IR disconnected from biography – even where methodologically robust – can never be more than anemic.

Index

9/11 terrorist attacks 201
Aberystwyth, University of, BISA Poststructural Politics Group Workshop 3–4
academic distance 104
academic practice, Western bias 48–9
academic prose 5–6
academics, snobbery 16–7
acting ethically 83–5
Adorno, T.W. 15, 17, 125
affairs 173–4
Afghanistan 29; Inayatullah's essay 1–2, 8; warm indifference 2
African-American experience 118–34; and the blues 122–6
African-American literature 118–20, 129
African-American music 122–6, 129, 130–1
Afrodiasporic musics 133
Agamben, Giorgio 28
agency 156
Ahmed, Sarah 105–6, 115
Alaska 104
Albania 103–4; education 113; the Hoxha regime 103; National Museum communist oppression exhibition 113–4; Tirane 103–4, 111–5; trafficking in women 104; travel restrictions 113; women in 104–5
Albanian Students Abroad Network 114–5
Algeria 176
Algiers, French invasion of 51
Ali, Muhammed 48
alienation 29, 160
alternative writing forms 6
Amangalle Hotel, Galle 157–8
American identity 122
American Studies 49–53

American University of Beirut 51–3
Amin, Idi 13, 14
Amy, Lori 103–16; academic distance 104; background 103–4; father 103–4; openness 115–6; return to Tirane 111–5; *Women and War* seminar 106–11
anecdotes 4–5
Angola 17
antiquated man 143
Aqoul blog 116n4
Arab world, US relations with 45–53
Arabian Peninsula, nomadic migrations 198
Arabian-American Oil Company (ARAMCO) 197, 197–8
Argentina 27
Asimov, Isaac 163
Asperger's Syndrome 168
authoritarianism 148
autism 161, 167–71; diagnosis 168–9; spectrum 168–9, 172
autobiographical awareness 9–10
"Autobiography as a Source for Exploring the Past and Anticipating the Future", ISA conference panel 5

Ba Vì, Vietnam 174–6
Baghdad 47, 51
Bangladesh 194
Baraka, Amiri 123
bare life 28
Batticaloa, Sri Lanka 37–9
Baudrillard, J. 89–90
BBC World Service 200
becoming, the classroom as site of 110–1
Beirut, American University of 51–3
belonging 87–9, 160, 191
Berlin 63
Berlin Wall, fall of 61, 78

Bin Laden, Usama 201
Birmingham 26
black body, the 41–4, 47
Black Skin, White Masks (Fanon) 29, 53
Black Talk (Sidran) 133
Blaga, Lucian 92n4
Bleiker, Roland 11n5
blues, the 122, 122–6
Blues People (Baraka) 123
Blyton, Enid 177
Bolshevik Revolution, the 142
Boston 126
Boyer, D. 137
Bridging Perspectives for a Shared Future conference, 2009 114–5
Brigg, Morgan 11n5
Bristol Royal Infirmary 21–2
British Expeditionary Force 20
Brown, James 134
Bucharest International Youth Festival 141–2
Burke, Kenneth 133, 134
Bush, George 45–53, 46, 53n1
Butalia, Urvashi 85
Byerman, Keith 134n1

Cambodia 27
Campbell, Joseph 163
Canada 87–9, 144–5
Cantemir, Dimitrie 82–3
capitalism 149
Casablanca 45
censorship 200
center, the 191–2
Challenger space shuttle 164
Chan, Stephen 13–8, 196–7
Chicago 124; ISA conference 3
Children's Encyclopedia (Mee) 177–8
China, martial arts movies 178–9
chorographic writing 4
chorography 4–5, 122
chronological accounts 3
cinema: black characters 41–2; Chinese martial arts movies 178–9; endings 171–2; and Gulf War I 46–7; impact 162–4; portrayal of USA in 41–53; war films 68
civic virtue 141
civil society 146
classroom, the, as a site bringing 110–1
Clinton, Bill 50
Clooney, George 46–7
Cold War, the 22, 103
collective memory 46, 53, 143

colonial power 182
colonialism 43, 152–60, 192
colonization 100
Commonwealth Secretariat, the 15
communal identities 34
communication 169; one-way 105; the possibility of hearing 105–6
communism 136–50; authoritarianism 148; collective memory 143; doctors as authority figures 139–40; fall of 78–91, 138; life simpler under 148–9; and mass conduct 142–3; memoirs 136–7, 138, 149; *ostalgie* 91, 137–8; and the post-communist generation 140–1; rule 146–7; vanguard organizations 142; view of human nature 142–3; Vrasti's experience of communism 138–40; work ethic 146–7
communist youth 141–3
community 155–7
concealment 30
confession 3, 8
Connolly, William 83
conscientious objectors 57, 64
context 36, 52
Convention on Certain Questions relating to the Conflict of Nationality Laws 63
Convention on the Reduction of Cases of Multiple Nationality and on Military Obligations in Cases of Multiple Nationality 63
Cosmos (TV programme) 164
creolized self, the 128–30, 133–4
Cuba 174, 176, 197
cultural difference 97–8
cultural expression 125, 133–4
cultural interaction 93–102
cultural knowledge 60
cultural narratives 108
culture 158–9; diminishment of 2; importance of 183–5; local 173–85
Czechoslovakia 78

Darlington 30
Darwish, Mahmoud 44, 52
Dauphinee, Elizabeth 11n5
democracy 146
dependency theory 191–2
Derrida, J. 29
despotism 146
development 189
Dhahran, Saudi Arabia 197
Diggle 20

dignity 44
Dinerstein, Joel 118–34, 196; African-American literature teaching interview 118–21; background 119–20; and the blues 122–6; creolized self 128–30, 133–4; midlife crises 130; novel 119–20, 120, 126–30; self-identity 120–1; *Swinging the Machine: Modernity, Technology, and African-American Culture Between the World Wars* 130–1
disappeared, the 27
disciplinary practices 29
displacement 106, 154
Dividing Practices: Race, Class, Religion and Global Economic Inequality, BISA Poststructural Politics Group Workshop 3–4
Djebar, Assia 51, 182
Dominican Republic 71–3
Donahue 126
Donzelot, J. 147
Doty, Roxanne 71–3
Drakulic, S. 85
Dresden, Germany 49–51
Du Bois, W.E.B. 47–8
dual citizenship: and international law 63; and military service 56–64
Dungeons&Dragons 170
Dupree, Louis 1
Dupree, Nancy Hatch 1

Easter Vigil celebration 166
Eastern Europe: and European integration 86; generation of transition 78–91
Ecology Party 22
Edkins, Jenny 3–4, 19–30, 197; brother 30; father 20–3, 25–6, 29, 30; grandfather 26; grandmother 19–20, 29; higher education 23–5; mother 25–6, 30; political activism 22–3; and trauma 27–8; and victims 28–9
Egypt 46
Einstein, Albert 122–3
Eisenstein, Zillah 1
El Alaoui, Khadija F. 41–53; American Studies 49–53; awareness of the black body 41–4; background 41–4; education 43–4, 48–9; and France 42–3; in Germany 49–51; grandmother 42–3; and Gulf War I 45–7; and US relations with the Arab world 45–53

Ellington, Duke 129
Ellison, Ralph 122, 124, 129
embodied mind, the 122
emigration, experience of 87–9
emotional consequences 106–11
emotional landscapes 193
emotions, hearing 108–9
empathetic knowing 202
empathy 18
encounters, meaningful 98
engagement 17–8, 107
Enlightenment, the 82–3
Eritrea 13–4, 17
ethical witnessing 103–16; Ahmed's *Women and War* seminar 106–11; emotional consequences 106–11; engagement 107–8; hearing 108–9; listening 110–1; openness 115–6; the possibility of hearing 105–6; the work of love 111–5
Ethiopia 13–4
ethnic violence: brutalization caused by 39; school fights 32–5; terror of 37–9; and theory 36–7
European integration 85–7
European Union 86
everyday dramas 183
exemplary memory 114–5
exorcism 31
expatriates 198–200
experiences, recording 15–6

facts, sterility of 192–4
Falklands War, the 23, 201
family background 19–30; Khan 190–1; Mandaville 197–8
famine 28
Fanon, Franz 21, 29, 30, 48–9, 52, 53
fear 35, 39
feminism 11n5
fictive distancing 5–6, 7
First World War 19–20
Flinders, C. 100
Floyd, Samuel 130
foreignness 80–3, 87–9
forgetting 52
Fort Bragg, North Carolina 70
Foucault, M. 29
France 42–3, 45, 51
freedom 90
Frisch, Max 61, 64n3
Fukuyama, Francis 200
Future of Cultural Memory, The, fourth annual conference 2

Galle Fort, Sri Lanka 152, 154–60
Gandhi, Indira, gift of buffaloes to Vietnam 175
Gender and History (journal) 11n5
genocide 27
geopolitical space 86
Germany 49–51, 62–3; military service 56–7, 63–4
Ghana 93–102; agriculture 93–6; Christianity 97; cocoa farming 95; Dawhenya 93–6; Morontuo 95; people's generosity 94; pineapple farming 96; rice farming 94–5
Ghosh, Amitav 182
good and evil, clash between 162–3
Good-Bye Lenin! (film) 91, 137–8
Gravity's Rainbow (Pynchon) 121
Great Britain: General Election, 1983 22; and Gulf War I 45; intellectual society 16–7
Great Depression, the 67
Greenham Common Women's Peace Camp 22
Guantanamo Bay 199
Guatemala 149
Guha, Ashok 183
Gulf Cooperation Council (GCC) 199
Gulf War I 45–7, 54n2

Hall, Stuart 25, 123, 125
Halliday, Fred 202
Harré, Rom 24
Hassan II, King 45, 46, 50
Hassinger Lumber Company 67
Hawai'i, ISA conference 3
hearing, the possibility of 105–6
Hedges, Chris 46
Heinlein, Robert 163
Hentoff, Nat 126
history 137
home, sense of 88
homesickness 88
Horkheimer, M. 15, 17
Hoxha, Enver 104
Hughes, Langston 47, 48, 129
Hülsse, Rainer: applies for bicycle division 57–8; called up for German military service 63–4; discharge from army 61; dual citizenship 56–64; higher education 62–3; joins Swiss Army 56–7; military reserve service 61–2; military training 58–61; visit to Berlin 63
human nature 142–3

Hungary 78
Hurston, Zora Neale 124, 129
hybridity 118–20
Hyderabad 174–5

I: importance of 202; multiple 184–5; retrieval of 6
identification 105
identity: American 122; communal 34; creolized 128; and dual citizenship 56–64; elite 59; group 58–9; political 125; religious 83–5; self 120–1
IMF 95
imperial encounters, US Army Dominican Republic deployment 71–3
imperialism 192
In Comes I: Performance, Memory and Landscape (Pearson) 4–5
inactivity 147
Inayatullah, Naeem 1–11, 30, 202
India: education 179–80; gift of buffaloes to Vietnam 174–5; Osmania University College for Women 179–80; partition 85; postcolonial 179
insight 202
instrumentalization 28
intellectuals 16
internal voices 105
international law, and dual citizenship 63
international order, structure 191–2
international politics, influence on biographies 56–64
International Relations 17, 196, 202, 203
International Studies Association 2–3, 5
interpellation by negation, power of 101
interpersonal relations 65–76
intertextual discourse 17
interviews 194
Ionescu, Nae 92n4
Iran 51
Iran-Iraq war 199
Iraq 29, 201; Gulf War I 45–7, 54n2; occupation of 53; US invasion of 51
Iraq War 192
Islam 51
Islamabad, Pakistan 190–1, 192
Israel 48; occupation of Palestine 45

Jackson, Michael 48
Jackson, Patrick Thaddeus 161–72, 202; as altar boy 165–7; Catholicism 164–7; education 163; impact of

Star Wars on 162–4; son 161, 167–71; son's autism diagnosis 168–9; son's stories 170
jazz 130
Jebel 139–40
Jelloun, Tahar Ben 87
Jinnah, Mohammed Ali 190
Johnson, James Weldon 125
Juneteenth (Ellison) 124
justice 29

Kakar, Sudhir 182
Kaviraj, Sudipta 182, 183
Khan, Sorayya 1, 187–95; employment at World Bank 189; family background 190–1; father 190–1; goals 189–90; higher education 189; mother 190; research in Pakistan 193–4; visit to Miani Sahib graveyard 187–8; writing 188–9, 191–3, 193–5
King, Rodney 47
knowing, empathetic 202
knowledge: colonial 182; global 178
Knoxville, Tennessee 66
Komsomol (*Kommunisticeski Soiuz Molodioji* - Communist Youth Union) 143
Konstanz, Germany 62–3
Korean War 197
Kozol, Jonathan 126
Kristeva, Julia 80–1
Kruzel, Joseph 11n5
Kumarakulasingam, Narendran 11n8, 31–40; Batticaloa trip 37–9; school fights 32–5; on violence 35–7
Kundera, Milan 86
Kuwait 45

language 32, 35, 43, 50, 154; and autism 169–70; colonizer's 182; and foreignness 88–9; French 180; learning foreign 179–80; military 70; multiple 183
learning disabilities 66
Lenin, V. I. 142
life: commodification of 28; vocational shape 161–72
life trajectories 2, 161–72, 187–95, 203
Lighthouse Hotel, Galle 158–9
literacy 44
literature 182; world 176–9, 179, 184
lived experience 93–102
Lives of Others, The (film) 91
local culture 173–85

local population, and the US Army Dominican Republic deployment 71–3
London 17; July 2005 bombings 27, 28
Lord of the Rings: Return of the King (film) 15
love, the work of 111–5
love and theft theory 125
Lowenheim, Oded 11n5
Lytham 20, 26

Maiden, Dr Colin 16
Malcolm X 47, 48, 49, 51, 126
Mandaville, Peter 196–203; anti-Americaness 200–1; education 200–1; expatriate life in Saudi Arabia 198–200; family background 197–8; life in Washington DC 201–2
Marx, Karl 29
Marxism 25
Mbembe, A. 185n4
meaning 172
Mee, Arthur 177–8
memory 114–5, 143
Menchú, Rigoberta 136
migrant laborers 199
military service: and dual citizenship 56–64; institutionalization 70–1; interpersonal relations 66–76
misery, chronicling 194
Missing Persons (Edkins) 27
mixtery 122
modernity 182, 183
moment, the 172
Montreal, ISA conference 2
Morgenthau, Hans 182
Morocco 41–4, 46, 49, 50, 51
Mountains of the Moon University, Uganda 13, 16, 18
Mozambique 17
Muppidi, Himadeep 11n2, 173–85; education 179–80; higher education 182–3; sringara 179–82
Murray, Albert 129, 133
Mutla Ridge massacre 47
mystory 4–5, 122

Nairobi 14
Nandy, Ashis 43, 182
narrative possibilities 194
Nazi Germany 27
Necroeconomics 153
Neo-liberal market economics 23
neoliberalism 50, 200

Netherlands, the 190
new man 143
New Orleans 131–2
new world order 46, 53n1
New York 119; ISA conference 5
New York Times 137
New Zealand 14–6
Noica, Constantin 92n4
nomadic migrations, Arabian Peninsula 198
normative internationalism 202
nostalgia 90–1, 136–50
numbers, sterility of 192–4

Oaxaca 174, 175
Obama, Barack 108–9, 111
objectification 19–30
objectivity 5, 107; myth of 13–8
objects 36
October Cities (Rotella) 134n1
oil industry 197, 197–8
Omni-Americans, The (Murray) 129
Open University, the 23, 24–5
Orientalism (Said) 50
Osmania University College for Women, India 179–80
ostalgie 91, 137–8
other, the 110, 111, 125, 129, 198–9
Other Side of Silence, The (Butalia) 85
Ottoman Empire 80, 81, 84
Ovid 88
Oxford, University of 14, 23–4

Pakistan: 1971 war 193–4; Islamabad 190–1, 192; Miani Sahib graveyard, Lahore 187–8; partition 190
Palestine 48, 51, 189; Israeli occupation of 45
participatory society 146
pattern 4
Pearson, Mike 4–5, 122
people, objectification 19–30
periphery, the 191–2
personal, the 4
personal connection 9
personal history, inability to escape 76
personal narratives, power of 201
personal origins 191
personal revelations 9
personhood 29–30, 153
Pervez, Kiran 3
Phạm, Quỳnh 173–85; at Ba Vì 174–6; and Chinese martial arts movie 178–9; father 174–6, 177; mother 178;

reading 176–9; sister 178; *tàijí* lessons 180–2
photographs 19–21, 26–7
Piano, The (film) 15
pity 36
place, and self 187–95
Poland 78
Politics among Nations 182
Popescu, Mariana 90
popular, the 4
postcolony, the 185n4
post-communist generation 140–1
Powell, Colin 46, 54n2
Pratt, Minnie Bruce 1
pre-colonial culture 158–9
pride 44
priesthood, status 164–7
primitivism 131
project development 1–5
projection 105
proximity 93–7
Putnam, Robert 141, 146
Pynchon, Thomas 121

racial politics: American 47–51; the black body 41–4, 47; cinema and 41–2, 46–7; and Gulf War I 45–7; and texts 52; Western bias of academic practice 48–9
racism 14
reading 100–1, 176–9
realism 182
reality, and theory 40
recording, experiences 15–6
refugees 14–5, 106
religion 164–7
remembering 114–5
Remembering the Past in Contemporary African American Fiction (Byerman) 134n1
Return of the Jedi (film) 163
Review of International Studies 202
Rich, Deacon 165–7
Roman Catholic Church 161, 164–7
Romania 78–91; 2008 90–1; Bucharest International Youth Festival 141–2; culture 92n2; the December Revolution 78–9; ethnic groups 80, 84; and European integration 85–7; francophilia 82; life in communist 79–83; Macedonian community 80–1; Muslim community 81–2; *ostalgie* 91; relationship with West 82; religious choice 83–5; school curriculum 82–3;

self-esteem 80; sense of Romanian-ness 84–5, 92n4; teenagers 144; Turkish community 80; *Uniunea Tineretului Comunist* (Union of Communist Youth) 143; volunteering 141
Rosenau, James 11n5
Rosenberg, Justin 202
Rotella, Carlo 134n1
Roxbury secession initiative 126
rubber-necking 28
Rumi, J. 102

Saddam Hussein 51, 54n2
Sagan, Carl 164
Said, Edward 50
St. Andrews University 200–1
Sajed, Alina 78–91; background 78; emigrates to Canada 87–9; and foreignness 80–3; francophilia 82; higher education 85–7; life in communist Romania 79–83; nostalgia 90–1; spiritual choice 83–5; visit to Romania, 2008 90–1
Samarawickrema, Nethra 152–60; father 156–7; higher education 155; response to colonialism 152–60; return to Sri Lanka 152–4; visit to Galle Fort 154–60
Samuelson, Paul 182–3
Saudi Arabia 197, 197–200, 203
Schwartzkopf, Norman 46
science-fiction 162–4
Scott, James 198
Second World War 67
security 39
Seeing Like a State (Scott) 198
self: creolized 128–30, 133–4; disclosure of 8; IR in relation to 202–3; and place 187–95; sense of 70–1, 73; spiritual choice and 83–5; transformation into the other 111
self-abnegation 8
self-disclosure 106–7
self-excavation 122
self-expression 125
self-indulgence 7–8
self-reflection 4
Sen, Amartya 183
Senders, Stephan 2
sex 179
sex industry 104
Shahrazad 46
Shakur, Tupac Amaru 48

Shamans, Mystics and Doctors (Kakar) 182
Sidran, Ben 133
social capital 141
social connectivity 39
social definition 124
social justice 121
Somerset House 26
Sorentino, Sara-Maria 93–102; breakdown 99–100; Independent Study Project 93–7; nasal polyps 98; reading 100–1; return from Ghana 98–9; visit to Dawhenya 93–6; visit to Ghana 93–8
souletariat 147
South Africa 107, 108
Sri Lanka 152–4; Amangalle Hotel, Galle 157–8; assassinations 38; Batticaloa 37–9; ceasefire 37; Colombo 37; communal identities 34; communalism 34; displacements 154; expatriates 157; Galle Fort 152, 154–60; history 33; Lighthouse Hotel, Galle 158–9; Muslims 38; public display of romance 155–6; school ethnic violence 32–5; school fights 32–5; Tamils 32–5, 38; tourists and tourism 158–9
sringara 179–82
Stalin, Josef 142
Star Trek (TV programme) 163
Star Wars (film) 161, 162–4, 172
Star Wars: The Clone Wars (TV programme) 171
Stark, Freya 44
Steele, Meili 2
Stomping the Blues (Murray) 133
storytelling 170–1
Strange Encounters (Ahmed) 105–6
strangeness, sense of 80–1
Strangers to Ourselves (Kristeva) 80–1
structures 191–2
Stump, Jacob L. 65–76; army recruitment 67; break with military 73–6; diary 73; Dominican Republic deployment 71–3; exhaustion 74; father 66–7, 75; graduation 66; higher education 76; joins up 69; military connections 68; military service 66–76; military training 66, 70–1; recruitment processing 68–9
style 4–5
subject matter, relation to 105–6
subjects 36

Subrahmanyam, K. 183
Suetsugu, Marie 30
Swinging the Machine: Modernity, Technology, and African-American Culture Between the World Wars (Dinerstein) 130–4
Switzerland 63; army abolition referendum 61; army bicycle division 57–8, 59–60; army discipline 58, 58–9, 64n3; cultural knowledge 60; military reserve service 61–2; military service 56–64; military service exemptions 58; military training 58–61
Sylvester, Christine 2, 17

tàijí 180–2
Tanzania 15
technological society, and African-American music 130–4
technologization 28, 29
telos 16
testimony, ethical witnessing 103–16
texts, questioning 52
Thatcher, Margaret 22
Their Eyes Were Watching God (Hurston) 124
theoretical framework 6–7
theoretical precision 6
Thesiger, Wilfred 198
Three Kings (film) 46–7
Tickner, J. Ann 11n5
Timişoaran Revolution 139, 140
Tirane, Albania 103–4, 111–5
Tocqueville, Alexis de 141, 146
Todorov, Tzvetan 114–5
toleration 84
tourists and tourism 157–9
traditions 170–1
trauma 27–8
triumphalism 8
Trotsky, Leon 142

Uganda 13–4, 15, 16, 18
Ulmer, Gregory L. 4
Unbearable Lightness of Being, The (film) 91
unfairness 153–4
uniqueness 8
United States of America: 9/11 terrorist attacks 201; academic study of 49–53; Afghanistan bombing campaign 1; African American music 122–6; African Americans 41–2, 47, 107, 109; African-American experience 118–34; African-American literature 118–34; African-American music 130–4; creolized 128–30; expatriate life in Saudi Arabia 198–200; film portrayal of 41–53; foreign policy 76; hybridity 118–34; imperialism 50, 54n2; invasion of Iraq 51; military service 66–76; Obama's election as president 108–9, 111; occupation of Iraq 53; race-based fear 108–9, 111; racial politics 47–51; relations with the Arab world 45–53; rice dumping 94; visa lottery 141; War on Terror 109; white ideals 42
urgency, sense of 7
US Army: Dominican Republic deployment 71–3; garrison life 73–5; recruitment 67; recruitment processing 68–9; training 70–1, 75, 76n3

Varela, Frank 122
Vassar College, NY 53
victims, treatment of 28–9
Vienna, Austria 194
Vietnam, Indian buffaloes 174–6
Vietnam War 68, 104
Village Voice 126
violence: Ahmed's *Women and War* seminar 106–11; brutalization caused by 39; emotional consequences of studying 106–11; encountering 108–10; field studies 35; Kumarakulasingam on 35–7; mastering 37; reality and theory 35–7; reality of 35; school ethnic 32–5; surviving 38; terror of 37–9; and theory 36–7; voyeurism 37; against women 104–5
visibility 153
vocational shape, of life 161–72
voyeurism 37, 197
Vrasti, Wanda 136–50; and communist youth 141–3; experience of communism 138–40; father 139; higher education 144–5; life simpler under communism 148–9; move to Canada 144; post-communist generation membership 140–1; volunteer tourism research 149–50; Western fantasies 145
vulnerability 116

Wales 22–3
Waltz, Kenneth 202

wanna-be's 183–4
war, Ahmed's *Women and War* seminar 106–11
War on Terror 109
warm indifference 2
Washington DC 67, 201–2
Weber, Max 161
Weldon, S. Laurel 11n5
Western culture 131
Western Europe 86
western privilege 93–102
Western values 182–3
Westernization 43
White, Hayden 16
white flight 119, 121
whiteness 128–30
Wilde, Oscar 147
Wolfe, George C. 128
women: Ahmed's *Women and War* seminar 106–11; trafficking 104; violence against 104–5

work ethic, the 146–8
world, structure 191–2
World Bank 95, 96, 189
World Trade Center, terrorist attacks 27, 29
World War II 197
writer: absence of 5–6; doubts of 31–2; presence 7
writers 191
writing 8–9, 161, 191–3; fiction 192, 193, 193–5; lack of control 31–2; power of 194–5; research 193–4

Zalewski, Marysia 11n5
Zambia, University of 14
Zehfuss, Maja 3–4
Zhang Sanfeng 180–2
Zimbabwe 13, 14, 15
Žižek, Slavoj 148

A World of Online Content!

Did you know that Taylor & Francis has over 20,000 books available electronically?

What's more, they are all available for browsing and individual purchase on the Taylor & Francis eBookstore.

www.ebookstore.tandf.co.uk

eBooks for libraries

Free trials available

Choose from annual subscription or outright purchase and select from a range of bespoke subject packages, or tailor make your own.

www.ebooksubscriptions.com

For more information, email
online.sales@tandf.co.uk

Taylor & Francis eBooks
Taylor & Francis Group

New eBook Library Collection

Taylor & Francis eBooks
Taylor & Francis Group

eFocus on Globalization

30 day free trials available!

This new **multi-disciplinary** collection approaches Globalization from a wide range of perspectives, including:

- Economics
- Business
- History
- Politics
- Geography
- Security
- Sociology
- Education
- Media
- Culture

Titles included cover the development impact on non western societies as well as on the west. The collection includes contributions which challenge the whole concept of Globalization as well as those that advance it.

Contributions from renowned authorities, the very best in academia...

Key authors include: **Ernesto Zedillo**, Yale University, USA; **Jeffrey Freiden**, Harvard University, USA; **Akbar S. Ahmed**, American University, Washington, USA; **Teressa Brennan**, **V. Spike Peterson**, University of Arizona, USA; **James Mittelman**, Helsinki University, Finland; and **Doug Guthrie**, Stern School of Business, New York University, USA.

The collection includes key works of reference:

- *A Dictionary of Globalization*
- *Globalization; Key Concepts*
- *Globalization*

As well as some **cutting-edge** works such as:

- *The End Game of Globalization* – **Neil Smith**, Graduate Center, City University of New York, USA.
- *A Globalizing World?* – **David Held**, London School of Economics, UK.

eFocus on Globalization is available as a subscription package of 80 titles with 10 new eBooks per annum.

Order now for guaranteed capped price increase.

Recommend this package to your librarian today!

For a complete list of titles, visit:
www.ebooksubscriptions.com/eFocusGlobalization
www.ebooksubscriptions.com

For more information, pricing enquiries or to order a free trial, please contact your local online sales team:

UK and Rest of the world
Tel: +44 (0) 20 7017 6062
Email: online.sales@tandf.co.uk

United States, Canada and South America
Tel: 1-888-318-2367
Email: e-reference@taylorandfrancis.com

ROUTLEDGE INTERNATIONAL HANDBOOKS

Routledge International Handbooks is an outstanding, award-winning series that provides cutting-edge overviews of classic research, current research and future trends in Social Science, Humanities and STM.

Each *Handbook*:

- is introduced and contextualised by leading figures in the field
- features specially commissioned original essays
- draws upon an international team of expert contributors
- provides a comprehensive overview of a sub-discipline.

Routledge International Handbooks aim to address new developments in the sphere, while at the same time providing an authoritative guide to theory and method, the key sub-disciplines and the primary debates of today.

If you would like more information on our on-going *Handbooks* publishing programme, please contact us.

**Tel: +44 (0)20 701 76566
Email: reference@routledge.com**

www.routledge.com/reference

Routledge Paperbacks Direct

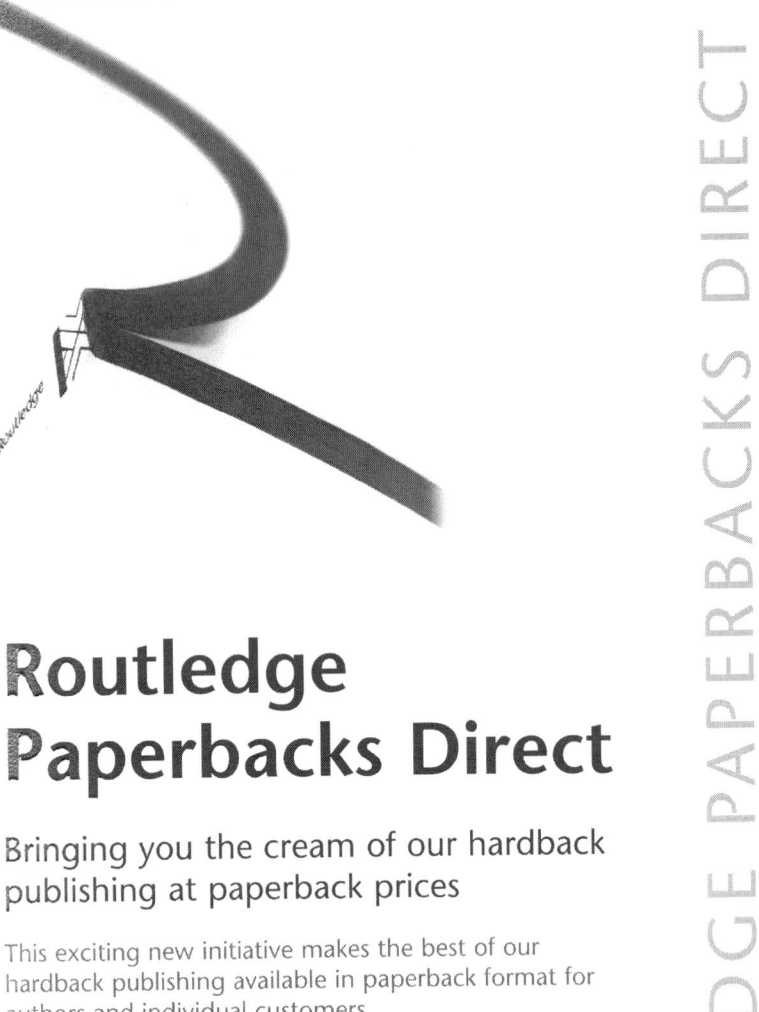

Bringing you the cream of our hardback publishing at paperback prices

This exciting new initiative makes the best of our hardback publishing available in paperback format for authors and individual customers.

Routledge Paperbacks Direct is an ever-evolving programme with new titles being added regularly.

To take a look at the titles available, visit our website.

www.routledgepaperbacksdirect.com

Routledge
Taylor & Francis Group